D0066094

Innovative Intelligence

GEORGIAN COLLEGE LIBRARY

GEOB-BK
#55.00

Innovative Intelligence

The Art and Practice of Leading Sustainable
Innovation in Your Organization

Best Wishes,

[signature]

David S. Weiss and Claude Legrand

Library Commons
Georgian College
One Georgian Drive
Barrie, ON
L4M 3X9

WILEY

John Wiley & Sons Canada, Ltd.

Copyright © 2011 by Dr. David S. Weiss and Claude Legrand

All rights reserved. No part of this work covered by the copyright herein may be reproduced or used in any form or by any means—graphic, electronic or mechanical—without the prior written permission of the publisher. Any request for photocopying, recording, taping or information storage and retrieval systems of any part of this book shall be directed in writing to The Canadian Copyright Licensing Agency (Access Copyright). For an Access Copyright license, visit www.accesscopyright.ca or call toll free 1-800-893-5777.

Care has been taken to trace ownership of copyright material contained in this book. The publisher will gladly receive any information that will enable them to rectify any reference or credit line in subsequent editions.

This publication is designed to provide accurate and authoritative information in regard to the subject matter covered. It is sold on the understanding that the Publisher is not engaged in rendering professional services. If professional advice or other expert assistance is required, the services of a competent professional should be sought.

Library and Archives Canada Cataloguing in Publication Data
Weiss, David S. (David Solomon), 1953-

Innovative intelligence : the art and practice of leading sustainable innovation in your organization / David S. Weiss and Claude Legrand.

Includes index.
ISBN 978-0-470-67767-4

1. Creative ability in business.   2. Organizational change.   I. Legrand, Claude P.   II. Title.

HD53.W44 2011   658.4'063   C2010-906458-5

ISBN 978-0-470-96407-1 (ebk); 978-0-470-96409-5 (ebk); 978-0-470-96408-8 (ebk)

Production Credits
Cover design: Joanna Vieira
Cover photo: ©iStockphoto.com
Interior text design: Mike Chan
Typesetter: Thomson Digital
Printer: Friesens

John Wiley & Sons Canada, Ltd.
6045 Freemont Blvd.
Mississauga, Ontario
L5R 4J3

Printed in the USA

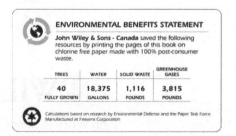

ENVIRONMENTAL BENEFITS STATEMENT

John Wiley & Sons - Canada saved the following resources by printing the pages of this book on chlorine free paper made with 100% post-consumer waste.

TREES	WATER	SOLID WASTE	GREENHOUSE GASES
40 FULLY GROWN	18,375 GALLONS	1,116 POUNDS	3,815 POUNDS

Calculations based on research by Environmental Defense and the Paper Task Force. Manufactured at Friesens Corporation

V007911_080718

To Norah and Joseph whose innovative intelligence is an inspiration.

—DSW

To Lauren and Sheila with love and thanks.

—CPL

Table of Contents

Acknowledgments

Innovative Intelligence had its inception in the similar ideas and experiences of the two authors, who have worked independently for many years. Our careers intersected when we were both teaching at the Schulich Executive Education Centre of York University. We want to thank Harvey Skinner, Dean of the Faculty of Health, York University, for introducing us and encouraging us to work together. After we met, we collaborated on a major innovative thinking development project for the senior leadership of a global pharmaceutical company. We then wrote an article titled "Innovative Team Learning,"[1] which gave us the confidence we could co-write effectively. We combined our areas of expertise to write this book, *Innovative Intelligence*. It has been a great journey together, and we are grateful to each other for the shared insights and collaborative team spirit.

A great deal of the development and refinement of our ideas for the book came from our association with the many clients throughout the world with whom we have worked. One of the joys of strategy, leadership, and innovation consulting is the privilege that comes from working with ambitious, dedicated, and intelligent leaders with the genuine desire to continually take their organizations to higher levels of performance. In particular, we thank our clients who had the confidence in each of us and the courage to champion the development of innovative intelligence, innovative thinking, and leadership capacity within their organizations. It

---

1. David S. Weiss and Claude P. Legrand, "Innovative Team Learning," *Canadian Learning Journal*, 2009.

was through their experiences that we gained the insights that helped us validate the ideas in this book. We are grateful to you, our clients, for your ongoing trust, support, and friendship.

We also thank our publisher, editors, and internal support staff, who contributed greatly to this project. A special thank you is extended to Karen Milner and the John Wiley & Sons team for their confidence and support of this project. We thank Mary Jo Beebe for challenging our ideas, her attention to editorial detail, and guidance in refining the thoughts throughout the book. Also, thank you to Sheila Robb for her editorial support and to Susan Beckley for her teamwork throughout this project.

We also would like to thank the people who have been a constant support and inspiration for our individual professional and personal learning.

On a professional level, special thanks to James Marchant for encouraging me to apply innovative thinking and write about it in my first book, *Beyond The Walls of Conflict*[2]; to Dr. Carol Beatty and Dr. Dan Ondrack for providing the University platform so that I could teach executive leaders and HR professionals these ideas; and to David Shaw for providing me with the opportunity to work as the Chief Innovation Officer of a multinational human capital consulting firm. On a personal level, my deepest appreciation is extended to my wife, Dr. Nora Gold, who is my inspiration as a writer and my best friend, and to our son, Joseph Weissgold, for his innate gift of innovative intelligence. Finally, to my late mother, Miriam Borenstein Weiss, I am always grateful for your endless support; and to my father, Moshe Weiss, I dedicate this book to you as my model of an inventive, resourceful, and clever thinker.

—*David*

A special thank you to all the people who, in different ways, shaped my work and my research in innovative thinking. First, to my wise, creative, and tremendously supportive wife, Sheila, who, for over 10 years, urged me to write this book, and to my daughter, Lauren, who has taught me many important things in her first 19 years and who will be a great

---

2. David S. Weiss, *Beyond the Walls of Conflict: Mutual Gains Negotiating for Unions and Management.* (Irwin Professional Publishing, 1996).

leader in the future. Both are constant sources of inspiration and intellectual challenge. To Ron Mandel, who introduced me to creativity; to David Hughes, who helped me shape many of the concepts; and to my partner, Rob LaJoie, who after 10 years as a great client has been an even better partner in Ideaction. Finally, to all the friends and clients who challenged me over the years to find the right questions, especially Genevieve Rouille, Chris Stamper, Mehbs Remtulla, and Brian Coupland. Each one inspired a part of my thinking for this book.

—*Claude*

To all of you, our thanks and love.

David S. Weiss and Claude Legrand
Toronto, Ontario, Canada
September 2010

Preface

Innovation has emerged as a key source of competitive advantage in today's knowledge economy—yet it is still quite elusive for many organizations. The evidence is clear that despite decades of effort, most established organizations have not figured out how to innovate systematically. We have not had sustainable solutions—practical and reliable programs that deliver long-term, predictable results. Instead, we have had an endless array of partial answers.

The observation that fueled our pursuit of this problem was the contrast between what so many established leaders were saying about the critical need for innovation and what so few were successfully doing. Most CEOs, government leaders, and consultants recognize the importance of innovation; and yet, innovation is still the exception, not the norm. Our question then is: Why is innovation not happening systematically when leaders demand it?

We have found that too many organizations try to improve innovation by focusing on one element at a time, particularly in the area of new products and services. They train individuals, hire more creative people, or create specialized innovation departments. Despite these investments, most organizations have disappointing results. They are left with an alarming innovation gap.

Innovative Intelligence responds to the question: *How can we make individuals and organizations systematically and sustainably innovative?*

We use a three-part approach as follows:

- *Part One* defines the root causes of the innovation gap and the role played by all individuals in an organization, including its leaders. We argue that many employees learned one thinking process in school; one that only accesses their analytical intelligence, which is based upon past knowledge and experiences. They did not learn a process or a set of techniques to access their innovative intelligence, which would help them to deal with the new ambiguities of work. This means that the majority of leaders and teams have no practical and reliable process to think innovatively when they are asked to do it. Only when leaders and employees can apply innovative thinking to access their innovative intelligence will organizations be able to systematically innovate.

- *Part Two* makes the case for focusing on leaders as the key lever to close the innovation gap. Most leaders have been trained and rewarded for thinking in a linear, non-innovative manner. Many leaders view it as their role to be the person who knows the answers to problems and can guide or tell employees what to do. However, the kinds of problems that leaders face in the knowledge economy are increasingly complex and often cannot be solved only with past experience or knowledge. Leaders need to focus more on understanding the depth of the question rather than on trying to have all the answers. Their new added value is to facilitate innovative thinking processes that uncover the questions and assumptions so that the leaders and employees understand the depth of the issues they are facing. Only then can leaders start exploring and discovering what could be potential innovative solutions to today's new complexities. This book presents the practical approaches that will enable leaders to become highly skilled in innovative thinking as well as to help others think more innovatively.

- *Part Three* clarifies that innovative thinking is not sufficient to close the innovation gap in organizations. The organizational practices and the culture have to make innovative thinking easier. In most organizations, however, the practices and culture make innovative thinking more difficult and can actually block leaders' and employees' access to their innovative intelligence. This book defines the changes required to develop a culture where innovating is the norm, and it presents the practical techniques to build organizational practices that make innovating easier. We also explain how to develop an organization-wide innovation plan that can help leaders and executives focus on the important innovations that are needed to close the innovation gap.

Some of the specific characteristics of *Innovative Intelligence* that distinguish it from other works are:

- It identifies that a primary way to close the innovation gap is to enhance the ability of leaders to resolve complex problems and to make their teams more innovative.
- It explains how leaders need to have access to multiple intelligences in addition to their current IQ-based analytical intelligence. Specifically, leaders need to have access to their innovative intelligence, emotional intelligence, and analytical intelligence to succeed.
- It emphasizes that a primary role of leaders in the knowledge economy is to enable their employees to access their innovative intelligence and to achieve business success by applying innovative thinking.
- It introduces a four-step innovative thinking process with tools and templates as a practical guide for leaders and organizations.
- It describes the preferred culture to support innovating and the organizational practices needed to make innovating easier. It also identifies the cultural and organizational barriers that might prevent an organization from successfully developing their leaders' innovative thinking capabilities and how to overcome these barriers.
- It reinforces the executive accountability to build and sustain innovative thinking in organizations.
- It concludes with a call to action to organizations, governments, and the school system to contribute to the development of leaders so that they will have access to innovative intelligence and be able to engage in effective innovative thinking with their employees and teams.

A DESCRIPTION OF THE BOOK
INNOVATIVE INTELLIGENCE

We present in this section a brief overview of the three parts of the book and a description of each chapter.

Part One: Closing the Innovation Gap

Part One of *Innovative Intelligence* (Chapters 1 to 4) describes the root causes and the challenges of the innovation gap, the need to enhance capabilities of leaders to lead through complexity, and the importance of accessing innovative intelligence to close the gap.

Chapter One: The Innovation Gap
This chapter defines innovation and innovative thinking. It then describes how the innovation gap impacts organizations and explains that there is an urgent need for innovation by all leaders, employees, and teams, in order to close the gap.

Chapter Two: Leading Through Complexity
The knowledge economy has created new demands for leaders to lead through much more complex issues and problems. Yesterday's "right" answer does not work anymore. All leaders need to engage employees, teams, peers, and customers in order to gain better insight into the complexities they face and to discover the best ways to proceed.

Chapter Three: Accessing Innovative Intelligence
To be effective in the knowledge economy and contribute to closing the innovation gap in the workplace, leaders need to draw out their employees' and teams' innovative intelligence. Leaders need to understand when analytical thinking is the best process and when they need to apply innovative thinking in order to access the team's innovative intelligence.

Chapter Four: Eclipse of Innovative Intelligence
This chapter describes three scenarios that can obscure or eclipse one's innovative intelligence and offers suggestions for removing or reducing the impact of each eclipse.

Part Two: Innovative Thinking

Part Two of *Innovative Intelligence* (Chapters 5 to 9) introduces the innovative thinking process necessary to access innovative intelligence. It describes how leaders and employees can apply innovative thinking techniques and tools effectively in the workplace.

Chapter Five: Innovative Thinking: An Overview

This chapter provides an overview for the entire Part Two. Specifically, Chapter 5 explores the characteristics of an effective innovative thinking model and the key success factors of innovative thinking.

Chapter Six: Step 1: Framework

The framework is the foundation of successful innovative thinking. This chapter presents the six essential tools and techniques needed in order to create an effective framework. The first five together help leaders and teams understand and define "the problem." The sixth tool is the plan, or project charter, which guides the process of gaining insight into an issue and discovering meaningful innovative solutions.

Chapter Seven: Step 2: Issue Redefinition

Issue redefinition is fundamentally concerned with identifying the root causes and sub-parts to shape and reshape an issue. Step 2: *Issue Redefinition* helps identify the best angles from which to solve the overall problem or opportunity.

Chapter Eight: Step 3: Idea Generation

Idea Generation is the step in the innovative thinking process that relies most intensely on innovative intelligence. This chapter explains the four stages of group idea generation and then describes how they can be applied by individuals.

Chapter Nine: Step 4: Implementation Planning

In Implementation Planning, leaders guide groups through the process of confirming the preferred ideas, engaging in a risk analysis, presenting the innovative solution for approval, and ensuring there is a proper handoff to an implementation team.

Part Three: Making Innovation Happen

Part Three of *Innovative Intelligence* (Chapters 10 to 14) explains how leaders can guide innovative teams. It then explores how to shape a culture of innovation, design organizational practices that promote and embed innovative thinking in an organization, and develop an organization-wide innovation plan.

Chapter Ten: Making Innovation Happen: an Overview

Innovative thinking is necessary but not sufficient for innovation to occur in organizations. This chapter provides an overview of the four essential enablers that are fundamental to making innovation happen.

Chapter Eleven: Leading Innovation

Innovation rarely happens and certainly cannot be sustained without the active commitment and involvement of effective leaders of innovation throughout the organization. This chapter explores the four areas of innovation leadership: leading self, leading innovation teams, leading intact work units, and leading innovative enterprises.

Chapter Twelve: Culture of Innovation

This chapter explores how culture impacts innovation and how to accelerate the transformation of a culture so that it enables and sustains innovation. It concludes with a challenge to leaders to actively create a culture that supports innovation rather than letting the existing organizational culture prevent innovation.

Chapter Thirteen: Organizational Practices for Innovation

This chapter explains the importance of implementing organizational practices that help individuals and teams to innovate. It explores all the organization processes and recommends how they can be improved to support innovation.

Chapter Fourteen: The Innovation Plan

This chapter focuses on the specific elements that should be included in an enterprise-wide innovation plan and the process to develop and measure its success. The final section of this chapter focuses on "pulling it all together." In that section we integrate the ideas presented throughout the book and extend a challenge to governments, education systems, and multinational companies to do their part to help organizations close their innovation gaps.

WHO SHOULD READ THIS BOOK

The book has been written for leaders who are dissatisfied with the current innovation gap in their organizations and are hungry for practical information, ideas, and techniques to advance innovation. *Innovative Intelligence* is very helpful both conceptually and practically. All the ideas and the practical tools presented in this book have been "road-tested" in engagements with our clients over the past few years and are already helping large organizations close their innovation gap. In particular, the following groups will find the book beneficial:

- Executives and managers at all levels who are seeking to understand how to enable innovative thinking and how to create a culture that supports innovation in their organizations.
- Boards of directors who understand their businesses' continual competitive advantage depends on their capacity to innovate.
- Human Resources, talent management, and leadership development professionals, internal and external to an organization, who are interested in understanding how to build the leadership capability as innovative thinkers.
- Members of associations that are concerned with leadership innovation issues.
- Members of the academic community interested in a well-researched and practical text to teach their students about the need for innovative intelligence and about the changing role and expectations of leadership.
- Students in business schools, engineering, organizational behavior, and Human Resources programs, looking for a fuller understanding of the challenge of building organizational and leadership innovation capacity.
- Management consultants seeking ideas to provide advice to organizations about how to develop leadership innovation to drive business results.

HOW TO READ THIS BOOK

Most readers will benefit from reading the book cover to cover. However, others will find they can dip into the book for specific ideas and information, and it will add value. Here are some alternative ways this book can be read:

- Some readers—those responsible for the development of innovative leaders—may want to use the book as a study guide for use in training. A suggested approach is to ask the leaders to read Part One for the first discussion and Part Two for the second discussion. Part Three should probably be read and discussed one chapter at a time.

- Some readers may want to explore the topic of innovative thinking and how it is done, which can be found in Part Two (Chapters 5 to 9).
- If the readers are primarily interested in systemic change to create an organization that supports innovation, they may want to focus on reading Part Three (Chapters 10 to 14), which describes the key enablers and disablers of innovation in organizations.
- Finally, readers may want to study a topic of their own interest. A detailed index has been prepared for referencing specific topics. For example, the topic of "individual innovative thinking" is referenced in several chapters of the book. Readers can combine the ideas about a topic area to form their own analysis of the material.

Our intent is that readers of *Innovative Intelligence* will be convinced that innovative intelligence is essential for organizations to close the innovation gap. The book provides business leaders with the logic and the tools to enhance innovative intelligence in the workplace.

To this end, *Innovative Intelligence* presents the case for a new focus for leadership, centered on innovative thinking and fostering a culture that supports innovation. Our hope is that *Innovative Intelligence* will become the road map for executives and leadership professionals who are exploring how to develop innovative leaders who can close the innovation gap for business success.

PART ONE

CLOSING THE INNOVATION GAP

CHAPTER ONE

THE INNOVATION GAP

"The problem is much more complex and challenging than we thought," the CEO declared to his executive team. "Initially, we thought our challenge was to sustain our leading position in the new competitive environment. We thought we were an innovative pharmaceutical company—but really we're only an innovative R&D company. And now our R&D pipeline has almost ground to a halt. Healthcare regulators are not approving our new products. Generic drug companies are contesting our patents through intense litigation. Doctors don't have the time to see us. We're facing unprecedented political pressure to reduce the costs of our drugs. It's obvious that we must become innovative throughout our company and not just in R&D. But how do we do that quickly?"

"We've trained our best leaders to focus on short-term problems and 'making' the numbers. We haven't trained them to think innovatively. Our few innovative leaders have left to join healthcare start-ups that appreciate their innovative thinking. So we don't have the skilled innovative leaders who can help lead us out of this mess."

The CEO raised his voice and challenged his executive team, "I'm not the only leader here. Together, we must radically change our culture and champion innovative leadership throughout our business to compete in our industry. Are you with me?" The executives saw the panic in the CEO's eyes and nodded in agreement—but they didn't believe they would make any meaningful changes—not because they didn't want to, but because they just didn't know how to do what the CEO wanted. And they didn't believe the CEO knew either.

It is stories like this one that motivated us to write this book. Many organizations are caught in the turbulent world of the knowledge economy. They may have good intentions to become more innovative—but not many of their leaders know how to do it. They recognize that innovation is a key source of competitive advantage. However, despite extensive efforts to change, many organizations are having difficulty achieving the levels of innovation they require. This dynamic is an *innovation gap.*

Innovation Gap = The difference between the stated importance of innovation and the actual results in an organization

---

Our purpose in *Innovative Intelligence* is twofold:

- To provide business leaders and senior HR executives with an accelerated strategy to close the innovation gap.
- To supply a series of practical and implementable frameworks and tactics for developing leaders who can drive innovation in their organizations.

THE INNOVATION CHALLENGE

Let's begin with the challenge of *innovation.*

Frequently it is only after the crisis has occurred—after the competition has captured market share, after the market has dried up, after organizations have slashed costs—that organizations react. Then they say they need to "innovate"—as best they can under the pressure of the crisis. Too often, they overreact and confuse systemic innovation with unbridled creativity. This kind of creativity merely produces high-risk ideas with no pragmatic means of applying them and no built-in process to sustain them.

Organizations face three major challenges as they attempt to respond to the innovation gap:

1. *Lack of a common understanding of what innovation is, how it happens, and what prevents it.* Despite many attempts at defining innovation, a lack of consensus on a common definition still exists. Too often, leaders define innovation only in terms of technology or scientific research, yet organizations require innovation in almost all areas.

2. *Lack of innovative leaders.* Most leaders have never learned how to be innovative and how to lead an organization so that it becomes more innovative. They may understand that they have a key role in innovation, but they do not know how to systematically generate new and better solutions. They also do not know how to reinforce the right innovative skills for their direct reports and teams.

3. *Lack of enabling organizational practices and cultures to reinforce innovation.* Many organizations inadvertently discourage innovation through their organizational practices (e.g. planning, budgeting, rewards). In addition, many organizations have cultures that drive short-term results and risk avoidance. Without changing some organizational practices and building a culture of innovation, leaders will not close the innovation gap.

Today, innovation is often extolled; however, on closer investigation, far more talk than action occurs. In this context, the old adage "talk is cheap" actually becomes "talk is expensive," because organizations pay a hefty price if they do not practice what they preach. Failure to innovate can be terminal.

WHAT IS INNOVATION?

Let's first define innovation. Then, we'll explain the innovation gap dynamic and substantiate it with our evidence.

Most use the concept of "innovation" as either an *outcome* or a *process*. This book is not about innovation as an *outcome*, although a great deal of research describes the innovation gap that is associated with the lack of innovative outcomes in organizations.

Instead, our approach focuses on the *process* of innovation and how innovation happens. Here are some key aspects of the innovation process:

*   The innovation process applies to everything an organization does or could do, as well as how it does it. For example, innovation applies to how the organization develops and implements strategies, creates new products and services, manufactures products and services, and ensures that internal functions support the business.

- It is an essential enabler of business strategies and goals—but it is not, in and of itself, the strategy or the goal.
- It is simply about innovating. It is a process that enables the organization to deliver on its strategies and its goals, in the same way that manufacturing, marketing, or accounting enables the organization to achieve its goals—no more and no less.

We use the word *innovation* in a very different way than the way we use the word *creativity*. Here are some comparisons of creativity and innovation:

- Creativity is about having new ideas, relevant or not, useful or not, implementable or not, while the output of innovation achieves defined value for an organization.
- Creativity is a stand-alone output, not a sustainable business outcome. On the other hand, *innovation* is directed toward achieving a sustainable outcome that can improve what people do or how they do it.

Our definition of *innovation* in a business context is as follows:

Innovation = Applied creativity that achieves business value

The confusion between innovation and creativity has been costly to many organizations. Once, a CEO of a successful bank indicated he did not want more innovation (because it would be too disruptive). What he was actually referring to was not innovation but creativity without boundaries, direction, or a rigorous process for application.

It is difficult to blame executives for their anxiety with unbridled creativity. Many executives are focused on risk mitigation and ensuring that the formula for success for their organization can be repeated continuously. Uncontrolled creativity could put an organization at risk, and although some executives say they want new ideas and innovation, they do not always support it when it occurs.

Even the expression "unleashing creativity" reflects this anxiety. To "unleash" implies that creativity was formerly restrained on a leash because it was dangerous. As a result, many executives do not focus on developing the innovation skills of their leaders because they are concerned that it will introduce uncontrollable risk.

Of course, managing risk is important—but concern with risk should not stop the innovation process. In fact, not taking risks and not changing is often the biggest risk of all, even if it is not immediately obvious. We need both innovation and risk mitigation at the same time.

We need both innovation and risk mitigation at the same time.

It is similar to the perceived oxymoron that higher quality can occur with lower cost. But it is true—better quality can be less expensive. The same is true for innovation: greater innovation can occur within acceptable levels of risk. Risk management should always be built into the innovative process.

Executives are correct in assuming that unbridled creativity could be disastrous—but focused innovation within acceptable risk levels can yield outstanding benefits for the business. To reduce associated risk, innovation needs to operate within clear boundaries and to be focused on achieving specific business outcomes.

The issue is that leaders often do not know how to foster innovation or how to manage risks on an ongoing basis. Risk is, just like innovation, an area that is spoken about frequently but with very little understanding or action. Risk is usually carefully evaluated for large projects or investments, but the discussion of risk for smaller projects is usually minimal. In most cases it is just glossed over, only to be discovered if something goes wrong later.

INNOVATIVE THINKING MAKES INNOVATION HAPPEN

Although there are many ways to understand innovation, most experts agree that innovation happens when people use innovative thinking.

Our definition of *innovative thinking* is as follows:

Innovative thinking is the process of solving problems by discovering, combining, and arranging insights, ideas, and methods in new ways.

The process of innovating is done by individuals or small teams that engage in innovative thinking. Computers, systems, cultures, or organizations do not innovate—only people do. However, the role of organizations and systems is critical; they are key enablers or potential blockers of innovative thinking by individuals and teams.

The Challenge to Innovate in the Knowledge Economy

The shift from the industrial economy to the knowledge economy has changed the nature of work more in the last 20 years than it changed in the last century. In the industrial economy, an organization could ask a few elite leaders to be innovative and focus everyone else on simply doing the work. When a problem happened, it was escalated to the elite "thinkers," who solved the problem and communicated the "right" decision throughout the organization.

In the knowledge economy, there is a need for all employees to use their intellectual potential because the nature of work is constantly changing and presenting complex challenges at every level of organizations. In this new economy, better solutions can only come from new ways of thinking—innovative thinking—not from conventional linear analytical thinking alone.

We need innovative thinking in our schools and businesses, in our health care and justice systems, and throughout our public institutions, in everything from politics to parenting. Even in manufacturing, the traditional hub of the industrial economy, all employees need to contribute to innovative thinking.

Unfortunately, in the context of today's collapsed time and increasing work complexity, many complain that there is little time for innovating, and too few people are able to dedicate time to thinking, let alone innovative thinking.

Almost no organization has a culture that allocates thinking time for employees as Google reputedly does[1]—and "lack of time" is the most common obstacle cited by workers when asked why they are not more innovative. Employees who designate office time to think about problems and issues are often assumed to be wasting time—as one bank

---

1. Boston Consulting Group, "Innovation 2007: A BCG Senior Management Survey," August 2007. http://www.bcg.ch/fileadmin/media/pdf/innovation 2007.pdf

employee told us: "When I think, I feel guilty because I am not doing." Some employees cannot think at work because they spend so much time in meetings, and they believe more in an "open door policy" (whereby anyone can disturb them at anytime), than in allocating time for dedicated "closed door" thinking.

In addition, the recent proliferation of smart phones has placed an even greater premium on instant reactions and instant solutions, to the detriment of well-thought-out decisions. As a result, some employees sneak away from their offices, just to have a few moments of undisturbed innovative thinking time.

We need to value thinking at work and create a climate where innovative thinking is legitimized and valued in meetings and during dialogue, and where we confront and understand complex issues that we encounter in the work setting.

Organizations need to value thinking at work and create a climate where innovative thinking is legitimized and valued.

THE EVIDENCE IS IN—WE ARE UNDERACHIEVING

While innovation is often heralded as a key source of competitive advantage, many organizations are woefully underachieving when it comes to innovation. When they need it most, they have seldom been able to achieve the type of innovation that anticipates, adapts, and leads change rather than following it. This is particularly true when an organization compares its actual business achievements to the potential of its individual workers and teams. Few organizations leverage the full potential of their employees and teams.

Many articles and researchers[2] focus on innovative organizations such as Apple, Google, Toyota Motor Corp., General Electric, and Microsoft. There are also other, less visible, innovative organizations in the private sector, social enterprise (non-profit) sector, and public sector. However, for every organization that succeeds at innovation, there are many more that

---

2. Boston Consulting Group, "Innovation 2007: A BCG Senior Management Survey," August 2007.

are either not engaged in it or not doing enough. One executive director of a creative dance company said it best in his presentation to encourage his management team to be more innovative: "Have we had innovation? Of course. Incremental improvement? Yes. Big ideas? A few. Sustainable innovation? Seldom. Enough innovation? Not even close." This observation is true for many organizations today.

What has emerged in organizations is a wide-ranging and potentially disastrous innovation gap. To validate the dynamic of the innovation gap, we reviewed a number of survey reports on innovation published over the past five years in North America and Europe. We also conducted our own research on innovation in the workplace to validate some of the findings that already existed, to test some of the underlying assumptions that appear to be the basis for much of the research, and to explore some additional questions.

What the Research Shows

The first overriding result in almost every research report is that there is a significant gap between innovation expectations and performance.[3] The dynamic is as follows:

- *Innovation Expectations:* Most executives believe innovation is "very important" or "important" for the future success of their organizations, and it is among the top priorities for their businesses.
- *Innovation Results:* Most executives are not satisfied with the innovation results their organizations are achieving.

Research validates these findings. The first survey we led[4] targeted senior leaders in 500 large organizations. We found the same dramatic differences

---

3. Accenture, "Overcoming Barriers To Innovation," 2008, and Boston Consulting Group, "Innovation 2007: A BCG Senior Management Survey," August 2007. Boston Consulting Group reported that innovation is a top strategic focus for 66% of 2468 executive respondents—most at C-Suite levels—ranking it one of the top three priorities, and 67% will increase spending on innovation; IBM researchers reported in the book *Rethinking Innovation* (Fast Thinking Books, 2008) that most believe innovation is a key priority; however, many are not satisfied with the results of their innovation efforts. The same result emerged in the report by the Delta Organization and Leadership (a Member of Oliver Wyman) in "The Global Leadership Imperative: Building and Innovation Engine," 2007.
4. *Globe and Mail* and the Schulich School of Business survey conducted in 2007.

between innovation expectations and innovation results. The results of the following two questions illustrate the point:

- "Innovation[5] is important for our future success" = 88 percent of respondents
- "Our organization is effective at innovation" = 33 percent of respondents

Another question we asked was, "Who was responsible for innovation?" The findings (Table 1.1) showed that 78 percent believed the executive team was responsible for innovation (and not specifically the CEO).

Table 1.1: Who is Responsible for Innovation?[6]

Executive Team	78%
CEO	47%
R&D Executive	16%
HR Executive	12%
Others	12%
No One Specifically	11%
Chief Innovation Officer	8%

Of course, there are high-profile examples of innovative CEOs who have almost single-handedly led their organizations to new industry innovations—however, these types of executives are few and far between. These unique innovative leaders are often found in owner-operated companies where the CEO may have launched the company after discovering a breakthrough concept, service, or product and retains that position of being the primary, and sometimes exclusive, generator of innovative ideas.

We also conducted a survey[7] of 550 HR professionals (including 130 HR executives) focusing on the Human Resource professionals' perception of the innovation gap. This research compared the results

---

5. The survey defined innovation as: Implemented ideas that create value in everything you do and how you do it (to the exclusion of R&D).
6. Respondents were permitted to select more than one response category.
7. Based on the research by Ideaction and the Human Resources Professionals' Association (HRPA) in Ontario, Canada, 2008.

of the respondents who said their organization was innovative (referred to as "innovative organization") to the ones who said their organization was not innovative (referred to as "non-innovative organization"). These results clearly showed that the HR respondents believed leadership was the single most discriminating factor for innovation success (see Table 1.2).

Table 1.2: The Role of Leadership in Innovative and Non-Innovative Organizations

	All Respondents	Executives Only	Innovative Organizations	Non-Innovative Organizations
Innovation is important for the future success of our organization	87%	93%	95%	79%
All our executives believe that innovation is crucial	53%	59%	86%	24%
Our executive team is an excellent example of teamwork	33%	44%	67%	12%
Our executives understand the process of innovation	29%	34%	68%	6%
Our executives role-model innovation practices in their own actions	28%	39%	68%	2%

In our research, innovative organizations differed from non-innovative organizations in some key ways:

- Typically, in innovative organizations *all* the executives believed innovation was crucial to their future success. It was not enough to have only the CEO formally promote innovation. To succeed, the organization needed to align all the top leaders.
- Most innovative organizations viewed executive teams as good examples of teamwork and as role models of innovation.
- Most innovative organizations understood the process of innovation and had a well-defined innovation strategy.
- All leaders were directly accountable and responsible for the success or lack of success of innovation in their organizations.

Another key finding in our research was that middle managers were very concerned about innovation in their organizations. Middle managers indicated the following:[8]

- There are greater barriers to innovation in their companies than C-Suite[9] executives realize.
- They have a much less optimistic view of the executives as supporters of innovation than the executives have of themselves.
- Not enough is being done by executives to help middle managers become innovative leaders.
- Accountability for innovation needs to be distributed throughout the leadership ranks.

Our research findings support the assertion that there is a need for organization-wide innovative thinking that becomes part of the way of working for all leaders and employees, at every level of the organization.

Our findings indicate the following about the role of a CEO in innovation:

- The CEO is not to be the chief innovator, but rather the champion of a culture and structure that incessantly encourages, celebrates, and grows innovation.
- The CEO must eliminate obstacles, including individual leaders who block innovation.
- The CEO needs to be a driver of innovation in the organization and should not be the person with exclusive accountability to discover innovations—that accountability extends far beyond the CEO.
- The direct responsibility of the CEO is to ensure that the executives and the entire organization actively support the innovation agenda.

What is required is leaders, from CEOs to frontline managers, who understand and accept the need to generate innovations. The executives need to

---

8. Schulich School of Business and the Human Resources Professionals' Association (HRPA)—research conducted by Ideaction.
9. C-Suite refers to the executive team of a company. The "C" refers to the popular designation of "Chief," as in Chief Executive Officer (CEO), Chief Financial Officer (CFO), Chief Marketing Officer (CMO), Chief Technology Officer (CTO), etc.

value small and large innovations, and they need to emphasize that everyone has a role in innovative thinking and in implementing innovative ideas.

The CEOs must be accountable for making sure all other leaders implement innovation, but they can't be the only leaders doing it. They must be taught how to use a systematic process of innovative thinking, how to role-model innovation, and how to create a climate of innovation for all leaders, employees, and teams.

Overall, the studies we conducted indicate that the key to overcoming the innovation gap is a strong leadership emphasis on innovation throughout the organization. Our research and our experience also support the following:

- *Many executives have an overall lack of understanding of how innovation happens and how to create an innovative organization.* They believe they are personally innovative, but they lack an understanding of how to create a culture that encourages innovation. They also do not know how to create effective organizational processes that support innovation, nor do they know how to foster skills development among leaders, employees, and teams so that they become able to be innovative.
- *Leaders at all levels (not just executives) need to be committed to innovation.* The leaders need to be taught how to apply innovative thinking, how to encourage others to use it, and how to create a climate of innovation for their employees and teams.
- *Organizations need systematic innovation plans.* Organizations are becoming more and more complex, and they need organization-wide innovation plans to govern the innovation agenda and to create a culture of innovation that enables and encourages individuals and teams to think innovatively.

TRY IT ANOTHER WAY

The business approach that has worked for many leaders in the past is often an obstacle to innovation in the current knowledge economy. It is time to try another way.

Some leaders believe they can fix any problem if they return to their former successful ways of operating. For example, some executives assume that new product and service innovations are their primary source of innovation, based on their past experiences. However, the new frontier for innovation extends well beyond product and service innovations. Some organizations are generating great value from other areas, including process innovations, customer innovations, business model innovations, marketing and sales innovations, and HR and IT innovations. There are many new areas of focus for innovation that require attention. Relying on product and service innovation alone will not be sufficient.

Some of these leaders may be suffering from "tunnel vision"[10]—a pattern of human thought that proceeds as follows: When a specific kind of performance leads to success and that success leads to meaningful rewards, then it is very likely that the person will repeat the original performance again. If this pattern occurs numerous times, the person may become complacent and be deceived into believing that repeating the same performance, even when the context is radically different, will produce the same success and rewards. Some leaders believe their past methods are the only way to achieve successful outcomes, even when conditions around them change. When leaders exhibit tunnel vision, it often results in missed opportunities and, in some cases, disastrous results.

Leaders need to have the humility to never believe they have found the absolute performance formula for success. They need to retain the flexibility to do the right thing based on what they face currently and not on how they responded in the past, regardless of how successful their past performance may have been. All leaders, including executives, need to be open to the current context and to be willing to try it another way to ensure continual organizational vitality. This expectation of executive leadership is consistent with Jim Collins' concept[11] of "level 5 leadership," which emphasizes that the most effective leaders are humble and persistent. It is not about the leader; it is about organizational success. Personal humility lets leaders be open to new contexts and eventualities. It helps them look forward and discover new innovations rather than looking backward and incorrectly applying what worked in the past to the current context.

Organizations need innovation to be the responsibility of all leaders. Executives need to listen to middle managers to uncover the barriers to innovation and discover innovative approaches to resolving them.

---

10. David S. Weiss, *High Performance HR: Leveraging Human Resources For Competitive Advantage* (John Wiley and Sons, 2000).
11. Jim Collins, *From Good to Great: Why Some Companies Make The Leap … And Others Don't* (HarperCollins Publishers, 2001).

CONCLUSION

It should be clear by this point that the innovation gap is a major problem for organizations and that there is an urgent need for an effective approach to innovation in the work place. Most leaders know that innovation is essential for their success; however, they do not know how to generate it.

Chapter 2 explains the changing expectations of leadership in responding to the challenge. Chapters 3 and 4 explore why accessing innovative intelligence is a key success factor in this leadership transformation and why leaders trying to meet the new expectations may encounter many obstacles. The remainder of the book provides the strategy, frameworks, and practical techniques for leaders to develop their innovative intelligence and to drive innovation throughout their organizations. So read on and enjoy!

CHAPTER TWO

LEADING THROUGH COMPLEXITY

Many executives do not recognize the need to develop innovative leaders who can lead through complexity until it is too late. Clayton Christensen was quoted as saying, "Managers are the smartest people in the world, on average [but] . . . are CEOs smart enough to seize the innovation moment? Their own jobs are at stake—and much, much more besides."[1] As long as executives fail to recognize the critical importance of developing innovative leaders throughout their organizations, they will impair their capacity to respond to complex business challenges. They will also erode their competitive capability and undermine their potential for new growth.

Complexity is not a new management concern; rather, it is a predictable outcome of the shift to the current globalized knowledge-based economy. A shift of similar importance occurred with the advent of the industrial economy in the twentieth century, which introduced a complicated work environment and drove the development of new methods and processes, such as Taylorism and Six Sigma. The recent knowledge economy shift has introduced even greater complexity. This complexity is characterized by constant change and unpredictable course corrections that often have direct or indirect impacts on businesses and entire industries.

Our fundamental premise in this chapter is that the root cause of the innovation gap is the inability to effectively manage the complexity inherent in the knowledge economy. Enhancing the ability to *lead through complexity* will

---

1. David Churbuck, "The Innovation Moment," *Forrester Magazine*, Issue #1, 2005, p. 51.

dramatically contribute to closing the innovation gap. We also argue that the biggest obstacle to leading through complexity is the way leaders think today, and the most effective way to lead through complexity is to apply innovative thinking to tap into the innovative intelligence of leaders, their employees, and their teams.

The most effective way to lead through complexity is to apply innovative thinking.

As a result, new leaders need to:

- Be skilled in using innovative thinking to respond to complex problems
- Build an organizational climate that supports the systematic use of innovative thinking by leaders, employees, and teams
- Be able to remove obstacles that block the use of innovative thinking in the organization.

To close the innovation gap, leaders throughout the organization must be effective at leading through complexity and developing innovative solutions for business success.

WHY COMPLEX ISSUES ARE SO CHALLENGING

Many leaders succeeded in the past because they were excellent at solving problems through the application of their prior experiences and logic. They responded to a complicated problem by breaking it down, simplifying it, solving the smaller problems, and then putting the parts back together again. They applied what they had learned, used "best practices" that worked elsewhere, and hired the right consultants who knew the solutions to the new problems they encountered. This approach worked best in the industrial economy, where success depended on streamlined and repeatable processes and the environment was relatively slow changing and predictable. Many organizations put in place systems and mechanisms to develop this kind of leadership.

However, now the world of work has been transformed to a knowledge economy, and many of the approaches of the past are no longer as effective. The new complexities of the knowledge economy make work less predictable and constantly demand new and innovative solutions. Yesterday's answers are often not good enough anymore.

Rather than looking for similarities, the new innovative leader needs to encourage teams to uncover the unique aspects of problems that distinguish them from previous problems. This requires an intellectual capability that goes beyond logic and that often conflicts with what made leaders successful in the past. Some organizations are finding that they do not have internal leadership talent who can lead effectively through this kind of complexity. Unfortunately, they also are not successful at sourcing it externally. Apparently, leaders who can help an organization deal with complexity are in short supply.

Almost all organizations have undergone changes in their business environments, which are characterized by increased complexity. This includes organizations in the knowledge economy, as well as manufacturing and the rapidly growing service sector. It also includes social enterprise (non-profit) and public sector environments, where the metrics and outcomes are unclear and the various stakeholder interests may be conflicting. For example, at a time when the future appears less and less predictable, leaders in the public sector need to answer the very complex question: "What is in the long-term good of the public?" They need to systematically assess how to balance multiple stakeholder interests and to look into the future to identify the long-term implications of their decisions. These changes are also affecting internal organizational departments, such as Marketing, Information Technology, Finance, and HR, which are facing increasingly complex challenges in their attempts to support the business strategy.

The need for leaders who can lead through complexity is a challenge throughout the world, as one of the authors[2] learned when he spoke at a conference in India. Many leaders in India are effective within their own country. However, as companies in India globalize, either in support of global companies or as global players themselves, there are new expectations

2. David S. Weiss, "HR Value Proposition," Presented at the *Asia Pacific Human Resources Association Conference*. Mumbai, India. February 13, 2008.

of them. They must learn to interact cross-culturally and deal with new complexities. Many leaders initially attempted to respond to the complexity by seeking simple solutions based upon what worked in the past. However, times have changed. The "old" leadership thinking approach is not generating the kinds of solutions that are required for the new complex work situations. Problems in the current work environment require new ways of thinking that extend beyond what the leaders know and how they were trained to think.

One senior executive, reminiscing about the good old days, reflected on the changes in the kinds of challenges she experiences now and said: "It seems like we no longer solve problems—we only manage dilemmas." She was quite correct. The luxury of having a simple problem and a simple solution is rare in our current business environment.

If a leader approaches problems assuming they can be simplified (when that is not the case), then that leader will likely make errors in decision making. Most issues that leaders encounter today are extremely complex and require sophisticated and innovative approaches to gain insight into the real issue and to discover the best course of action to take.

COMPLICATED VS. COMPLEX ISSUES

We use the term *issues* to refer to both problems and opportunities. There are essentially three kinds of issues:

- Those that are simple and need to be solved quickly
- Those that are complicated and need to be simplified
- Those that are complex and need to be addressed through innovative thinking processes.

Simple issues are tasks that require a single solution that remains constant. Examples include how one turns on a light or boils water.

Table 2.1 summarizes some of the characteristics of complicated and complex issues and the thinking approach that would best address those issues.[3]

---

3. Ralph D. Stacey, *Strategic Management and Organisational Dynamics: The Challenge of Complexity to Ways of Thinking about Organisations* (Prentice Hall, 1993).

Table 2.1: Complicated vs. Complex Issues

	Complicated Issues	Complex Issues
Characteristics	Multi-faceted repeatable problems that need to be simplified and organized	Ambiguous and somewhat unique problems and stakeholder relations that need to be understood
Thinking Approach	***Traditional Analytical Thinking:***	***Innovative Thinking:***
	Leverage existing expertise to develop a repeatable solution that simplifies and solves the complicated problem	Use innovative thinking to deal effectively with the ambiguity and gain insight into the complexity that makes this problem unique, before discovering potential solutions

Let's explore the characteristics of complicated and complex issues in greater detail.

Leading Complicated Issues

Many leaders excel at applying their past experiences to resolve complicated issues that need to be simplified and organized. A prototypical example of a complicated problem is a manufacturing process that needs to be simplified so that workers can perform their part of the process more effectively. Many of the processes and procedures in the industrial economy were designed to simplify or streamline complicated problems. In the industrial economy, an efficient organization could be compared to a machine where consistent processes produced predictable outcomes. As long as the "machine" analogy worked well in the workplace, this approach was extremely effective.[4]

Some of the implications for organizations that encounter a wide array of complicated issues are as follows:

- *Leaders who master complicated process are promoted.* Many organizations select or promote people to leadership roles because they understand the entire complicated process and can fix the process or tell others how to fix it if something goes wrong.

---

4. Brenda Zimmerman, Associate Professor of Policy, Schulich School of Business, York University in Toronto, Canada, uses the machine analogy to describe complicated problems.

- *Leaders focus on knowing the answers.* Leaders are "answer people," and employees seek them out for their decisions about what to do. Most of the complicated problems have repeatable solutions, so the leaders apply their knowledge and logic to simplify and solve the complicated issues.
- *Experts combine their knowledge to resolve complicated issues.* The most complicated issues are resolved by having a group of experts who understand the complication sort through the issue, simplify it, and figure out how to fix the problem.
- *Best practices are very helpful.* Often, best practices and benchmarks are very useful because a solution to a complicated problem that surfaced elsewhere can be applied to the complicated problem that the leaders are experiencing here and now.

Leading Complex Issues

Some of the important aspects about the new complex problems at work are as follows:

- They are not as predictable as complicated problems and require new innovative approaches.
- They are unique problems that are often not repeated.
- They often have many uncertain and ambiguous components that need to be understood without artificially simplifying them.
- They may involve aligning multiple stakeholders.
- They require innovative thinking in order to first gain insight into the uniqueness of the issue and then to discover the most effective solutions.

Some examples of complex issues include:

- Stakeholder, shareholder, or government relations
- Responding to emerging technologies and non-traditional competitors
- Understanding changes in customer purchasing patterns
- Leading within a diverse cultural and multi-generational workforce

Complex issues need leaders who are effective at innovative thinking and who are able to build climates that will foster the use of innovative thinking by everyone. Expertise in a past problem can cause leaders to jump to conclusions and assume that the new complex problem is the same as a past problem. That's because the leader viewed the complex problem as a complicated one. Instead of focusing on the uniqueness of the complexity, which distinguished it from previous problems, the leader assumed that the problem was not unique, that the ambiguity could be ignored, and that a quick answer that was used before would suffice.

Some of the implications for organizations and leaders facing a wide array of complex issues are as follows:

- *Who is selected or promoted to leadership positions.* Organizations need to select, develop, and promote to leadership roles people who can think innovatively and ask the right questions to reveal underlying assumptions and to discover the root causes of the complexity.
- *Leaders focus on facilitating the process.* A leader needs to excel at facilitating innovative thinking rather than being the most innovative person. A leader's role is to raise the overall innovative thinking capacity of employees and teams so they understand a complex issue thoroughly before even considering a resolution. Employees seek out their leaders to discuss and think through what they might do. Most complex problems are unique, so a leader needs to excel at asking questions to expose the underlying assumptions and uniqueness of the issue that created the complexity.
- *Diverse groups work better on complex issues.* Complex issues require people with diverse opinions and professional backgrounds to approach the issue from different perspectives and to uncover alternative solutions not considered in the past.[5] A diverse group looks at the issue in different ways and can more easily challenge assumptions and discover the underlying complexities in the issue. This is much preferred to a group of homogeneous experts who may all arrive at a similar understanding of the problem and potentially the same answer—which may be simple, but is often wrong.
- *Best practices can be misleading*[6]. Often, best practices and benchmarks can lead an innovation team astray because the team may select the external solution before understanding the unique complexity of the

5. IBM, *Rethinking Innovation* (Fast Thinking Books, 2008).
6. For a more elaborate discussion of this issue see David S. Weiss, Vince Molinaro & Liane Davey, *Leadership Solutions: The Pathway to Bridge the Leadership Gap* (Jossey-Bass, 2007, p. 18–19).

issue they are facing. The best practice that worked well in another organization may not be an adequate solution to the current complex problem. For example, when traditional industrial-type organizations attempt to be more innovative, their first instinct is to look for examples of other companies that have been successful at innovation. However, the examples they are trying to emulate were developed in a different business context, with different leaders and different stakeholders and customers. In a complex environment, each of these distinctions reduces the ability to generalize best practice solutions.

Of course, few issues are purely complicated or purely complex. Most complicated issues have elements of complexity, and most complex issues have elements of complication. On top of it, most of them involve people who augment the degree of difficulty and unpredictability. Nevertheless, it is a very useful practice for leaders to consider whether an issue is predominantly complicated or predominantly complex and then apply the proper thinking approach, depending upon the nature of the particular problem.

There are some useful clues to help leaders know if a problem is mainly complicated or complex. In general, complicated issues can be broken down into distinct parts, and machine and systems analogies are often used. Complex issues usually are problems for which:

- There are some unchallenged assumptions.
- Past solutions do not seem to work.
- Many stakeholders are involved.
- There are significant elements that are unpredictable and ambiguous.

Leaders must know whether to approach a problem as an expert simplifying a complicated problem or as an innovative thinker trying to discover the underlying complexities of a unique dilemma. Leaders need to be able to approach different parts of problems with different thinking approaches.

Many managers and leaders (and indeed, executives) have difficulty with innovative thinking. In part this is because (1) they do not know how to separate complicated and complex issues because they have never considered the difference and (2) even if they correctly identify the issue as complex, they may not know how to use innovative thinking processes to gain insight into and discover a solution to the complex problem. They were not taught how to be innovative thinkers or how to lead through complexity. Unfortunately, leaders often do not innately include innovative thinking as one of their thinking styles.

All leaders need to be capable of applying their own and their team's innovative thinking to complex issues, and they need to see innovative thinking as a core characteristic of their work. They also need to engage employees, teams, peers, and external stakeholders in open dialogue about the complexities in order to understand them and discover the best way to proceed.

COMMON MISTAKES

Here are five common mistakes that occur often when leading through complexity.

Common Mistakes When Leading Through Complexity
1. Talking more than doing
2. Solving complex issues with approaches used for complicated issues
3. Focusing on creativity and games
4. Expecting the leaders to be the most innovative people
5. Assuming that leaders do not need to understand how innovation happens

---

1. **Talking more than doing**

    The most common mistake is that some executives believe that if they tell leaders to be innovative, they will become innovative and more effective at solving complex issues. Unfortunately, it does not work. Often, an executive team may initially identify that their organization needs more and better innovation. They then repeat the message to their leaders and employees, hoping that they will act upon it. In some cases they may ask the training department to teach employees to be more innovative, but isolated training programs without ongoing support and reinforcement have little impact. Executives need to do more than say they want innovation; they need to become the role models of innovative thinking and foster an organizational climate that promotes innovation and innovative thinking.

2. **Solving complex issues with approaches adapted to complicated issues**

Responding to complex issues by applying a process appropriate for complicated problems is an error. When leaders try to simplify complex problems, they often miss the underlying complexity and end up solving the wrong problem, which, many times, is only a symptom of the real issue. The solution may look simple and effective at first, but it will most likely fail to achieve the expected result. For example, some organizations engage in "budget-based strategic planning," whereby they simplify strategic planning down to an exercise of completing financial spreadsheets. These spreadsheets are based on the assumption that the future will be a linear extension of the past. The solution may appear logical, but strategically it is wrong because the executives did not thoroughly consider the complexities of the evolving business environment.

The corollary of this mistake is that it would be an error to apply an innovative thinking process to a complicated problem that just needs to be simplified. Innovative approaches can sometimes make solving a complicated problem more challenging than it needs to be.

3. **Focusing on creativity and games**

Although this mistake has lost some of its appeal recently (and rightly so), some organizations still believe this solution works. Here is an example:

The CEO heard an enthusiastic talk on the need for more creativity in the workplace and made an impassioned speech to his Executive Team: "We know we need more ideas, but we continue to identify inadequate answers. I just heard this great speaker, and I want him to train our employees in creativity. He can show employees how to discover creative ideas." All the executives nodded. The training department was put in charge of this project, and they did help employees generate some creative ideas. However, most of the executives were not on board with the program and made excuses not to attend. When the employees returned to their offices and started proposing creative ideas, most senior managers questioned the thoughtfulness of the ideas and told the employees to stay focused on their jobs. The few ideas they tried were not tested, so they were not well executed. The ideas didn't answer the major issues of the company, and most attempts at creativity were rejected because the ideas generated were too risky. Within four months, the creativity program became history, and the organization returned to the way it was before the infamous speech.

What made this company's error even more damaging was the impact it had on the reputation of creativity and innovation in this company. Some leaders discouraged employees from further attempts at creativity and innovation. The employees stopped offering ideas to improve the organization, the best and most creative individuals began to leave the organization, and new executive-sponsored initiatives were labeled as "flavors of the month" and really did not receive the attention they deserved. Unfortunately, this organization was not able to initiate a good innovation initiative until the corporate memory of the event had faded.

4. **Expecting the leaders to be the most innovative people**
    In the industrial economy, leaders were expected to be the smartest people who had the best answers. So it should not be a surprise that many executives expect leaders to be the most innovative in order to lead through complexity and create an innovative business. However, this is not an appropriate expectation. Leveraging the innovative thinking of their employees and teams maximizes the innovative potential of the entire group. This should be the primary role of leaders when they lead through complexity. Just educating leaders about how they can be more innovative is not enough. They also need to excel at creating and sustaining an innovative climate that encourages innovation among their employees and teams.

    This was demonstrated in a study by Akkermans, Isaksen, and Isaksen.[7] They found that the most important role for leaders is to influence and build an innovative organizational climate, and the organizational climate will contribute to greater innovative productivity. They also found that leaders who demonstrate innovative

---

7. Hans J. L. Akkermans, Scott G. Isaksen & Erik J. Isaksen, "Leadership For Innovation: A Global Climate Survey," Creative Research Unit Technical Report, Fall 2008.

behavior themselves but do not build an innovative climate do not have a strong correlation with greater innovative productivity. The implication of this research is that it is more important to teach leaders how to lead innovation, how to create an innovative climate, and how to facilitate innovative thinking than it is to teach leaders how to be innovative themselves. Leaders who are innovative thinkers themselves can function as good role models for an innovative climate, and they can become more effective participants in innovative teams; however, they must be careful not to overwhelm the teams they lead with their own innovative ideas because that might stifle the group's innovative thinking.

Organizations need many teams with well-developed innovative thinking capabilities and leaders who can draw out the innovative talents of their employees and teams. Leaders need to work with their teams to gain insight into the underlying complexity of an issue, to think innovatively to discover potential solutions, and then to mitigate the risks of the recommended innovative solutions.

5. **Assuming that leaders do not need to understand how innovation happens**
One reason for the lack of systematic innovation in organizations is that most executives have not learned how innovation happens and do not have a plan for it. Most of the current leaders and executives never studied innovation and do not understand how it happens—organization-wide innovation is not considered a proper academic discipline in most business schools.

The result is an over-reliance on ready-made, pre-packaged innovation solutions. If executives chose their accounting or legal advisors the way they choose their innovation suppliers, by picking the first one that promises results, more organizations would fail. Instead of trying to understand how innovation really happens, too many executives try to eliminate the problem by implementing a solution that appears to make sense to them at the time. They also tend to choose the simpler solution, whether it works or not and whether it has the potential to create long-term benefit or not.

CONCLUSION

Many organizations have not fundamentally changed their approach to innovation, even though the pace of the knowledge economy and the nature of work has radically changed. Although many organizations continued to deliver new answers and develop new tools, they did this within the context of the old industrial economy. Organizations developed new solutions perfectly adapted to the old economy, without dealing with the fact that the context was changing dramatically. A profusion of new answers flowed forth, but results were, at best, partial and short-term.

Many organizations found that their efforts at innovation did not work well because they ignored the new context, did not fully understand the problem, and churned out great solutions to the wrong problems. The pervading corporate culture operated on the premise that if they threw enough corporate intelligence at a problem, they would find an answer; consequently, they focused on finding quick answers rather than on questioning the question. In turn, this created an environment that made it tough for innovative leaders to address the larger context of a problem when the demand for short-term results was so strong, so persistent, and so lucrative. Many believed that it was easier and more profitable in the short-term to recommend solutions than it was to attempt to unravel the complexity of the problem and prolong the wait for answers.

We have found that the challenge is better served if leaders excel at struggling with the complexity and understanding its underlying assumptions—rather than leaping to solutions. Effective leaders do not need to be the innovators or the ones who come up with the solutions. Rather, leaders in the knowledge economy need to understand and model the process of innovative thinking and be able to reinforce its use by their direct reports, their teams, and everyone in the organization. They also must create organizational culture and practices that reinforce the use of innovative thinking by individuals and teams, and at the same time they need to systematically remove obstacles to the application of innovative thinking and the implementation of new and valuable ideas to resolve complex issues.

The next chapter provides the missing ingredient that explains why it is often so difficult for leaders to lead through complexity by thinking innovatively—the inability of leaders to access and develop their *Innovative Intelligence*.

CHAPTER THREE

ACCESSING INNOVATIVE INTELLIGENCE

A military officer in a combat zone detects an approaching enemy attack. He immediately searches his mental database to find a similar situation he has encountered previously, either in battle or in training. He remembers a somewhat similar situation and, regardless of the limited points of similarity, he automatically makes the prior situation fit his current one. He immediately acts on the answer he has applied before—but, unfortunately, the answer is wrong, and disastrous results occur.

This thinking process is the antithesis of what the military wants or needs today. Modern military leaders need to know when it is time for consolidation and when it is time for innovation. They need to know when it is time for discipline, conformity, tenacity, and action and when it is time for reflection, questioning, and independent thought. What needs to be instilled in military leaders is the good judgment to determine which kind of "intelligence" is required in any given situation.

The same challenge exists for leaders within any business organization. Every leader has the innate potential of innovative intelligence, the proof being that most children are able to develop new and creative ideas. The challenge for leaders is to access and put to organizational use the innovative intelligence they previously were able to access as children.

We define *innovative intelligence* as the human cognitive ability to look at problems or opportunities in new ways and to discover new implementable solutions. To respond to complex challenges effectively, leaders need to access their innovative intelligence and to drive the use of innovative intelligence throughout their organizations. If leaders are not able to do this, then their chances of closing the innovation gap will be minimal.

Innovative intelligence is the human cognitive ability to gain insight into problems or opportunities in new ways and to discover new and unforeseen implementable solutions.

INTELLIGENCE: WHO KNOWS?

We need to explore selected aspects of the very challenging construct of *intelligence* in order to understand how we approach *innovative intelligence* in this book.

There are many theories and books about what intelligence is and how it manifests in human beings. Despite the extensive literature on the subject, there is no universal agreement or clear definition of human intelligence. For example, a number of years ago, two dozen prominent theorists were asked to define intelligence, and they gave two dozen somewhat different definitions.[1]

Some experts assert that intelligence cannot be observed, only measured, which means that any definition of intelligence is characterized by, and limited to, how it is measured. There is no better example of this than the century-old measure commonly referred to as IQ (Intelligence Quotient).

In essence, intelligence as measured by IQ (we will refer to it as "analytical intelligence") assumes that our intellectual brain operates on logic and an immense registry of information and employs the premise that most of yesterday's facts will be today's and tomorrow's truths. It operates primarily on a system of rote computation based on a finite inventory of learned information and experiences. It is a powerful system, one that discovers and understands such complicated principles as the Pythagorean Theorem[2] and those as simple as $1 + 1 = 2$.

Thinking is the process we use to access our intelligences, in addition to our stored knowledge. In the past, the belief that intelligence and

---

1. Robert J. Sternberg and Douglas K. Detterman, *What is Intelligence?: Contemporary Viewpoints on its Nature and Definition* (Ablex Publishing, 1986).
2. Pythagorean theorem is that the square of the hypotenuse of a right-angle triangle is equal to the sum of the squares of the other two sides.

thinking were the same often led to the conclusion that people with high analytical intelligence (higher IQ scores) were automatically good thinkers and that people with weaker analytical intelligence (lower IQ scores) were not good thinkers. Of course, highly intelligent people can be good thinkers, but this does not follow automatically. In addition, intelligence is not just inborn but can increase with experience; thus, high intelligence is both innate and socially influenced, and thinking is a skill that can be developed.

Edward de Bono offers a helpful metaphor. The relationship between intelligence and thinking is like that between a car and the driver of that car. Someone may drive a powerful car badly and waste its potential. Another individual may drive a less powerful car well and fully utilize its potential. The power of the car is the potential of the car, just as intelligence is the potential of the mind. The skill of the car driver determines how the power of the car is used. The skill of the thinker determines how the potential of intelligence is used.[3]

Notwithstanding the logic of this explanation, differences of opinion about how to define intelligence are still widespread.

Our approach to innovative intelligence in this book relies on these three premises:

Premises About Intelligence

Premise #1: Humans have multiple intelligences.

Premise #2: Intelligences exist in potential until we access them.

Premise #3: Context determines whether intelligence potential is realized.

Premise #1: Humans Have Multiple Intelligences

It was commonly accepted throughout most of the 1900s that there is only one intelligence and that it can be measured by IQ. Since 1983, a number of theorists have argued the concept that humans have multiple intelligences. For example, Howard Gardner argued that "there are multiple intelligences rather than a unitary concept of intelligence" and proposed the notion that

---

3. Edward de Bono, "de Bono's Thinking Course," BBC Active, 2006.

humans have seven intelligences.[4] Robert Sternberg[5] argued that humans have three intelligences: analytic (academic), practical, and creative, which he refers to as the "Triarchic Mind." Daniel Goleman's concept of emotional intelligence also is dependent on the premise that humans have multiple intelligences. We accept this premise of multiple intelligences and use it when we introduce the multiple intelligences required of leaders at work.

Premise #2: Intelligences Exist in Potential until We Access Them

Gardner indicates that intelligences are "potentialities or proclivities which are realized or not realized depending on the cultural context in which they are found."[6] We accept this perspective as a premise that humans are born with intelligence "in potentiality." The notion of understanding intelligence as potentiality is very important for our work. It suggests that intelligence can exist without it being used. We use this premise to argue that leaders in organizations already have innovative intelligence in potentiality; it just needs to be developed into reality so they can access it when they need it.

Premise #3: Context Determines whether Intelligence Potential Is Realized

The potential of intelligence is developed (or not developed) within a context. As Gardner indicates, "intelligence cannot be conceptualized apart from the context in which individuals live."[7] In this book, we focus our attention on the context of the work setting and demonstrate that it is possible to change the work context by influencing organizational practices and culture, as well as the talent that is brought in and developed.

Our intent in this book is to teach how to develop leaders' innovative thinking to enable them to realize their innovative intelligence potentiality. Our purpose is also to show how an organization can create the context and enhance the ability of both leaders and teams to access their innovative intelligence.

---

4. Howard Gardner, *Multiple Intelligences* (Basic Books, 1993), p. 8.
5. Robert J. Sternberg, *The Triarchic Mind: A New Theory of Human Intelligence* (Viking Press, 1988).
6. Howard Gardner, *Multiple Intelligences* (Basic Books, 1993), p. 221.
7. Howard Gardner, *Multiple Intelligences* (Basic Books, 1993), p. 223.

LEADERS REQUIRE THREE INTELLIGENCES

We argue that there are three primary intelligences that are essential for leaders in organizations, as shown below in Figure 3.1. These are:

1. Analytical intelligence
2. Emotional intelligence
3. Innovative intelligence

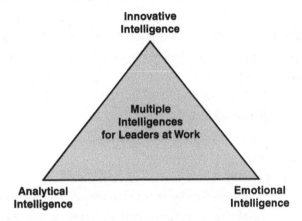

Figure 3.1: The Three Essential Intelligences for Leaders in the Workplace

Here is a description of the three essential intelligences for leaders at work:

- Analytical Intelligence
  Most leaders require analytical skills that are developed through standard school-based academic courses of study.[8] Analytical intelligence is often measured through IQ or IQ-equivalent testing. When leaders fulfill their potential for analytical intelligence, they have the ability to do the following:
    - Apply their literacy and numeracy skills.
    - Apply their memory of solutions to solve many complicated problems at work.
    - Apply logic to problem-solving situations that are extensions of problems solved in the past.

---

8. Robert J. Sternberg, *The Triarchic Mind: A New Theory of Human Intelligence* (Viking Press, 1988).

- Emotional Intelligence
  Emotional intelligence[9] governs self-knowledge and self-adaptation. It refers to the area of cognitive ability involving traits and social skills that facilitate interpersonal behavior. Emotional intelligence involves being "emotionally adept—knowing and managing feelings well, and being able to read and deal effectively with other people's feelings."[10] In work settings, people manage their emotions so that they are expressed appropriately and effectively, enabling them to work smoothly with others toward common goals. It is widely accepted as an essential intelligence for leaders, and it is an important predictor of success in the workplace.[11] The four major skills that make up emotional intelligence are:
  - Self-awareness
  - Self-management
  - Social awareness
  - Relationship management
- Innovative Intelligence
  We define innovative intelligence for leaders as the *capability of gaining insights into complex problems or opportunities and discovering new and unforeseen implementable solutions.* When leaders have access to their innovative intelligence, they can solve the real issues, produce better solutions, and help others become more innovative. The two components of innovative intelligence are problem insight and solution discovery.
  - *Problem insight*
    Leaders are able to use their innovative intelligence to generate insights in a variety of situations, including the following:
    - *Insight within an issue:* Leaders think through the unique complexities of the problem in order to understand it fully before engaging in problem resolution.

---

9. The concept of emotional intelligence was first introduced by Peter Salovey and John D. Mayer in *Emotional Intelligence. Imagination, Cognition, and Personality,* 9 (1990) p. 185–211. Another model of emotional intelligence is in Reuven Bar-On, *The Development of a Concept of Psychological Well-Being,* Ph.D. dissertation, Rhodes University, South Africa, 1988. The concept was popularized by Daniel Goleman, *Emotional Intelligence: Why It Can Matter More Than IQ* (Bantam Books, 1995).
10. Daniel Goleman, *Emotional Intelligence: Why It Can Matter More Than IQ* (Bantam Books. 1995), p. 36.
11. See Wayne Payne, A *Study of Emotion: Developing Emotional Intelligence* (1985). This doctoral thesis is the first reference to emotional intelligence in the literature (taken from the website "TechTarget").

- *Insight outside of an issue:* Leaders gain insight from external and diverse ideas to formulate new ways of understanding the issue.
- *Insight before an issue exists:* Leaders generate insights to forecast potential problems or opportunities before an issue arises.
- *Insight after encountering an issue:* Leaders see and understand patterns of experiences and events to contribute to insights about future issues.

- *Solution discovery*

Leaders are able to use their innovative intelligence to discover a range of possible new solutions and to identify the most effective solution under the circumstances.

- *Discovery through divergence:* Leaders fully explore possible solutions by generating, combining, and arranging existing and new ideas, elements, and methods without any judgment.
- *Discovery through convergence:* Leaders refine ideas and choose the best aspects of each to create a "best-fit" solution to resolve the complex issue.

Table 3.1 on the following page describes the characteristics of the three intelligences, how they are accessed, and their strengths and weaknesses.

Leaders need access to all three intelligences (analytical, emotional, and innovative), and they also need the ability to discern which intelligence or combination of intelligences best fits the issues they encounter. However, many organizations do not give sufficient attention to all three intelligences. Our assessment of the current state of leadership development in the three intelligences is as follows:

- *Analytical intelligence:* Most leaders enter the workforce with acceptable levels of analytical intelligence based on their academic training, and they continue to develop their analytical skills through their work experience. For many leaders, well-developed analytical skills often lead to promotions and career opportunities. Organizations often enhance leaders' analytical thinking by providing challenging projects,

Table 3.1: The Three Intelligences, How They Are Accessed, Strengths, and Weaknesses

	Analytical Intelligence	**Emotional Intelligence**	**Innovative Intelligence**
Characteristics	• Always one right answer • Ability to combine logic and existing knowledge to retrieve the "right" answer	• Ensuring emotions (of self and others) are considered • Awareness of self and others and their interactions	• Identifying the solution that is the best fit to resolve the complex issue at this time • Ability to combine multiple sources in new ways to identify a better answer perfectly adapted to the real issue
How we can access it	IQ thinking or its equivalent • Apply literacy and numeracy skills • Apply memory • Apply logic	Emotional awareness • Self-awareness • Self-management • Social awareness • Relationship management	Innovative thinking • Identify the issue • Generate ideas • Generate solutions • Plan the implementation
Strengths	Works well if an issue is linear and predictable and the issue has previously been solved successfully in a similar context	Makes us aware of the emotional (people) side of every issue, complex or complicated	Essential if an issue is complex, in particular when the issue is ambiguous, there is minimal precedent, and when stakeholders disagree
Weaknesses	Can lead to wrong solutions when the context is changing, the outcome is unpredictable, and where stakeholders disagree	May divert the focus to interpersonal variables that may not be relevant for issues that are exclusively scientific or technical	Can waste time when an issue is complicated, in particular when the issue is predictable and has a clearly defined precedent in a similar context

learning programs in areas such as strategy, planning, critical thinking, and through business processes.

• *Emotional intelligence:* In the past decade the concept of emotional intelligence[12] has been widely accepted, and many organizations have explored how to develop their leaders' emotional intelligence. The language of emotional intelligence is now commonly used, and people have a greater awareness that it is a key factor in the success of leaders

12. Peter Salovey and John D. Mayer, *Emotional Intelligence. Imagination, Cognition, and Personality*, 9 (1990) p. 185–211; Daniel Goleman, *Emotional Intelligence: Why It Can Matter More Than IQ* (Bantam Books, 1995).

and executives. Many organizations focus their leadership development courses on the assessment and development of leaders on a personal level, which sometimes includes the explicit development of their emotional intelligence.

- *Innovative intelligence:* Very few organizations have invested in the development of leaders' innovative intelligence or in their ability to access it. We suggest this lack of investment is a primary contributor to the innovation gap in many organizations. Also, very few organizations focus their development on the integration of the three intelligences to develop holistic leaders.[13] This book, *Innovative Intelligence*, was written to help rectify these oversights.

Leaders also need to be aware of the impacts of combining more than one intelligence to address an issue. Table 3.2 summarizes the impact of the combination of analytical, innovative, and emotional intelligences.

Leaders also need to be able to create a working climate in which all employees and teams can access their three intelligences—analytical, emotional, and innovative—in order to deliver maximum value to their customers, stakeholders, and employees.

Leaders are accountable for maximizing the access to and use of the full potential of the innovative intelligence of all of their employees and teams.

To deliver business value, leaders need to maximize their teams' and employees' innovative intelligence potential. The practical techniques described later in this book clarify how leaders can do this by:

1. Facilitating the innovative thinking process so that individuals and teams can access their innovative intelligence. Leaders need to assist employees and teams as they apply their innovative thinking to resolve problems or take advantage of opportunities.

---

13. The topic of holistic leadership is explored in depth in David S. Weiss, Vince Molinaro & Liane Davey, *Leadership Solutions: The Pathway To Bridge the Leadership Gap* (Jossey-Bass, 2007); and in David S. Weiss and Vince Molinaro, *The Leadership Gap: Building Leadership Capacity For Competitive Advantage* (John Wiley & Sons, 2005).

Table 3.2: Interactions of Analytical, Innovative, and Emotional Thinking

Combination of Intelligences	Positive Impact	Potential Negative Impact
Emotional intelligence and Analytical intelligence	• Adds the "people" side to every problem-solving situation • More rigorous process to look at emotional issues • An excellent combination for complicated problems with people involved	• Maximum value for complicated problems is not gained if the two intelligences are not balanced • A person's emotional adeptness can enhance influencing skills even if they are promoting the wrong solution, which could result in the adoption of an invalid solution
Emotional intelligence and Innovative intelligence	• Very effective for complex issues with a strong people component in the issue or in the implementation of a solution • Helpful to enhance interpersonal maturity of innovative teams	• Need to balance the two intelligences to get maximum value for complex issues • May restrain spontaneity and playfulness when brainstorming creative ideas
Innovative intelligence and Analytical intelligence	• An effective combination for issues that include both complicated and complex elements	• Conflict between the priorities of the two processes. The analytical thinking wants to get to the solution, while the innovative thinking wants to "stay" in the problem as long as necessary
Innovative intelligence and Analytical intelligence and Emotional intelligence	• Best combination for business as it taps into the leaders' full potential • This combination works best when the process of innovative thinking is used as a driver and analytical and emotional "tools" are applied when appropriate	• Possibility of getting overwhelmed by the different signals from the three intelligences • Possibility of conflicts between the tools and processes used for analytical intelligence and innovative intelligence

2. Engaging in conversations with employees and teams to assist them in the discovery of new implementable solutions to existing or anticipated problems or opportunities.

3. Leveraging organizational practices, cultures, and processes that enable and encourage individuals and teams to innovate, rather than inhibiting access to innovative intelligence.

Here is an example of how a leader was able to maximize the innovative intelligence of her team, which resulted in a competitive advantage for her organization.

This leader's team met to consider how to launch a new product line similar to a line that a third-party contractor was providing. One of the team members believed the company could generate new revenue by becoming a third-party contractor for their own customers. He felt strongly that they needed to proceed down this path immediately. However, in the team discussion, many argued that if they followed this path, they risked alienating their current third-party contractor and that other employees would perceive this idea as borderline unethical behavior. Some on the team felt the risk was potentially too damaging for the team to recommend. The leader facilitated an innovative thinking process with the team to explore the complexity further rather than abandon the idea entirely. The team proceeded to challenge several assumptions about the new initiative, uncovered the underlying complexity of the issue, and then clearly redefined the problem. The leader then facilitated a brainstorming process that generated many ideas. They combined various insights and crafted a way to partner with the current third-party contractor rather than competing with them.[14]

By helping the team engage in innovative thinking, the leader in the above example maximized the team's ability to access their innovative intelligence. By tackling this issue jointly, the team maintained the internal trust, kept the service provided by the third-party contractor, and delivered a credible product to the marketplace.

LEADERS NEED TO THINK ABOUT THINKING

Becoming aware of thinking about the way they think and understanding how to make choices about which intelligence to apply in any given situation is critical for leaders. Specifically, they need to know how to use their innovative intelligence in the workplace for themselves, their employees, and their teams.

Here is our definition of "thinking" in the work context—thinking in organizations is an integrative process that helps employees and teams solve problems.

---

14. This example first appeared in David S. Weiss and Claude Legrand, "Innovative Team Learning: Maximizing the Value of Learning and Working Together," *Canadian Learning Journal.* Volume 13, Number 1, Spring 2009.

Thinking is a complex cognitive process by which leaders access their intelligences, knowledge, and experiences in order to solve problems (small or large, known or unknown, current or future). Thinking can be applied to elements as diverse as:

- Setting a course for the organization
- Working on the structure and culture
- Making teams more effective
- Solving large and small customer issues
- Improving processes at all levels.

Thinking is a process of solving problems or identifying opportunities, of challenging what is known, and arguing for what is needed by mixing different forms of intelligence with logic, knowledge, reason, beliefs, or emotions.

Leaders need to be aware of how they think, reflect on how to improve their thinking, and be competent at choosing how they will think and which intelligence to access in any given situation. This expectation of leaders implies a prerequisite that they think about thinking—which, unfortunately, most leaders do not do.

We often test this assumption when we speak at conferences or at our *Leading Innovation* sessions. Consider this interaction that recently occurred during one of our conference presentations. It began with the posing of some simple questions:

The presenter asked: "Do any of you think about how you think?" Most people were stunned by the question, so he elaborated: "Do you think about your process for solving problems or about how you analyzed a situation and reached a solution?" When there continued to be silence, the presenter then asked a more provocative question: "Do you think?" After some laughter, the presenter suggested that most people do not choose to think in one way or another; they simply follow automatic patterns. Yet most people are fully capable of deciding which style of thinking to use and how to think for any given issue they encounter.

On some occasions, participants do describe how they would like to think or how they believe they thought the last time they were confronted with a major challenge. However, their professed method of thinking often is not the same as the way they actually think. Table 3.3 presents an example of the professed way of thinking versus what is often the actual way of thinking.

Table 3.3: Professed Way of Thinking Versus Actual Way of Thinking

Professed Way of Thinking	Actual Way of Thinking
A supervisor or a client identifies an issue or a problem.	A supervisor or client gives me a problem which I accept unquestioningly as THE problem; it would be inappropriate to challenge or question it.
I analyze all the relevant facts and the boundaries to understand the problem clearly.	I recognize the problem as quickly as possible. If I do not recognize it as is, then I look for a "close enough" problem that I had in the past.
I understand and separate the symptoms from the root causes.	I am encouraged to take action rather than think. I immediately look for a solution that best answers the problem. If I do not have a ready-made solution, then I take the first one that occurs to me.
I brainstorm the possible ways to address the challenge.	I stop thinking after I find one solution. I assume that there is only one answer to a problem.
I develop a series of possible alternative solutions, assess risks associated with each solution, and select the best solution among the range of options.	I implement the solution as quickly as possible. I hope the solution fixes the problem and its symptoms.

In the previous scenario, the employee eventually may be told to fix the inadequate solution. The employee often does not go back to the root cause of the poor work, assuming instead that rework is just part of work. When we ask employees how much of their time they spend on rework in an average week, the most common response is between 20 and 50 percent, which validates the actual process of thinking described above. When employees say they have no time for innovative thinking, the first step should always be to look at the amount of rework in their particular environment. The reasons for rework vary greatly and are usually dependent on the area of the organization. The most common factors are:

- Someone (usually the supervisor) changed his or her mind
- Working on the "wrong" problem
- Someone not liking the answer
- Too many (or the wrong) people making decisions
- Unconnected decision layers, the facts changed
- Someone forgot to mention an important fact until after the solution had been given.

Here is an example of a team that used innovative thinking to reduce rework.

The leaders in a bank's marketing department identified that employees needed to engage in more innovative thinking. They oriented the employees to an innovative thinking program, but the employees were very resistant. They complained that they did not have time to think, let alone engage in innovative thinking. The leaders were surprised with their response, so they decided to explore why the employees were so busy. They asked the employees how much time they spent redoing things, and, to their surprise, the answer was between 30 and 50 percent of their time. The employees considered that as part of their jobs and as the normal way of working. So the leaders decided to proceed with the innovative thinking program with a targeted focus on how to reduce rework within their department. The employees felt that if rework could be reduced, it would be a useful business outcome of the program. Within one month, working with only a few teams, they were able to eliminate the most common causes of rework and reduce significantly the time spent on it.

At work, thinking about thinking is fundamental to each person's ability to choose how to consider and resolve issues. It also is the foundation of the work of all leaders and executives. However, there are major impediments that can block leaders' capability to exercise choice in the way they think. These are described in the next chapter.

Our contention is that it is possible to make individuals and organizations systematically and sustainably more innovative and that this process will improve productivity and the ability to close the innovation gap. Our solution is for all employees to learn a more innovative thinking approach, for leaders to maximize their teams' potential by accessing their innovative intelligence, and for organizations to reinforce the new behaviors continuously in their practices and culture.

CONCLUSION

In the knowledge economy, the ability to tap the innovative intelligence of leaders and employees is critical to productivity and competitive advantage. The journey begins by improving how leaders and individuals think and how they access the full potential of their intelligences.

Leaders need access to their analytical, emotional, and innovative intelligences to be effective in the knowledge economy and contribute to closing the innovation gap in their workplace. In addition, they must draw out the innovative intelligence of their employees and teams. Effective leaders also excel at being able to choose which intelligence or combination of intelligences to apply to any given situation. However, some leaders have difficulty reconciling the potential conflicts among their intelligences and integrating them so that they work in synergy with each other. The next chapter explores three dynamics that can block leaders' access to innovative intelligence and provides approaches to respond to these dynamics.

CHAPTER FOUR

ECLIPSE OF INNOVATIVE INTELLIGENCE

At times, leaders may experience interference that can block their ability to access their innovative intelligence. It is similar to an eclipse that occurs when one celestial body obscures all or part of another. In a total lunar eclipse, the moon still exists, even though it cannot be seen. Similarly, when a dynamic or an interfering intelligence obscures access to innovative intelligence, it still exists and is theoretically accessible.

In this chapter we describe three "eclipse" scenarios that can obscure a leader's access to his or her innovative intelligence. We also provide some suggestions to prevent this from occurring or to mitigate its impact.

ECLIPSE #1: THE SCHOOL SYSTEM MADE ME DO IT

Leaders may face obscured access to innovative intelligence as an unintended consequence of the school systems they experienced. For most, school systems focus on transferring skills and knowledge from teachers to students so that students can use that knowledge as they encounter current and future problems. Students learn a repeatable process of how to access their analytical intelligence. At best they also learn *critical thinking*, an evolution of analytical thinking that looks critically at the possible answers.

The characteristics of the process are as follows:

- Relies on past information and experiences
- Operates in a linear fashion

- Focuses on answers
- Does not like ambiguity and uncertainty
- Emphasizes speed
- Seldom questions the question

In school, teachers always ask the question and require their students to have the "right" answers. The more successful students are very analytical and logical or are good at memorizing and therefore are able to access the right answers. The students who give the right answers tend to perform better on tests and receive better grades. Usually, they are rewarded (by teachers, parents, or peers), and the faster they give the right answer, the smarter they are considered to be.

At the outset of the twentieth century, the industrial economy was a complicated environment that needed people with good memories and good logic to be able to replicate a system and resolve complicated problems. Our current school system was developed at that time. It prepared students to function effectively as employees and leaders in the industrial economy, as it answered the industrial demand for people who could "intelligently" replicate mass production models.

However, in the current knowledge economy, workers cannot rely only on memory and logic to succeed. Within the knowledge economy, the "half life" of knowledge and skills (the period of time within which 50 percent of what a person knows or is able to do will become obsolete) is diminishing rapidly. It is estimated that half the new knowledge learned by students in the first year of a four-year post-secondary technology program is obsolete by the time they graduate.[1] Students are often asked to be innovative at school, but they are rarely taught innovative thinking skills. Schools need to give at least equal emphasis to educating students about how to think, how to access all of their intelligences, and how to self-learn. The focus should not be just on content and skills, some of which may be irrelevant by the time the students reach the workforce.

In many cases, the students who have the opportunity to learn from the more innovative and passionate teachers are the students identified as "gifted." However, students are often designated as gifted by some form of analytical intelligence or IQ test (or equivalent), which measures logic and memory, rather than assessing their innovative intelligence. Nothing is wrong

---

1. George Gilder, *Telecosm – The world after bandwidth abundance*, quoted by the author of the video "Did You Know."

with teaching creativity and innovative thinking to gifted analytical thinking students; however, the students who have strong innovative intelligence and only average (but not exceptional or gifted) IQ scores are often not exposed to the "gifted" classes and the most innovative teachers. They will have to follow the standard school curriculum that most often does not teach them to access their innovative intelligence.

Of course, there are alternative schools and some mainstream schools that are introducing innovations in learning and teaching children how to learn.[2] These are important developments. Most good teachers will indicate that they try to develop their students' ability to think differently and innovatively. In addition, new technologies embedded in the Internet and gaming can also help students develop their abilities to learn and access their innovative intelligence independently. All of these developments are part of longer-term educational solutions. However, the current workplace requires more immediate interventions to help leaders and employees overcome the way they have been taught to think in school.

The current workplace requires more immediate interventions to help leaders and employees overcome the way they have been taught to think in school.

Counterbalance the School System Influence by Anchoring an Alternative System at Work

Productivity in the knowledge economy requires leaders to be better thinkers and to have access to all their intelligences, including a well-developed innovative intelligence. It demands thinking that is more flexible and better adapted to each new situation. Leaders need to stop responding automatically, and instead ask themselves what is the best way to think about a specific circumstance. They need to determine which intelligence or combination of intelligences they should access: innovative, emotional, and/or analytical.

The thinking process promoted by school systems is so deeply ingrained in most leaders that they develop a natural proclivity to apply that thinking approach to all problems. However, it is possible to counterbalance this by repeatedly "anchoring" an alternative system. This can be done by embedding specific organizational practices and creating a work culture

---

2. For example, Montessori schools, and secondary schools in Singapore, among others.

that systematically and continuously encourages and validates access to all three intelligences. Organizations also need to simultaneously promote innovative thinking and invest in innovative thinking development programs for employees, teams, and leaders.

Table 4.1 depicts our approach to building an innovative work system that counterbalances the school system and maximizes leaders' access to their innovative intelligence.

Table 4.1: Building an Innovative Work System to Maximize Leaders' Access to their Innovative Intelligence

	People Initiatives	Systemic Initiatives
Internal Motivation	Develop innovative thinking for all leaders and employees.	Build a self-sustaining culture of innovation.
External Motivation	Develop the leaders' ability to access the innovative intelligence of their employees and teams.	Implement organizational practices that systematically reinforce innovative thinking.

If an organization is serious about asking all leaders and employees to use their innovative intelligence to counterbalance the impact of the school system and to close the innovation gap, it needs to implement a full-scale approach. This will require extra effort to create and foster an environment that enables innovation.

To effectively counterbalance the deeply ingrained school system way of thinking, four practices are needed in a work system:

1. *Develop all leaders' and employees' innovative thinking* to ensure that they can think innovatively even without direct support and that they can participate in teams engaged in innovative problem solving (see Chapters 5 to 9).

2. *Develop the leaders' ability to access the innovative intelligence of their employees and teams* to reinforce their innovative thinking and to help the leaders fulfill their accountability to maximize the sum total of their team's innovative intelligence (see Chapter 11).

3. *Build a self-sustaining culture of innovation* to enable and sustain the commitment to innovative thinking and to counterbalance the tendency toward operating with a school system–based culture (see Chapter 12).

4. *Implement organizational practices that systematically reinforce innovation* to externally motivate employees and leaders to access their innovative

intelligence and engage in innovative thinking, and reward them (see Chapter 13).

ECLIPSE #2: THE ANALYTICAL INTELLIGENCE PARADOX

It seems logical that if someone is well developed in one intelligence area, that person is equally strong in all three intelligences. However, this assumption is not empirically supported. In fact, some of the best analytical thinkers have difficulty with the process of innovative thinking.

A root cause of the problem is what we refer to as the *analytical intelligence paradox*, which states:

The Analytical Intelligence Paradox
The more that individuals have a dominant and successful analytical intelligence, the less likely they will have easy access to their innovative intelligence.

For years, the analytical intelligence that many leaders use has proven to be effective, efficient, and powerful. In fact, excellent analytical thinkers have been responsible for unprecedented growth in developing industrialized economies. Leaders who excel at analytical intelligence can often handle massive amounts of information. The flip side is that analytical intelligence can be too well trained, too fast, too dominant, and too good, so much so that it can seriously impede leaders' access to their innovative intelligence.

Analytical intelligence depends on memory and logic. This means that the more leaders know, the better they are able to recognize a problem, and the faster they can arrive at an answer. Those who excel in analytical intelligence have vastly superior retained knowledge. However, with the exponential growth of knowledge and information, leaders have to specialize in their knowledge area in order to be experts. This narrow focus limits their potential for new thinking—the knowledge is so specialized that there is little cross-fertilization with other areas of knowledge, a key in innovative thinking. The age of the "renaissance" person who combined knowledge from many disciplines is gone, and yet we need a true renaissance in leadership thinking, where more leaders can add another dimension to their thinking.

These leaders have a problem of too much knowledge—which limits their access to other insights and discoveries.

Norman Doidge[3] alludes to this phenomenon when he describes the "plasticity paradox," which he refers to as "one of the most important lessons" of his book, *The Brain That Changes Itself*. Doidge argues that human beings have "plastic brains." He says that humans have the potential to "develop into increasingly flexible children and stay that way through their adult lives," constantly learning and developing. He cites numerous examples of people who were able to regenerate cognitive capabilities they were believed to have lost. Doidge's concept should give one confidence that even though executives and leaders may have been schooled in one way of thinking, they still have the *neuroplastic capacity* to be flexible and learn different ways of thinking, including how to think innovatively.

However, Doidge then observed what he referred to as the "plasticity paradox," which states that "the same neuroplastic properties that allow us to change our brains and produce more flexible behaviors can allow us to produce more rigid ones." This means that if a person practices one way of doing things repeatedly, the plasticity of the brain can actually rigidify and, paradoxically, the person will become more rigid and less able to change. We quote Doidge's example of the "plasticity paradox":

Neuroplasticity is like pliable snow on a hill. When we go down the hill on a sled, we can be flexible because we have the option of taking different paths through the snow each time. But should we choose the same path a second or third time, tracks will start to develop, and soon we tend to get stuck in a rut—our route will now be quite rigid, as neural circuits, once established, tend to become self-sustaining. Because our neuroplasticity can give rise to both mental flexibility and mental rigidity, we tend to underestimate our own potential for flexibility, which most of us only experience in flashes.

The analytical intelligence paradox is a specific application of the plasticity paradox. As leaders strengthen their analytical intelligence, they become more rigid and reduce their ability to access their innovative intelligence. Leaders with highly developed analytical thinking are so focused on finding the "right" answer that they do not systematically access their insight and divergent thinking, which would give them the potential to be innovative.

---

3. Norman Doidge, *The Brain That Changes Itself* (Viking Press, 2007), p. 242–243.

They also do not deal well with uncertainty because they focus on "one problem, one answer," and they may not explore alternatives outside of what they already know. Unfortunately, many experienced executives of larger, established organizations developed their analytical thinking at school and at work. It may be difficult for many of them to accept that another type of intelligence is required to succeed in the knowledge economy.

The limitations of analytical intelligence are striking in these situations:

- When a different perspective is needed.
- When knowledge must be configured in a different way than it is in a schoolbook or a training manual.
- When an issue is complex and the answers that are needed have little or nothing to do either with yesterday's solutions or memorized knowledge.

Leaders need a better way of accessing their potential for innovative intelligence when they need it.

Leaders' strength in analytical intelligence can contribute to their weakness in accessing their innovative intelligence.

The core problem is their overdeveloped analytical intelligence and, more specifically, the means by which they access the other intelligences. It has been incredibly useful in the past, but now it is getting in the way. In the twenty-first century, there is a dire need for excellent leaders to tap *all* their intelligences in order to find the best solutions to complex problems.

Use Analytical Thinking as Part of the Approach to Innovative Thinking

In the future, if leaders want to respond successfully to ambiguities, and experiment when necessary, they must continue to respect analytical thinking while also embracing the need for innovative thinking.

One way for leaders to more readily accept the need for innovative thinking—and at the same time overcome the analytical intelligence paradox—is to use a logical and rigorous process to engage in innovative thinking.

Most creativity educators focus on non-linear exercises to expand the thought process for leaders. Although these exercises are usually fun and the techniques are sometimes useful, in order to be effective, they need to be compatible with the thinking process that most leaders currently use—which is an analytical thinking process. Therefore, organizations need to present innovative thinking using a logical and systematic foundation. When it is first introduced, innovative thinking needs to look like or mimic the analytical thinking approach leaders currently use. Within this approach there often are many opportunities for non-traditional techniques and thinking processes, but the foundation has to be familiar or else the leaders who excel at analytical thinking will not engage in innovative thinking long enough to make it "stick." (Chapters 5 to 9 describe this approach in greater detail.)

This approach increases the chance that the leaders who excel at analytical thinking will not block their innovative thinking, and it will help them apply innovative thinking to appropriate situations, such as when they are faced with ambiguity, when stakeholder relations are unclear, or when yesterday's answers are failing.

ECLIPSE #3: IMPACT OF HIGH NEGATIVE STRESS

Eclipse #3 occurs when leaders are under high negative stress[4] or other types of significant emotional pressure that obscures access to their innovative intelligence. For the majority of leaders under this kind of pressure, only long-term, repeatedly used knowledge and processes are available at that moment, because they have been imprinted at a deep level of the brain. Any knowledge or process acquired recently or used infrequently is not available.

To explain this phenomenon, we use the "Triune Theory" of the brain, developed by Dr. Paul D. MacLean.[5] This is a theory that has been used by military forces in many countries to make the right type of thinking available to an officer at any time in battle.

---

4. Note that we are referring specifically to negative stress, and not positive stress that can actually heighten capacities and can be constructive. See Hans Selye, *Stress Without Distress* (Lippincott Williams & Wilkins, 1974).
5. Dr. Paul D. MacLean was Chief of the Laboratory of Brain Evolution and Behavior at the National Institute of Mental Health in Bethesda, Maryland, part of the National Institutes of Health (NIH), which is part of the U.S. Department of Health and Human Services.

The Triune Theory separates the brain into three levels:

1. *The first level is the Reptilian (or Animal) level of the brain.* It is the level of the automatic, instinctive reactions such as "fight or flight." Every living being has this level of the brain. It is the brain that humans use to respond when someone shouts, "Watch out!" and they instinctively duck, without taking the time to assess the situation.
2. *The second level is the Limbic (or Emotional) level of the brain.* It is the seat of human emotions, and also where thoughts and emotions are imprinted. The limbic level is the dominant brain until age eight to ten (the "age of reason"). After that age, new information or processes can only be included at that level of the brain through high emotions or multiple repetitions.
3. *The third level is the Intellectual level (or cortex) of the brain.* It is the level where humans store all the knowledge and processes that they acquired after the age of reason that has not been imprinted at the limbic level through intense emotion or repetition.

When leaders encounter normal, non-stressful situations, they should be able to access everything they have learned. For example, if leaders attend a learning program or read books on innovative thinking, they should be able to use the skills and processes they have learned.

However, when leaders encounter negative stress, they only have access to the reptilian and limbic levels of the brain to solve problems or make decisions. In these negative stress situations, even if the leaders have taken many innovative thinking learning programs, if they have not practiced innovative thinking repeatedly in their work, they will not have access to their new learning. The leaders will automatically revert to their dominant thinking process (usually the analytical thinking process) available at the limbic level of the brain.

Here are some examples of situations where individuals tend to revert to using a specific level of the brain:

- In a case of crisis or panic, most people use only the Reptilian brain, whereby they either fight or run away when they feel a threat approaching. The Emotional and Intellectual brains are not available at that instant. Use of these brains in a threatening situation is often a good coping mechanism, because if individuals think too much, they might respond too slowly to the danger.

- As we have pointed out, when encountering high negative stress, many people have limited access to the intellectual level of their brain. For example, some contestants on television quiz shows ring the bell to indicate they know an answer but then freeze and cannot "access" the response. Another example is people who say inappropriate things under negative stress, only to regret them later. The issue is that when experiencing negative stress, people have trouble accessing the part of the brain where that correct answer is stored.

When leaders experience negative stress at work, they can only access the thinking processes that are imprinted at the limbic level of the brain. Here is how this applies to analytical, emotional, and innovative intelligence:

- *Access to analytical intelligence.* Most leaders have access to their analytical intelligence through analytical thinking patterns that they learned, practiced, and imprinted at the limbic level of the brain during their school years.
- *Access to emotional intelligence.* Leaders who have access to their emotional intelligence can retain access to their emotional thinking even during highly negative stress. That process was usually developed and imprinted in family interactions at home or from participation in team sports. As leaders, they can access their emotional intelligence at all times and are usually more successful in business.
- *Access to innovative intelligence.* Very few leaders have full-time access to their innovative intelligence when they experience negative stress. In our empirical research with highly innovative teenagers,[6] we identified that most of the teenagers developed and imprinted their innovative thinking in their family before the age of 10. Some also developed it through music and team sports, but almost always during their younger, formative years. None of the teenagers indicated that they developed this capability at school. Although it is helpful to imprint innovative intelligence by the age of 10, it is possible to learn how to

---

6. Survey conducted in 2001 with focus groups of over 100 innovative high school students in grade 11 who had been selected for their results and their innovativeness to attend the SHAD valley program that offers them advanced summer education programs in Canadian universities. www. shad.ca.

access it and to imprint it at the limbic level of the brain as an adult; however, it takes more time and practice.

Leaders also can have a negative impact on their employees and teams by being the source of the negative stress. Here is an example:

The VP had promised the CEO innovative ideas for a new plan for the organization. He simply had forgotten to tell his staff about this promise. The VP needed to present the ideas in two days, so he gathered his most innovative employees and told them, "We're under lots of pressure to find great ideas for the new plan by tomorrow night! I know there is not much time, but you all have experience on this subject, and I know you always have great ideas. I'm counting on you!" And then he departed.

The employees were stunned. Eventually, they started throwing ideas on the table, as fast as possible. By the next day, they had 50 ideas and an overall recommendation that they presented to the VP. Some of their ideas were good, but none of them solved the organization's main challenges.

Two lessons from this example are, unfortunately, too common:

- The first is that innovative thinking is not instantaneous, and you cannot turn innovative thinking on and off like a tap. As we will see in Chapter 7, understanding the issue is an essential prerequisite for generating innovative ideas, and it requires reflection and insight.
- The second lesson is that high negative stress can block access to innovation. This is because highly charged emotional responses create the negative stress that can in turn limit one's ability to access innovative intelligence.

Negative stress can block innovative responses even for the most sophisticated leaders. For example, there are occasions when leaders are under stress and they say or do something and then afterward think, "I shouldn't have said or done such-and-such." That's because, at the time, their thinking was one-dimensional. Or at other times, leaders may look back on a meeting and think of several innovative ideas they wish they had thought to put forward, but did not because they were not able to access their full innovative intelligence while they were experiencing emotional pressure.

What leaders need is a means of accessing their innovative intelligence—in fact, all their intelligences—no matter how stressful or emotional the situation.

Imprint the Innovative Thinking Process at the Limbic Level of the Brain

Many leaders have attended learning sessions on how to be more innovative—through workshops, seminars, or training. However, most of these courses are taught at the intellectual level and have no sustained impact. As a result, when the crunch time comes and the pressure is on and leaders need to be more innovative, they cannot access all that knowledge. They revert to accessing what they "know"—the tried and true. And, because they are not using them, the innovative tools they have been taught are soon forgotten. Consequently, there is no lasting change.

To access their innovative intelligence at any time, even while under negative stress, leaders must imprint the innovative thinking process at the limbic level of the brain. Otherwise, they might understand the logic of a situation but be unable to manage it innovatively. It becomes apparent that the problem is much more a question of processing than a question of potential. Many leaders have the capacity, but they are not able to access all of their potential when they experience intense negative stress. The innovative intelligence may be there, but they just cannot access it.

Imprinting innovative thinking at the limbic level is the only way leaders can access their innovative intelligence on a consistent and reliable basis, even when under intense negative stress. It is somewhat analogous to computer programming, whereby, if the instructions are not embedded in the operating system (the limbic level) then one cannot access the required information and knowledge.

There are two ways that leaders at work can imprint innovative thinking at the limbic level of the brain:

1. *Through a highly charged emotional experience.* This method can imprint innovative intelligence rapidly, but it is not often feasible in most workplaces. A few leaders who are shocked by a layoff experience or by negative performance feedback can rebound with greater openness to alternative ways of behaving and thinking.

2. *Through leaders investing time and engaging in repeated practice of innovative thinking.* Repetition is one reason why people with a lot of experience in a particular subject or task (whether a veteran athlete, a seasoned public speaker, or a senior leader) are usually better under stress—because they

have imprinted a process for accessing all they know at the limbic level. However, repetition can only happen if done in an environment that facilitates this method and where the individual is motivated to carry out repetitive activities. We have found that for innovative thinking to be accessible at any time, even under negative stress, leaders need to practice it repeatedly for a minimum of four to six months. They also benefit from peer support and significant external reinforcement and encouragement.

Both ways are highly dependent on the organizational context. For example, fighter pilot training involves repetitive training of very stressful situations in simulation cockpits. The training imprints the correct response in the limbic levels of the pilots' brains so that it is available even when they are under extreme stress. As a result, it should not be surprising when the tape from a recovered flight black box reflects the pilots' calmness just before a plane crash. As a result of their repetitive training, the pilots have embedded that reaction deeply within the limbic level of their brain, which results in clear assessments of the situation—even when the outcome is fatal.

In a business context, where the objective is to make teams more innovative, team leaders must create the conditions that make innovative thinking possible. Some may *impose* the new behavior. However, because the new behavior does not come naturally, it is essential that it be repeated often. The more it is intensified through urgency, speed, stress, and motivation, the more effectively it will be imprinted at the limbic level of the brain. Once the access to innovative intelligence is imprinted, leaders and employees will be able to access it even under stressful conditions.

There is no miracle solution. Leaders need to learn the theory and the process and then practice it systematically over an extended period of time. The need for repetition explains why so many one-time learning programs fail to have any sustainable impact. Leaders also have a very important role to provide reinforcement and encouragement to their employees and teams in order to help them access their innovative intelligence and imprint the new innovative thinking process.

While imprinting innovative intelligence is not an easy task, the modern military focuses on imprinting an equivalent of innovative thinking every day. Here is what they have done:

The military often uses the acronym, O.O.D.A. (Observe, Orient, Decide, Act),[7] *which has become a trained and imprinted thought process at the same level as analytical thinking. Under extreme stress (the ultimate emotion, fear of dying), soldiers must avoid thinking with the natural response of the limbic level of the brain (fear, panic, overreaction, or inaction) or with their analytical intelligence (past experiences). Instead, they must use their innovative intelligence by observing the situation, orienting themselves based on their mission, deciding on the best course of action, and only then acting or executing as trained—usually in an instant. Their initial response focuses on clearly seeing and assessing the problem before deciding on an action, and it requires a thought process that is imprinted at the emotional level and is accessible at times of extreme stress. They achieve much of this imprinting of innovative intelligence through intense and extensive training at boot camp and with constant repetition and continual reinforcement.*

We believe that leaders of organizations must recognize (just as the military does) that they cannot make fundamental changes in the way they and their employees think without a clear methodology for doing so. They must educate themselves and their employees in specific ways and with processes to imprint innovative intelligence at the deep limbic level in order to override their ingrained, one-way thinking. Only then will leaders have equal access to their innovative intelligence during times of pressure. Only then will they have the ability to choose whether accessing their analytical intelligence, their innovative intelligence, or a combination would be most appropriate for a challenging situation.

CONCLUSION

This chapter described three scenarios that can obscure or eclipse one's innovative intelligence and offered suggestions of how to remove or reduce the impact of each eclipse. The second section of the book (Chapters 5 to 9) describes innovative thinking and how leaders and employees can apply the innovative thinking techniques and tools effectively. The third section of the book (Chapters 10 to 14) explains how leaders can lead innovative teams and how to shape an innovative culture and design organizational practices that promote and embed innovative thinking in an organization. The book concludes with a systematic method of developing an organizational innovation plan to help leaders and employees access their innovative intelligence and thereby contribute to closing the innovation gap.

---

7. Presentation by John Boyd, *Organic Design for Command and Control* (May 1987). See http://www.citizenstrategist.com/4the-john-boyd-archive.html

PART TWO

INNOVATIVE THINKING

CHAPTER FIVE

INNOVATIVE THINKING: AN OVERVIEW

In her yearly "State of the Union" address to all employees, the CEO of a mid-sized company talked about the need for innovation in everything they do. She went on to discuss "the need for new ideas to create positive change." The executive team nodded in agreement—however, some interpreted the CEO's remarks as confirmation of the need for innovation to drive growth, while others thought the CEO was giving them free rein to cut costs substantially.

The middle managers and supervisors, who had heard the CEO speak less frequently, had no idea what she meant by "thinking innovatively," but they understood "new ideas" and "change," and they feared it would disrupt their way of working. Some took it to mean gradual change in someone else's area. Others decided to wait and see if this new initiative would blow over, just like all the previous commitments to dramatic change.

The front-line employees, who rarely heard the CEO speak, also had mixed opinions about the notion of thinking innovatively. Some became very anxious, as they feared this could be another program like the quality initiative that had resulted in layoffs. Others were excited because they had many ideas for improvements.

The result? Confusion. The reason? A total lack of common understanding of what the CEO meant by "thinking innovatively" and by "ideas to create change."

This story illustrates the confusion that can result when a common understanding of innovative thinking is lacking. As we showed in Section I, innovation only happens when individuals and teams systematically apply innovative thinking, and innovative thinking is the only sustainable way to close the innovation gap. Innovative thinking by itself is not a strategy—rather, it is a different way to solve problems and to take advantage of opportunities to achieve business objectives.

The focus of Section Two of *Innovative Intelligence* is to ensure that leaders and employees at every level understand what innovative thinking is and how to put specific innovative thinking tools and techniques into action. We conclude each chapter in Section Two with an explanation of how to apply innovative intelligence in combination with emotional and analytical intelligence. We also include recommendations to help leaders lead and manage that step of the innovative thinking process.

CHARACTERISTICS OF AN EFFECTIVE INNOVATIVE THINKING MODEL

For most people, innovative thinking is not the natural way of thinking—using it has to be a deliberate choice in order to overcome the preference for analytical thinking. Innovative thinking will only be readily adopted by individuals if it has the following characteristics:

- **One common definition of what it is and where it should be applied**
  Employees at successful innovative organizations have a shared definition of innovative thinking and use the same innovative thinking process. Leaders and employees both must understand the innovative thinking process, know when to apply it, and be able to contribute to it effectively.

  If different areas or departments adopt their own versions of innovative thinking and use their own sets of tools and techniques, confusion will occur. Cross-functional teamwork will be a challenge because different teams will use different innovative thinking approaches. A single model, used regularly and consistently, with common tools and techniques, will accelerate the adoption of the innovative thinking process in an organization.

  In Chapter I, we defined innovative thinking in organizations as follows:

Innovative thinking is the process of solving problems by discovering, combining, and arranging insights, ideas, and methods in new ways.

This definition emphasizes that organizations most often use innovative thinking to solve problems and discover opportunities. It also emphasizes that innovations are mostly derived from linking together separate ideas in new ways to gain insights into issues and to discover new solutions to problems.

We recommend that employees use innovative thinking as the preferred way to approach complex problems. The starting point is to define which thinking process is best suited to each issue's level of complexity.

- If a problem is simple or merely complicated, rather than complex, the analytical thinking process will probably be an effective thinking approach. It can be supplemented with specific innovative thinking techniques, such as idea generation brainstorming, which can improve analytical thinking effectiveness. Idea generation brainstorming and other innovative thinking tools are explored in Chapter 8.
- If a problem or opportunity is complex, the innovative thinking process will deliver better and more sustainable results.[1] Complex problems or opportunities are often characterized by their uniqueness, ambiguity, and uncertainty.
- If a complicated or a complex issue also includes different views among key stakeholders, then it is important to apply innovative thinking and to use emotional intelligence as part of the process. Applying emotional intelligence will be useful in understanding the impact on people, which will ensure the solution will be successfully implemented.

- **A scalable approach that can be used for all kinds of issues that require innovative thinking**
  The process selected needs to be scalable, which means it can be used by individuals or teams on all types of issues, large and small, short- or long-term, and for all types of solutions, incremental or revolutionary. The four-step innovative thinking model we introduce later in this chapter satisfies all the requirements of scalability.

---

1. The tools that facilitate the process are described in the next four chapters of this book.

- **A process that can coexist with analytical thinking**
  For the innovative thinking process to coexist with the dominant analytical thinking process, compatibility between the two thinking processes is essential. A fundamental error in innovative thinking over the past 40 years has been the attempt to promote creative processes that require totally different thinking approaches from the dominant analytical thinking process. The efforts to teach innovative thinking as a totally new thinking approach were never sufficient. As a result, only a few people who were naturally inclined continued to use the new innovative thinking process.

- **Consistent application of innovative thinking tools and techniques**
  An effective innovative thinking process needs simple, flexible tools and techniques that can be applied to any complex issue. The consistent use of the same set of tools and techniques accelerates the adoption of the overall process. The tools and techniques also accelerate imprinting the innovative thinking process at the limbic level of the brain.[2] This is where it is accessible under any conditions, and especially under high levels of negative stress.

- **Innovative thinking processes, tools, and techniques need to meet the following criteria:**
    - Enable access to all the capabilities of our innovative intelligence
    - Be practical, simple, and memorable tools that can be used by team members in any circumstance and at any level of complexity
    - Be recognizable and compatible with the dominant analytical thinking approach so that they are more easily accepted but, at the same time, different enough from the analytical thinking process to avoid confusion
    - Be rigorous enough to ensure systematic and implementable results
    - Be supported and used by leaders to demonstrate their commitment to innovative thinking.

---

2. See Chapter 4, "Eclipse Number 3," to understand why imprinting is important to innovative thinking.

KEY SUCCESS FACTORS FOR INNOVATIVE THINKING

Innovative thinking involves a number of key success factors.

Key Success Factors for Innovative Thinking
1. Use a step-by-step innovative thinking process.
2. First diverge, then converge.
3. Balance individual and group work in a team.
4. Mitigate risk within the innovative thinking process.
5. Ensure an effective handoff between discovering the innovative solution and change implementation.

Use a Step-by-Step Innovative Thinking Process

In a culture of "just do it" thinking, leaders may view carefully planning an approach to thinking as counter-intuitive. Why should leaders spend time thinking about an issue and identifying possible obstacles when they could put a few people together and generate immediate solutions?

The reality of the complex knowledge economy is that problems are always changing. The innovative thinking process enables us to fully access our innovative intelligence to generate deeper, more useful actionable insights into a situation and to discover and implement new and better solutions.

Innovative thinking is effective because by applying it we see new possibilities, we can create new connections between previously unconnected knowledge, and we can look at an issue from new and different points of view in order to improve our understanding of it. An innovative thinking process must make it possible to look at unique elements as well as common traits in an issue, to hold conflicting thoughts simultaneously without judging, to work with ambiguity without trying to eliminate it, and to allow deeply held beliefs to be challenged.

Our four-step innovative thinking process[3] appears on the following page in Figure 5.1.

---

3. The four-step innovative thinking process was originally developed by Claude Legrand's firm, *Ideaction*.

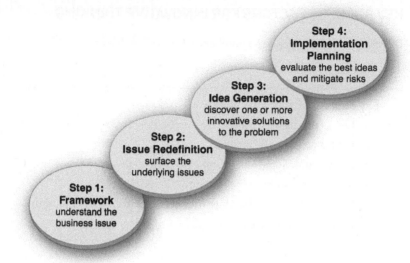

Figure 5.1: The Four-Step Innovative Thinking Process

Here is a brief description of each of the four steps of the innovative thinking process. Chapters 6 to 9 describe these steps in detail and provide practical techniques for leaders and employees to use in applying the steps to the complex issues (problems or opportunities) they encounter.

- *Step 1: Framework*

  The purpose of this step is for the team to identify the following:
  - The objective or goal of the work
  - The type of solution required
  - The real boundaries and assumptions for a good solution
  - The real decision maker or owner
  - The most effective approach to achieving the objective.

People rarely give this critical first step the importance and time it deserves, despite the fact that it is impossible to consistently deliver innovative solutions without a well-thought-out framework. In fact, many innovative or creative thinking approaches combine Steps 1 and 2, which dramatically reduces the impact of this step.

The deliverable for Step 1: *Framework* is a project or team charter defining the problem or opportunity the team will explore. It includes a clear definition of the objective, the problem's boundaries, and how success will be measured. Chapter 6 describes the tools and techniques for this step in greater detail.

- *Step 2: Issue Redefinition*
  In this step, the team gains insight into the complexity and the underlying root causes of the issue. This is essential in order to improve the potential of finding the right solution to the problem or opportunity. It often involves collecting facts, breaking the issue down into distinct subsets, looking at it from both rational and emotional points of view, and understanding the root causes of the issue, as well as identifying any obstacles to the implementation of a solution.

  The deliverable for Step 2: Issue Redefinition is a question (or series of questions) that is distinct, clear, and manageable, and that addresses the core of the issue to be solved. It should be based on the work done in Step 1: Framework. Chapter 7 will describe the tools and techniques for this step in greater detail.

- *Step 3: Idea Generation*
  In this step, the team identifies one or many possible answers, depending on the objectives established in the framework and confirmed during the issue redefinition. To be effective, idea generation is a step that demands planning and rigor. This is contrary to the unstructured "lob some ideas into the air" approach leaders and teams often take.

  The deliverable for Step 3: Idea Generation is one or a range of implementable ideas that are within the boundaries set during the framework step. Chapter 8 describes the tools and techniques for this step in greater detail.

- *Step 4: Implementation Planning*
  In this last step, the plans for the best solution are successfully developed. This is where the leaders responsible for the process must stop and critically assess the risks associated with their proposed solution. The challenge in this step is to "check twice and move once"—leaders need

to think through the solution, assess its risks, and plan its implementation thoroughly before rushing to action.

The deliverable for Step 4: Implementation Planning is a well-thought-out change implementation plan that will take the idea from concept to successful implementation. Chapter 9 describes the tools and techniques for this step in greater detail.

First Diverge, then Converge

Applying divergence and convergence perspectives sequentially at every step and within each technique in the innovative thinking process is critical for effective innovative thinking. Here is a description of what we mean by divergence and convergence perspectives:

- *Divergence perspective* is the process of exploring freely all the aspects of an issue, without criticism or censorship, to create a set of options. There can be several objectives, such as:
    - To develop different possible solutions during a brainstorming process
    - To develop different possible points of view on an issue
    - To uncover all the possible boundaries for good solutions
    - To identify all the things that could possibly go wrong with the selected solution
    - To challenge dominant paradigms without being negative. This freedom from judgment encourages greater participation by people who may otherwise censor their valid ideas before sharing them.

The concept of divergence was first developed in the 1950s by psychologist J. P. Guilford,[4] who saw divergence as a major component of creativity. He associated divergence with four main characteristics:

- *Fluency:* The ability to produce a great number of ideas
- *Flexibility:* The ability to use different approaches to address a specific problem

---

4. Joy Paul Guilford, "Creativity," *American Psychologist*, 1950, Volume 5, Issue 9, p. 444–454.

- *Originality:* The ability to produce original ideas
- *Elaboration:* The ability to organize the implementation of an idea.

• **Convergence perspective** is the process of selecting the best possible options from the range of possibilities identified during divergence. These could include identifying:
    - The best angle from which to attack an issue
    - The key boundaries that define a good solution
    - The best solution
    - The significant issues that must be addressed to ensure the successful implementation of the preferred solution.

The convergence perspective is the perspective most people are comfortable with because it has many similarities to analytical thinking. It requires the skills of selection, evaluation, and judgment. The objective of convergence is to review all the options developed during divergence and select the best option available at that time. When using convergence to select one or more solutions that best fit a problem or opportunity, the team should always use the framework created at the outset of the process as the criterion.

The innovative thinking process requires a clear separation of the divergence and convergence perspectives. Everyone is capable of thinking from both perspectives, although many are naturally more comfortable with, or have developed a preference for, one perspective over another. The key to innovative thinking is to make the formal separation of divergence and convergence perspectives systematic so that it becomes intuitive every time a complex issue is encountered.

Many leaders profess that they separate divergence and convergence perspectives when problem solving; however, few leaders actually do it in business situations. The standard explanation is that they cannot afford the time to apply divergence and then convergence. However, they and their teams always find the time to revisit topics already discussed and decisions already implemented. This rework usually occurs because hurried analytical solutions are not effective at resolving the root causes of complex issues.

While divergence is most often associated with Step 3: *Idea Generation*, it can and should be used as part of every step of the innovative thinking process. Table 5.2 describes how the divergence and convergence perspectives are applied to each of the steps of the four-step innovative thinking process.

Table 5.2: Divergence and Convergence Perspectives Applied to the Four Phases of Innovative Thinking

	Divergence Perspective	Convergence Perspective
Framework	What are all the possible objectives, types of thinking, and boundaries?	Which objective, type of thinking, and boundaries do we want to focus on?
Issue Redefinition	What are all the possible ways to look at the issue?	What is the best or easiest way to solve the issue?
Idea Generation	What are all the possible (and impossible) solutions?	What solution best fits the objective, type of thinking, and boundaries?
Implementation Planning	What could go wrong with the implementation of the solution?	What can we do to minimize the risks and maximize the likelihood of success?

Here are some tips for applying *"first diverge, then converge:"*

• **Formally separate the divergence and convergence perspectives at each step**

Leaders must formally separate the divergence and convergence perspectives at each step of the innovative thinking process. It is important to do this because it stops the automatic tendency to jump to a conclusion about an issue or a solution. The process works best if the individual or team focuses on one task at a time, first by looking at the problem or opportunity from a divergent perspective. If the team members raise convergent ideas before considering all the possible divergent perspectives, make note of those perspectives so they can be reviewed later, during the time allocated to the convergence perspective.

Focusing on the problem and separating divergence and convergence perspectives are the most effective ways to prevent the analytical thinking process from taking over. Also, spending time on the divergence perspective is the part of the innovative thinking process where innovative intelligence is accessed directly.

- **Define in advance a specific amount of time for divergence and convergence**

  The most effective way to manage the process is to define a specific amount of time to be spent on each perspective and to tell team members the allocated time in advance. Analytical thinkers often find the unstructured thinking in the divergence perspective part of Step 3: Idea Generation frustrating and want to find "the" answer quickly. A fixed amount of time prevents the premature closure of divergence. Other team members find divergence so interesting and fun that they prefer to continue, leaving no time for convergence. The fixed time ensures that convergence is effectively addressed as well.

  When defining a problem that has proven intractable before, the team should spend more time on the divergence perspective. This will help the team members to better understand everything possible about the problem by looking at it from every possible angle, whether it appears relevant at first or not. The objective is to identify any parts of the problem that have not been considered and determine why. After exploring the divergence perspective, the team will find it is then possible to combine the analytical, innovative, and emotional intelligences to converge and select the most effective way to look at the problem. In Step 3: Idea Generation, the objective may be to find one practical solution that can be implemented quickly. If this is the case, the team can spend less time on divergence, generating a few possible options, and more time on convergence to refine the solution and ensure it can be implemented quickly and successfully.

- **Apply "first diverge, then converge" to all group meetings**

  The process of separating divergence and convergence perspectives also applies outside of innovative thinking. Most meetings need discussions from both of these perspectives. However, because meetings are often not structured, divergence and convergence perspectives can be voiced at any moment, almost at random throughout the meeting. One or two individuals may be looking at new alternatives (divergence perspective) while other participants may have already made up their minds about a few solutions and be trying to come to a conclusion (convergence perspective). As a result, team members work at cross purposes and become frustrated without being aware of why.

The preferred approach is to allocate time within agenda items to consider both perspectives. For example, if a team has one hour to decide on the selection of a new supplier, it is more effective to formally separate the time allocated to the divergence and convergence perspectives. Initially, the team can use 30 minutes to diverge and discuss all the options, listen to everyone around the table, and look for innovative ideas to consider. In the remaining 30 minutes, the team can converge to identify the strengths and weaknesses of each option and select the best alternative.

Balance Individual and Group Work in Teams and in Meetings

Innovative thinking is a very effective process for individuals, but in the context of business, it is particularly valuable as a team process.

The definition of innovative thinking focuses on solving issues by *discovering, combining, and arranging* existing and new ideas. A team is always more effective than an individual in this process because the sum of a team's collective knowledge is greater than the knowledge of any one individual. The challenge is to ensure that the collective knowledge of the team is shared and combined efficiently to create new insight and to discover new solutions.

The ability of a team to promote and discuss different points of view on an issue is invaluable. An innovative thinking process must encourage looking at a known problem in different ways. It must increase the potential of discovering new connections by stretching each team member's thinking and preventing the dominant analytical thinking from censoring intriguing combinations that could lead to new insights and new solutions.

While working in one team is a highly effective and efficient approach to accessing innovative intelligence, sometimes applying individual innovative thinking is very helpful as well. Some activities, such as brainstorming, benefit from creating the time and space to hear the innovative ideas from the quieter, more reflective individual thinkers. Also, specific subject matter experts may be added to a team for some steps of the process to offer their insights, knowledge, and experiences to the innovative thinking process.

It is important to balance independent work with group work in order to maximize the value of an innovative thinking process in a team. The process is straightforward and needs to be reinforced by the team leader or facilitator. Here is the process:

- The leader or facilitator asks a clear question and makes sure everyone understands it.
- The participants work individually for a few minutes and write down their ideas about the question.
- The leader or facilitator asks each participant to give one idea at a time. If necessary, the process can be repeated a few times. Ideally, all the ideas are recorded on a flip chart so they can be discussed.
- At this point, the team has a variety of divergent ideas. The group then begins discussion by generating additional ideas and exploring the common and different points identified.

This simple process avoids the situation where a group is dominated by one or several participants, and it creates a much more open discussion in which the participants hear all points of view and value all the ideas.

Mitigate Risk within the Innovative Thinking Process

Some leaders are concerned that innovative thinking can create uncontrolled risk for the organization. This observation usually reflects a lack of understanding of the innovative thinking process and the role leadership should have within it. An effective innovative thinking process must include risk management to assess how much risk can be taken and in which areas.

There are specific ways to manage the risk in each of the four steps of the innovative thinking process:

- *Step 1: Framework* includes clearly defining boundaries that a solution must adhere to in order to be implemented. Boundaries can include items such as: "do not impact short-term financial results," "do not negatively impact the customer experience," or "the IT system cannot be modified in any way." If the boundaries are well set, the risk is already limited before ideas are generated.
- *Step 2: Issue Redefinition* involves analyzing the root causes of the issue and ensuring that you are working on the right part of the complexity that needs resolution.

- *Step 3: Idea Generation* includes using the convergence perspective to assess which are the best ideas and ensure that the selected solution is within the boundaries set in the original framework and can be implemented.
- *Step 4: Implementation Planning* includes a series of tools to assess the potential risks associated with the solution, and it includes methods to actively mitigate those risks. These tools and techniques are more fully explored later in Chapter 9.
- *Owner's Review After Each Step:* The owner or decision maker must review the outcome of each step in the innovative thinking process. This is the most effective way to de-risk innovation, as it ensures that the team is not proceeding in a direction that is not approved formally.

Ensure an Effective Handoff between Discovery and Implementation Teams

Innovation and change are highly interdependent. To create value, innovative solutions always require successful change implementation. A very important stage of *Step 4: Implementation Planning* is identifying how the chosen solution to the complex problem will be implemented and who will take ownership of the implementation process.

Sometimes an innovative thinking team will continue their work on the problem through to implementation, and in other situations the innovative thinking team does a *handoff*—they give the resolved problem to a team that focuses on change implementation.

When there is a handoff to another team, the transfer of roles and responsibilities must be achieved seamlessly. Without a seamless handoff, the outcome of the innovative thinking process will only be ideas. While possibly brilliant, if they remain ideas and are not successfully implemented, they do not create any value for the organization.

The innovative thinking team should use their experience on the project to create a simple and clear *implementation planning report*. This ensures that the handoff is effective and seamless. The implementation planning report should highlight the key milestones, the project's first steps, and the key elements of the recommended change management plan. In particular, the implementation planning report needs to be clear on the potential weaknesses of the ideas as well as possible risk mitigation strategies.

CONCLUSION

This chapter provided an overview of the innovative thinking process. The process works best when leaders and team members attempt to gain insight into and discover solutions for complex issues. It is augmented by effective emotional intelligence thinking, especially when there is stakeholder disagreement or different interests among the team members. Analytical thinking also augments the innovative thinking process, particularly when teams converge the many ideas to select specific solutions.

The next four chapters describe each of the four steps of the innovative thinking process and provide the processes, tools, and techniques for employees and leaders to think innovatively in a systematic way. Each chapter concludes with a discussion of how emotional intelligence and analytical intelligence can augment the innovative thinking process in that step and how leaders can facilitate that step of the innovative thinking process.

CHAPTER SIX

STEP 1: FRAMEWORK

The CEO of a property management company knew that time was running out for the organization if they did not quickly implement bold new solutions to meet customer needs.

He decided to ask his top six middle managers to work as a dedicated team on a one-month project to turn the company around. The CEO told the team members to be boldly innovative, to think way out of the box, to redesign the value proposition, to break new ground. The mandate seemed clear, and the excitement of the team was palpable. The team believed the CEO had instructed them to create the new path for the organization. When the team leader asked if there were any specific issues to focus on or any limits or "non-negotiables," the CEO replied that there were none that really mattered.

Inspired, the team went to work right away to understand their customers better and to analyze best practices. They asked the best consultants to help them and ran multiple brainstorming sessions. Finally, they had it—the magic answer that got everybody on the team incredibly excited. It would be the major breakthrough the organization needed. It would also mean dramatic changes—new skills the organization did not have currently and lots of capital to fund the research, the design, the new technologies, and the implementation. The team was confident their plan would achieve the required turnaround and that the CEO and executive team would approve it.

During the presentation of the plan, the CEO and his executive team sat silently until the end. The team was convinced that the silence meant the CEO was thrilled with their brilliant plan. Then the questions started coming: "How are we going to do this?" "Do we have any of the skills necessary?" "How are we going to find the capital to fund the project?""How long will it take?" The innovation team was stunned, and their team leader replied: "You told us to be boldly innovative, to think way out of the box. This is as good as it gets. We didn't know we had a specific budget or time limits."The CEO responded, "But you know our executives *and managers are very traditional. You know our results are not great and that we need to find answers quickly. Your concept is great, but it's too expensive. Go back and focus on how we can retain our customers for the next two years and do it for $1 million instead of $20 million." The team left the room dejected, without any desire to continue to work on the project.*

In this example, the CEO chose not to give the team any clear directions or limits because he did not want to stifle their creativity. He was hoping for a miracle solution that would fit within his unspoken boundaries. The team made an attempt to validate what the original directive really meant, but they were unsuccessful. Had the framework for the problem been clearly established up front, the team might have found an implementable innovative solution within the defined boundaries. Instead, they were disappointed by the outcome of their work. The time, money, and resources invested in the project were all wasted.

These kinds of stories occur too frequently. Leaders believe they are being helpful by asking for bold solutions while providing vague directions without limits. But this approach often sets up talented leaders and teams for failure. Complex problems can have many possible solutions and leaders need to invest time into defining the framework before asking a team to solve a complex project. This chapter explains how that framework can be established to increase the probability of innovative thinking success.

Chapter 5 introduced the four-step innovative thinking process, depicted in Figure 6.1. This chapter focuses specifically on the tools and techniques for Step 1: *Framework*.

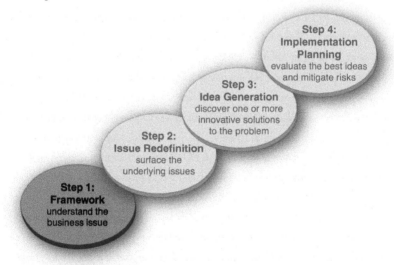

Figure 6.1: The Four-Step Innovative Thinking Process

UNDERSTANDING FRAMEWORK

Step 1: *Framework* establishes a clear project charter. It is an essential step in the innovative thinking process because the detailed process and the best techniques required to resolve complex issues differ from problem to problem. This step is also the most effective way to stop the analytical thinking reflex of jumping to conclusions about the problem and accepting the first solution that appears reasonable.

A clearly defined framework
greatly increases the probability of a successful outcome.
No framework or an unclear framework
almost guarantees failure or sub-optimal results.

Ideally, the problem's owner or decision maker should prepare the framework and give it to the team at the outset of the process. If the owner has prepared the framework, the first task of the leader and the team is to review and challenge each element of the framework to ensure it is as clear and accurate as possible. If the team perceives any gap in knowledge or understanding, they must address it before proceeding.

In some cases, the owner may not have the time to develop a defined framework to give to the innovation team. In that case, the first task of the team must be to create a full framework based on their collective understanding. They must then validate it with the owner, ensuring that the owner gives it full attention.

There are six essential tools in the framework process. The first five together define "the problem." The sixth tool defines the "project charter," which guides the process of gaining insight into the issue and discovering a meaningful innovative solution that can be implemented.

Essential Tools in the Framework Process
1. The context
2. The "How to . . . ?" question
3. The boundaries
4. The type of solution
5. The owner or decision maker
6. The project charter

THE CONTEXT

The first technique in establishing the framework is understanding the context for the problem or opportunity. Although it may seem obvious that the context is a critical element of a problem or opportunity, many leaders and teams believe that when they need to be innovative, the past and the context do not really matter. In fact, they often believe that looking at what the organization has tried before will taint their thinking.

The opposite is true. If a leader or a team is not aware of the past and current context for an issue, they are bound to repeat the same mistakes that have been made in the past. The context should include all the elements that are relevant to the necessary level of understanding of the issue. On a major revolutionary innovation project, hundreds of pages of research and analysis may be necessary to describe the context. A simple problem may require only a few paragraphs.

Understanding the background, what has been tried in the past, what worked and what did not work and why, are critical pieces of the thinking necessary to be successful. Other elements of the context can be:

- What is the higher purpose or the strategy that this problem or opportunity fits within?
- Why is it a problem or opportunity, and what is the history?
- What will happen if it is not resolved?
- How much support will the executives and other key parts of the organization give to the project?
- What other current or future activities or projects can impact the project or the implementation of ideas?
- What laws, rules, or regulations will impact the implementation of ideas?

Taking time to share (or "level-set") the context and the collective knowledge is even more important when working as a team. Team members will have different knowledge relevant to the issue because of their functions or their personal experiences. Collecting and mapping all the collective knowledge to create a shared context is one of the cornerstones of any successful project. The differences of opinion among team members on any element of the context are useful indications that there is more to an issue than what first appears. The team should explore these differences of viewpoint. The team should not try to reduce the differences to achieve a soft consensus but rather accept them, learn from them, and understand the real complexity of the situation. In the opposite situation, when there is too much consensus on a key issue, the team should consider the possibility that the beliefs and assumptions that create this unique picture are so strong as to be suspicious and need to be challenged.

Once the team understands the context and urgency for the issue, they can be more specific and define the specific problem statement to explore.

THE "HOW TO . . . ?" QUESTION

The second technique in Step I: *Framework* is to clearly define the problem that needs to be solved or the opportunity that needs to be exploited. This exercise ensures that each member of the team has the same understanding of the goal. The most effective approach is to phrase the problem as a question, starting with the words: "How to." The form "How to . . . ?" creates the right compromise between an imprecise statement such as: "We need to do something about . . ." or "We have a problem with . . ." and a very directive question such as: "What if we could do . . . ?" which suggests that there is one ideal end goal that simply needs to be validated.

A well-written "How to . . . ?" question unambiguously sets out the ultimate objective and how success will be measured. It is the touchstone to which the leader or the team can always refer to ensure the right problem is being solved. It is an important point of reference at various stages of the entire four-step innovative thinking process.

Asking the right question may seem intuitive, but in practice, analytical thinking does not generally lead to active consideration of a question's value. Frequently, the assumption is that simply because the question is being asked, it is the right question. This assumption is often reinforced during early school experiences in which teachers ask questions and students are expected to focus on providing an answer rather than questioning the question. Not many people are trained or have taken courses on how to phrase a problem unless they specialize in research or philosophy.

Asking the right question is critical to the entire innovative thinking process. The right question will address the real issue or opportunity, and the solutions will always be of value. With the wrong question, any answer, however innovative, will probably be faulty. In innovative thinking, as in life, simple answers to the right question are always preferable to brilliant answers to the wrong question. When there is limited time to clarify the framework, then the most effective technique to apply is the "How to . . . ?" question.

When developing a "How to . . . ?" question, leaders must first apply a divergent perspective, looking at all the possible ways to phrase the question. Subsequently, they should apply the convergence perspective and choose the question that best represents what they are trying to achieve.

Here is the recommended process an innovation team can use to develop effective "How to . . . ?" questions:

- Each team member writes a proposed "How to . . . ?" based upon the member's understanding of the context and view of the issue. Each writes the question starting with "How to" and ending with a question mark. Asking it in this format will immediately make the issue and the direction clearer.

- Each person then writes his or her question on a flip chart and explains the choice to the other members of the group.

- The team then discusses the "How to . . . ?" questions on the flip charts and integrates them into the preferred short list.

- Next, the team parses the short-listed "How to . . . ?" questions so that each more accurately reflects the real problem and makes it easier to solve. This requires looking at each word and each concept independently, making sure each is clear and unambiguous. If a word can have more than one meaning, the team writes down all the possibilities (divergence) and then selects the word or the concept that precisely captures what they really mean (convergence). This process does not require everyone on the team to agree, but everyone has to develop a common understanding of the question.

- The team then selects the "How to . . . ?" question or questions that best reflect the team's goal. If the team has difficulty reaching consensus on one definition, it most often indicates there is more than one "How to . . . ?" question for the issue.

Sometimes during the "How to . . . ?" question process, the team has serious debates about the nature of the problem and its priority. Some leaders worry about the lack of immediate team consensus, but in practice, early debate is preferable, and it may be the best thing that could happen to the team.

The open debate at this step of the innovative thinking process reduces the likelihood of destructive debate at the implementation planning step when individuals each favor a particular solution based on different interpretations of the problem. At the solution step of the process, team members will have strong emotional attachments to their solutions, and a reasoned discussion will be more challenging.

This is most evident in strategic planning, which should be approached as another form of innovative problem solving. At the outset of the strategic planning process, the team should have animated discussions on the context, the facts, the main business trends, and the key questions the strategic planning process must resolve. When debates on solutions occur at the end of the process, they are generally rooted in disagreements on the facts and questions up front, but by this point they are much more difficult to resolve.

This technique can also be used in reverse. When an employee or a team comes to the leader with a new idea, the leader should always ask what problem the solution solves. Systematically using this technique can eliminate many of the frivolous creative ideas that do not solve real business problems.

The "How to . . . ?" Questions Checklist

Here is a checklist to assess "How to . . . ?" questions:

☐ Is the level of the "How to . . . ?" question too lofty?

Example: How to succeed? How to achieve our objectives?

These problem statements are so amorphous that it is almost impossible to find anything tangible to hold onto in order to solve them. To improve them, identify the specific problems they imply—take them from the loftiest level to a more practical level. From that list, identify the best level from which to start. The problem could then become: How to reach $1 million in sales? or How to raise $10 million in capital?

☐ Does the "How to . . . ?" question lack specificity?

Example: How to increase sales from all customers?

In this question, "all customers" does not discriminate among good and bad or new and old customers. It is very unlikely that the same answer will work for all customer segments. Better questions would be: How to improve sales from our best customers? How to improve sales from recent customers by

10 percent? How to improve sales from local customers? How to improve sales in-store? How to improve sales on the web?

☐ Is the "How to . . . ?" question too tactical?

Example: How to execute a brochure for ABC? How to choose a supplier to do XYZ?
When starting at a tactical level, the team should make sure they have thoroughly thought out the tactic they want to implement (e.g., the brochure, the supplier). The best way is to ask: "What problem does the brochure (or the supplier) solve?" Or "Have you considered alternatives to the brochure?" If the team members have thoroughly examined the problem, they will have clear and obvious answers to these questions.

☐ Does the "How to . . . ?" question have two or more problems in one statement?

Example: How to encourage employees to register <u>and</u> use the service regularly?
When the words "and" or "all" appear in a question, it usually means that there is more than one problem, unless the intent is to combine more than one element. In the example question there are probably two or even three distinct, sequential questions: The end goal is: How to encourage employees to use the service regularly? Three sub-problems to resolve the goal could be: (1) How to encourage employees to register? (2) How to encourage employees to use the service once? and (3) How to get employees to use the service regularly? The key to improving possible multiple problem questions is to consider whether one single answer can solve the problem. If you need more than one answer, as in the example above, then you probably have more than one problem. There is nothing wrong with having more than one clear problem, if that is reality, but multiple problems require separate innovative thinking processes to solve them effectively.

☐ Is the "How to . . . ?" question wording inaccurate or imprecise?

Examples: How to <u>improve</u> the process? How to increase . . . <u>significantly</u>? How to minimize, if <u>required</u>, . . . ? How to <u>reduce</u> the cost?
A single plastic[1] word in a statement can derail the best team. Plastic words sound very precise but in isolation have no real common meaning. Some of the most obvious plastic words are: improve, sooner, better, future,

---

1. Uwe Poerksen, *Plastic Words* (University of Pennsylvania Press, 1995).

higher, expensive, more. These words have a very clear meaning for the person saying or writing them. They also usually have a clear meaning for the person hearing or reading them, but the two interpretations often differ considerably. Leaders must ensure that there are no plastic words in the problem they assign to a team. They should think carefully about the meaning and the intent of each word and be ready to explain what each term means.

The above examples could be rewritten without plastic words as follows: "How to accelerate the process by one day?" "How to increase . . . by 10 percent without increasing costs?" "How to create a contingency plan if X happens?" "How to reduce the distribution cost by 10 percent now?"

A simple way to reduce the use of plastic words is to make sure the listeners have permission to verify the intended meaning of each ambiguous or potentially ambiguous term. If every time a leader uses a plastic word, anyone can ask for a clarification, the language will become clearer, innovation efforts will be more focused, and results will quickly improve.

☐ Are some of the words in the "How to . . . ?" question unnecessary or in the wrong place?

Example: How to increase the production volume of Product A by 10 percent between January 1 and July 1 without increasing our cost?
A question should be as short as possible to clearly state what the team is trying to achieve and as long as necessary to be clear. The style should be as direct as possible by making sure the end goal is the first concept in the question. In addition, a useful method of keeping a question short is to use an asterisk (*) linked to footnotes to clarify what ambiguous or plastic words mean. The above example could be rewritten more simply as follows: "How to increase* production volume of product A? "The footnote would be as follows:" *By 10% between January 1 and July 1 without increasing costs."

It is important to remember that the framework is always more than a "How to . . . ?" question. It also includes the Context, Boundaries, and Type of Solution, and some of the details may fit better in one of these areas than in the "How to . . . ?" question.

THE BOUNDARIES

The opening example in this chapter illustrates the request to work on a project without boundaries. These kinds of projects are doomed to failure, rework, misunderstanding, or aggravation even before they start.

The boundaries in innovation are the formal limits that define which solutions will be acceptable and what a solution must not include. If team members understand the boundaries, they are able to focus in the right direction from the outset and do not waste time on fascinating but unworkable directions.

Changing the boundaries of a problem often dramatically changes the process to resolve it. Consider the problem below and the implications of having very different boundaries for the process of problem resolution:

- *The Problem:* How to improve satisfaction for our best customers?
  Boundaries A: Impact in two months, no changes in information technology systems, $25,000 budget.
  Boundaries B: Impact within 12 to 18 months, information technology systems changes are possible, $500,000 budget.

In addition to setting boundaries for each problem, the team will find it useful to have overall boundaries that will apply for all innovation initiatives. We often recommend two kinds of overall boundaries for a department or an organization:

- One set should define the areas where innovation and improvement are sought and those that are restricted.
- The second set should define the process and the level of executive involvement required for each level of a project.

Global, Specific, and "Must Do" Boundaries

It is useful to separate boundaries into global, specific, and "must do" boundaries:

- *Global:* The global boundaries are outside the control of the project owner or the team. They can include legislation, corporate strategy, corporate image, or customer satisfaction, and so on.

- *Specific:* The specific boundaries are within the control of the project owner or decision maker and relate directly to the issue. Examples could include budget or return on investment, time available, negative impact on short- or long-term profits, resources, or impact on other areas of the organization.
- *Must Do:* The "must do" boundaries are the elements that must be included in any solution for it to be approved. Examples could include:
    - Must be different from the current answer
    - Must appeal to the very best customers
    - Must be fully integrated
    - Must be profitable within 12 months.

The Three Stages of Setting Boundaries

There are three distinct stages to setting boundaries:

1. Stage 1 applies the divergence perspective to setting boundaries. It requires the individual or the team to list all the possible boundaries that could apply to the project. Separating the global and the specific boundaries may be helpful, but when in doubt simply write the boundary down in either category.
2. Stage 2 challenges each boundary to ensure that it is a real boundary for the innovation project and not an obsolete assumption. It is also important to eliminate the plastic words in boundary statements. At this stage, common sense is often as useful as historical or specific knowledge
3. Stage 3 applies the convergence perspective. It is used to select the boundaries that will be most useful to separate the implementable solutions from the "brilliant-but-not-implementable" ideas.

Teams will find the boundary exercise very useful to ensure every member understands how to select solutions at the end of the process. Also, by working as a team, members find they can use their collective knowledge to identify whether a boundary is real or not. Often one team member will have specific new information that invalidates a boundary. For example, a team member representing the marketing department may believe that a certain path is unavailable, but a member of the technology team, with the most up-to-date information, may know it is actually possible.

The Difference between Boundaries and Obsolete Assumptions

The issue with boundaries is that there is no obvious visible difference between a good boundary that really defines your "sandbox" and an old, obsolete paradigm[2] or assumption. At times, bad assumptions are so strongly held that they become automatic and unwritten boundaries for a team. The assumptions can be individual or collective and are usually inherited from the organization's culture or previous leadership. This explains why, at the outset of the process, the team must always validate the boundaries to eliminate the most obvious assumptions or old paradigms.

What to Do if an Owner Says There Are No Boundaries

If an owner says there are no boundaries, it may be necessary to ask extreme hypothetical questions: "So if I really understand correctly, you are telling me that I can take 10 years and spend $1 billion to complete the project?" This question usually gets the conversation focused on the real boundaries, however tight or loose. If the owner or decision maker still does not want to identify the boundaries for a project or does not have the time to do this, the team should create its own best educated guess at possible boundaries. Then, they should validate the boundaries with the owner before proceeding with investments of time and resources.

Using Boundaries is a Key Method to Manage Risk in Innovative Projects

Many executives and leaders at every level, even in successful organizations, believe that in order to control risk, they should limit the number and scope of innovation initiatives. However, the risk would diminish dramatically if they were to mandate innovation within clear boundaries that are understood by everyone in advance. As indicated earlier, a leader can fundamentally change the nature of a problem and the level of risk a team can take by simply expanding or restricting the boundaries of the problem.

Establishing boundaries is one of the main differences between innovative thinking and analytical thinking, between innovation and creativity, and between successful innovation and solutions that create chaos or are

---

2. Joel Barker, *Future Edge* (William Morrow, January 1992).

never implemented. Using boundaries helps avoid wasting time and energy in useless directions, and it helps manage risk in the problem solving and innovation process. Ultimately, boundaries are the best way to make sure the team develops the best possible new solution within the defined sandbox.

Avoid the "Thinking Out of the Box" Dilemma

One phrase that has caused unnecessary problems for innovative thinking is "thinking out of the box." This phrase is taken from the classic creativity exercise that asks you to link all nine dots (as depicted below in Figure 6.2) by drawing four lines without lifting your pen. The solution is to draw the line outside the self-imposed frame of the nine dots, hence the phrase "thinking out of the box."

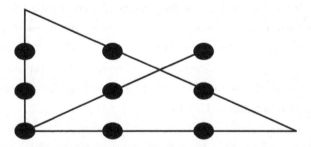

Figure 6.2: The "Think Out of the Box" Solution to the Nine Dots Exercise

This phrase has become synonymous with innovation, and it has been promoted for many years as the explanation for the lack of innovation afflicting organizations. Contrary to the objectives of the leaders who talk about it, it has created much damage. Typically, it is an attempt to be creative using analytical thinking, but with all the shortcomings we have described above, it rarely delivers useful or sustainable change. By virtue of its name and starting assumptions, it generally fails to consider the walls of the box, which are the boundaries, real or hypothetical.

What *really* happens when people engage in "thinking out of the box" in real life, not in creativity books, is that people's first reaction is to look for rules to break, whether the rules are real or not, whether they are obsolete assumptions or solid business boundaries. By thinking out of the box without trying to understand what the box is made of and how real some of its walls are, leaders and teams are most likely to jump right into another box that will look new and exciting but is still just another box. The team will break some of the real but unmovable boundaries, making the solutions fun and creative but also valueless for the organization. The team will be frustrated because their "brilliant" ideas will not be approved and innovation will take one or more steps backward for a few years.

So, while innovative thinking may not sound as exciting as "thinking out of the box," it does deliver value systematically and sustainably. Many start-up companies in the dot-com-boom era vanished because they really did "think out of the box," but they forgot that businesses have rules and consumers have their own ideas of how much they are ready to change their behaviors.

THE TYPE OF SOLUTION

In many ways, the word "innovation" is the ultimate plastic word. It can cover different types of innovation such as product or process innovation, short- and long-term innovation, implementable ideas and fuzzy concepts, as well as a continuum from continuous improvement to disruptive business models. One of the ways to clarify what is expected is to define upfront the type of solution required.

Identifying the type of solution helps the leaders and the teams improve their understanding of the desired outcome of the process. It is an excellent way to ensure that all team members share one common view of the objective. It can be customized for each type of business, but it has two parts:

* **Types of innovation:**
  It is important to clarify the type or combination of types of innovation[3] expected, from process to product, from sales to management. When a team works on a problem, the type of innovation may appear obvious, but if it is not clearly expressed, confusion can arise. For example, there are many ways a team can approach the following problem: "How to sell more cars in five years?"
    - They can focus on *process innovation* and look for better processes to design, manufacture, or sell the cars.
    - They can focus on *product innovation* and look for new features or a new style, such as a new engine or new finishing touches.

---

3. There are many models for the types of innovation; for example, we find the Doblin model useful (www.doblin.com).

- They can focus on *marketing* and *sales innovation* and find new ways to sell existing cars, as Saturn did with the "no haggle" policy, or by selling cars directly to the consumer.
- They can focus on *management innovation* and look for business model solutions, such as creating new partnerships and strategic alliances.

- **Types of outcomes:**

  An innovative thinking team needs to be aligned on the key dimensions of the outcomes, including: how many solutions are expected and whether they should be the following:
  - Incremental or revolutionary or somewhere in-between
  - Implementable or conceptual
  - Implemented or produce results in the short- or long-term
  - Implemented within tight or flexible boundaries.

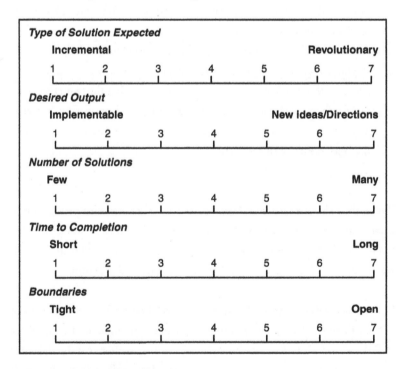

Figure 6.3: The Types of Outcomes Chart

A team can use the *Types of Outcomes Chart* to discuss the mandate and make sure team members are aligned. A team can also customize the *Types of Outcomes Chart*, depending on the type of business and the type of innovation. Here is a description of each of the elements in the *Types of Outcomes Chart*:

1. *The Type of Solution Expected:* This element identifies whether the outcome should be incremental or revolutionary innovation.
2. *Desired Output:* The second element identifies how finished the solutions should be at the end of the process. A rating of 1 indicates the solutions should be fully developed and ready for implementation "as is." A rating of 7 indicates the solution should be in conceptual form.
3. *Number of Solutions:* The third element identifies whether there should be one single solution (rating of 1) or if the outcome should include many different solutions (rating of 7).
4. *Time to completion:* The fourth element identifies the timing for the implementation of the solution, from very short term (rating of 1) to longer term solutions (rating of 7). Versions of this element can focus on the timing to start the process (immediately or later) or on the timing to be able to measure the actual impact or results.
5. *Application of the boundaries:* For a given project, a team may want to consider that the boundaries are firm, meaning that the team members must adhere to them without interpretation or leeway. On the other hand, they may agree that, if necessary, they can discuss and modify the boundaries with the owner.

In a team, each member should individually fill in the *Type of Outcomes Chart*. Then, they should post the results on a wall chart and discuss them. It is important to remember that there are no right or wrong answers, only different views of the same issue. The objective is to learn from the various points of view. Here is what can happen during the discussion:

- *Team members agree on the expected outcome.* The leader simply needs to confirm their understanding. It is particularly important to confirm their understanding of the *Time* dimension, as there can be different interpretations of short- or long-term. For each project, the result should be very specific.
- *Team members disagree on the type of outcome expected.* The discussion should first clarify the nature of the differences. The team members who have different views can debate why they believe the outcomes should be

different. The purpose is not to convince one person or prove anyone is wrong but to enlarge the discussion and ensure that the team members consider each point of view. The dissenters may know something the rest of the group does not, and the learning from the discussion can be very important. If the members still have a difference of opinion at the end of the discussion, the owner can choose one option or decide that two different teams will look at the two different options.

- *There are clearly two possible outcomes on one or more dimensions, and the team members agree on what the outcomes should be.* An example would be determining that there is a need for long-term and revolutionary solutions and also for short-term and incremental solutions. In this case, the owner must make a choice as to which problem the team will work on first. The second problem can be worked on either by another team or by the same team after they have completed the first project. The guideline is simple: work on one problem with one set of desired outcomes and boundaries at a time. The only incorrect process decision is to accept that the team should work on both short- and long-term options at the same time. This may not appear to be a major guideline, but it is one of the common sources of failure for innovation teams. By chasing two incompatible goals, innovation teams usually achieve neither well.

- *There is a "Z" pattern, showing a major incompatibility among the answers.* An example would be if the team wants many revolutionary, implementable solutions in the short term within tight boundaries. In this case, the group must ensure that they discuss and, if necessary, modify the desired outcome to make it manageable. If there is no consensus, the leader of the project must decide. It is preferable to have that conversation at the outset and debate any incompatibility up front, rather than to try to design a process to deliver on an impossible goal.

- *There is an incompatibility between the desired type of solution and the problem or the boundaries.* In this case, the leader and the team must identify the reason for the incompatibility and resolve it before the team can move forward.

The Type of Solution technique is very powerful for any team tasked with developing innovative solutions to a problem or an opportunity. It prevents rework and frustration by clearly establishing the type of solutions the team and leader (or owner) expect and by preventing the creation of multiple goals for the same problem. Depending on the issue and its urgency and importance, the goal may be an incremental innovation or revolutionary breakthrough. Only the owner can decide how far and fast the team can go to innovate, but the process and the overall steps the team uses to determine the solution will be the same.

THE OWNER OR DECISION MAKER

Some people believe that because they have been given a problem to solve, they can make any changes to the problem they believe necessary, without asking for permission. But the person who really owns an issue is the owner or decision maker. The owner is the person who will make the ultimate decision on whether the solution will be implemented or not. The owner must approve the solution and must also approve the intermediate steps that define Step 1: *Framework* and the outcome of Step 2: *Issue Redefinition*. Not validating the framework or the redefined problem with the owner before looking for solutions is a setup for innovation failure.

One example clearly illustrates the impact of ownership:

A large financial institution redesigned the processes in its communication department.

In the old process, the communication department would create a communication strategy (the framework) and get it signed off by the executives in the communication, marketing, and product areas. Based on the strategy, they would then produce communication material such as newspaper advertisements or brochures (the solutions). The process was mired in delay. The parties always approved the strategies quickly with very few comments, but the approval of the communication material almost always resulted in conflict and arguments. As a result, the materials were often rejected, and the work had to be done again. By their own estimation, the staff in the communication department spent between 40 and 50 percent of their time redoing things, sometimes multiple times.

In the redesigned process, one of the main implemented changes agreed to by all the executives was that when an executive in the product or marketing areas approved a communication strategy (the framework), they could not reject the resulting advertising material if it was on strategy. They had to take ownership of the strategy.

When the new process was first implemented, the executives still paid little or no attention to the strategy, as was their pattern. Soon afterward, a new advertising campaign was presented, and the executives did not like it, so they refused it, even though it corresponded to the approved strategy. The communication executive who had implemented the new process stood firm. The matter was escalated to the executive suite where it was resolved that if there was a process and everyone had agreed on it (even if they hadn't understood the full impact), then the new process should stand. From that point on, the strategies were always fully discussed.

The result was almost immediate. Within a few months, the amount of time the communication department spent redoing work was reduced by half. Employees now had an extra full day a week that they could spend thinking better. The department had over 50 employees, and the direct benefit represented the work of 10 full-time employees.

The onus is clearly on the owner to pay attention when presented with a framework or a redesigned problem. By not paying full attention and not investing the time that it takes to review the framework, owners are almost certainly guaranteeing significant rework for their teams as well as for themselves.

THE PROJECT CHARTER

Innovative thinking works best when each problem, however small or large, is treated like a project. Whether it is one person solving a simple problem in one hour or a team of twenty people taking twelve months to work on a major innovation, the results are more effective if there is a solid process.

The project charter provides an effective format to document the innovation project and the overall process, including the approval of the owner or decision maker. The project charter also is useful as part of the orientation of new members. It will help them understand what the innovation project is trying to accomplish and within what precise boundaries. The new members also can understand what has been accomplished, what still needs to be done, and how they fit into the project.

There are a number of elements to consider when developing a project charter:

- *The total time available to find a solution.* The total time available is always the first factor to consider and confirm when planning the process.
- *The complexity of the issue.* The more complex the issue, the more time and resources the team will need in order to understand the problem or opportunity before they look for solutions. If the problem is very complex, the team will also need to spend more time in the implementation planning step.
- *The "age" of the problem.* Real insight happens when you know you do not know enough. When the team believes it has a good understanding of the

situation because it has been a long-standing problem, significant effort needs to be applied in the framework and issue redefinition steps to break patterns and separate reality from myth and faulty assumptions.

- *The type of solution desired.* The more different or revolutionary the expectations, the more time the team should spend in Step 2: *Issue Redefinition* and Step 3: *Idea Generation.*

Table 6.1 presents an effective format to plan most innovative thinking projects. Some of the items on the project charter can be skipped for simpler or short-term problems.

Table 6.1: The Project Charter

The Project Charter

1. *Context*
   - a.   What is the overall project goal?
   - b.   What are the known elements, including what has been tried before?
   - c.   Why is the project urgent and important?

2. *Objective of the process*
   - a.   What is the "How to …?" question that defines the problem?
   - b.   What is the desired output and outcome?
   - c.   What is the work to be completed by this team and the timing?

3. *Scope of the project*
   - a.   What are the boundaries for the project (i.e., global, specific, and "must do")?
   - b.   What type of solution is required (i.e., type of innovation and type of outcome)?

4. *Owner and project leads*
   - a.   Who will make the decisions at every stage?
   - b.   Who will lead the process?
   - c.   What is the delegated authority of the innovation team?

5. *Team and resources*
   - a.   Who are the people required to successfully complete the project and what will be the time commitment for each?
     - • Internal
     - • Contract
     - • Others (partners, stakeholders, etc.)
   - b.   What other resources are required to achieve the deliverables (i.e., technology, financial, administrative, physical, etc.)?
   - c.   What is the budget?

6. *Deliverables*
   - a.   What will be produced at the end of the project and in what form?
   - b.   How will the team measure success and value?

7. **Approach and methodology**
   a. What are the steps for how the team will achieve the deliverables and what are the deliverables the team will achieve at key milestones?
   b. What is the approach to engage in critical inquiry (i.e., are we doing the right things and are we doing them the right way)?
   c. What are the possible alternative methods to achieve the same deliverable?

8. **Work plan and timeframes:**
   a. Framework
       - Is the framework documented?
   b. Issue redefinition
       - What techniques will be used?
       - How many sessions will be necessary?
       - Who needs to be involved?
   c. Idea generation
       - What techniques will be used?
       - How many sessions will be necessary?
       - Who needs to be involved?
   d. Implementation planning
       - What techniques will be used?
       - How many sessions will be necessary?
       - Who needs to be involved?

LEVERAGING THE THREE INTELLIGENCES IN THE FRAMEWORK STEP

Up to this point, we have focused on how to apply innovative thinking in the framework step of the innovative thinking process. Teams can augment the framework step by the appropriate application of analytical and emotional intelligence. This section describes some of the areas where leaders will find the combination of intelligences beneficial as they engage in innovative thinking.

Augmenting Innovative Intelligence with Analytical Intelligence

Chapter 4 describes a number of the challenges that can occur when leaders overuse analytical intelligence. However, there are some ways in which analytical intelligence can be helpful in the framework step. These include the following:

- *Setting the context:* Analytical intelligence can be useful in the process of collecting information about what the team members know about the context of an issue. It can also be helpful in identifying past experiences with this kind of issue.

- *Developing the "How to ...?" question:* Analytical intelligence can be helpful for collecting a team's preconceived ideas about what the question is. However, the key is to go beyond the first series of ideas by asking what else is possible, impossible, or improbable, forcing the team members to stretch their thinking beyond the obvious and the automatic.

- *Establishing boundaries:* Team members can find analytical intelligence helpful for identifying all the assumptions that may create real or artificial boundaries. However, it is important to emphasize that the team needs to challenge these assumptions in order to separate the real boundaries from the obsolete assumptions.

- *Developing the project charter:* The power of logic in the analytical thinking process can be very useful to organize the elements of the project charter. However, be aware that team members who tend to overuse analytical thinking may be motivated to skip the essential parts of the framework step and simply complete the project charter without applying innovative thinking to each of the elements.

Augmenting Innovative Intelligence with Emotional Intelligence

Emotional intelligence can augment innovative intelligence during the Step I: *Framework* by affecting these two elements:

1. The development of the content of the issue that the team must solve
2. The way the innovation team works together in the process of developing the framework.

How Emotional Intelligence can Affect the Content of the Issue that the Team Must Solve

The process of developing the content within the framework step can be facilitated by applying emotional intelligence effectively. Here are some ways that can be done:

- *Setting the context:* At this point, the team collects the facts. In addition, it is useful to consider what people feel about the issue and how they feel about different solutions that were tried before. It is important to consider the context from all the stakeholders' points of view, focusing on both their rational and their emotional perspectives.

- *Developing the "How to . . . ?" question:* Sometimes emotional characteristics can shape the core question that should be explored. For example, if the problem is to communicate a predefined new policy to employees in a department, the "How to . . . ?" question could be "How to engage the employees in the department so that they adopt and feel good about the new policy?"

- *Establishing boundaries:* Sometimes there are emotional boundaries in addition to the more obvious rational boundaries. For example, how do people feel about the last failed attempt at solving the problem? Any solution that would remind them of the previous, failed solution may be rejected outright because they may feel it will have almost no chance of being successful. There also can be emotional "must do" boundaries. An example of this would be "the innovative solution must not result in staff becoming disengaged."

- *Clarifying the role of the owner:* The ownership of an issue is often defined by hierarchical reporting relationships and accountabilities. However, sometimes emotional factors may further define the real owner of an issue. For example, the person accountable for a project may be the VP the team leader reports to, but that VP may be relying on the advice of a former VP who is now in a new role. It will be very helpful for the innovation team to understand this dynamic in order to ensure they involve and consult the right people throughout the process.

How Emotional Intelligence Affects the Way the Innovation Team Works Together in the Process of Developing the Framework

Using emotional intelligence to improve the effectiveness of the innovation team is also critical to its ultimate success. Here are two ways it can be done:

- *Choosing innovation team members:* When selecting an innovation team, it is important to consider the technical capabilities and diverse viewpoints and experiences of potential innovation team members. However, it is also important to consider emotional intelligence variables. For example, the team leader should think about the following:

- Do potential team members have the emotional intelligence to be open to viewpoints other than their own?
- Do potential team members use coercive ways to force their opinions on a team, which could undermine the team's trust and thought processes? On the positive side, does a potential team member have the emotional intelligence to facilitate open dialogue among the team members so that they can develop insights into issues and discover the best possible solutions?

- *Encouraging questioning and open debates:* Some leaders avoid debating because they feel it will have a negative impact on the team's morale. The opposite is often true. It is important for the leader to ensure that all team members can express their views on any issue. Team members benefit because they will feel they can be heard, be open to different viewpoints, and be supported as they question ideas and debate openly. Also, when team members can debate openly, they are much more likely to stand behind the direction the team leader chooses.

THE LEADER'S ROLES IN STEP 1: FRAMEWORK

There are two different roles for leaders in the Step I: *Framework:*

- The oversight role—the leader who is the owner of the innovation project
- The accountability role—the leader who is the team leader of an innovation team.

The Oversight Role

We define *oversight* as ensuring that those who hold the responsibility for an innovation team are held accountable for the team's actions and decisions. Senior leaders who are the owners of innovation projects should use Step I: *Framework* to do the following:

- Increase the probability that their innovation teams will discover innovative solutions in a systematic way
- Reduce the risk that the teams will develop unwanted or risky solutions.

The role of an owner-leader (the leader who owns the project) is to allocate the time required to the framework step and to pay thorough attention to each of the elements in this innovative thinking step. Owner-leaders who relate to the framework superficially and approve weak frameworks reduce the potential for the discovery of innovative solutions to important issues.

Here are some actions that the owner-leaders can take:

- As much as possible, the owners should prepare the framework themselves as part of the delegation process to the innovation team. If time is not available to prepare a framework, then the owners should ask the innovation teams to develop the framework and then validate it with them.
- Require innovation teams to develop an approved framework before permitting them to spend any time or resources on a project involving innovation.
- Encourage discussions and challenges to the framework. Also, ensure that the language in the framework has no ambiguity.
- Focus on the context, the "How to . . . ?" question(s), the boundaries, and the type of solution in the framework step, and avoid engaging in the premature exploration of possible solutions.
- Always ask what problem an unsolicited solution solves and within what boundaries.

The Accountability Role

The innovation team leader has specific accountabilities throughout the innovative thinking process. We define *accountability* as the obligation to answer for a responsibility conferred by the owner. The accountable leader has a number of specific roles in the framework step, which include the following:

- **Establish ground rules and norms for the innovation team**
  Leaders need to ensure that innovative teams establish norms for how the team members will work with each other, including a clearly defined role for the leader. Here is an exercise that often generates good innovative team ground rules. The leader divides the team into four groups, and they each respond to one of the following four questions:
    - What would make this team a *terrific innovative thinking team*?
    - What would make this team a *terrible innovative thinking team*?

- What would make the leader a *terrific leader* of an innovative thinking team?
- What would make the leader a *terrible leader* of an innovative thinking team?

Because the team members generate the responses to these questions, they often have a quicker level of acceptance to the team's ground rules. Also, if they identify ground rules for the team or the leader that the leader cannot accept, the leader can clarify what he or she is willing to do, or not do, in order to make the team process effective.

- **Clearly articulate the overall team goals**
  The leader needs to take the initiative to define the objectives for the process. The team is expected to discuss the ultimate objectives to ensure they fully understand the work they need to accomplish and the complex challenge that they need to explore.

- **Clearly establish boundaries**
  The leader may have received specific boundaries and must communicate these honestly and clearly so that the team knows precisely what the boundaries are for the entire process. Also, in some cases, the leader establishes additional boundaries that will be important to articulate to the team.

  Sometimes, leaders make the mistake of telling others what they should do and how they should do it. But in order to lead through complexity, it is more important for leaders to excel at defining the boundaries of complex issues for their teams. However, within the boundaries, team members should have the freedom and safety to explore the complexity of the issue and to identify the unique characteristics of it and the best resolution to it.

- **Clarify the ownership of the issue and the accountabilities**
  The accountable leader should share with the innovation team the accountabilities that have been conferred, the owner's oversight role, and the method by which the team leader will make decisions throughout the process. The accountable leader also needs to clarify the leader's delegated authority for the work on the complex innovation problem. For example: Does the leader have the authority to proceed with the

innovative thinking process all the way to implementation planning or is the leader expected to check with the owner at interim points to clarify that the team is proceeding in the right direction?

CONCLUSION

This chapter presented the tools and techniques leaders and teams can apply to create an effective framework, a necessary step to succeed at innovation. Leaders at the executive level need to be very familiar with this step of the process because they are accountable for the framework for key innovation initiatives. More junior leaders who receive the delegated request need to have the strength of character to ask the owner questions about the context, the key questions, the boundaries, the ownership of the project, and the type of solution expected. They also need to collaborate with their innovation teams to develop the project charter and to seek the owner's approval to confirm that the innovation team's understanding of the project charter is accurate.

It is also critical to remember that the various elements that compose the framework must be consistent between them. For example, a very tight budget and time frame in the boundary would probably be inconsistent with revolutionary or breakthrough solutions. If the team decides to recommend a few changes in any element of the framework, they must ensure that it is still compatible with and does not affect other elements of the framework.

The next chapter describes the Step 2: *Issue Redefinition* process. This step takes the framework developed in Step I and generates insight into the issue by uncovering the unique elements of the complexity and the root causes of the problem or opportunity.

CHAPTER SEVEN

STEP 2: ISSUE REDEFINITION

A team developed their project charter with the focus on the question: "How to increase sales of mutual funds to our current individual customers?" They began Step 2: Issue Redefinition, by looking at their current customers and recognized considerable differences within individual customer segments. They realized that no single solution could address the different needs of easy and difficult, young and old, recent and long-time customers. They decided to regroup them into distinct and actionable segments. After working on three different sub-problems, they were able to gain insight into the most complex challenges associated with each segment. Based on this analysis, the team was able to redefine the three issues and identify different solutions that worked well for each customer group.

By the time the team has completed the Step 1: *Framework*, they should be clear about the overall direction for solving the problem or opportunity. The framework defines the goal (the "How to . . . ?" question) and the type of solution desired, as well as the boundaries that must be respected. However, even after completing the framework process, the team will find that complex issues can still include many uncertainties and ambiguities and be multi-layered.

Thus, the objective of Step 2: *Issue Redefinition* is to strip the problem or series of problems down to root causes and make the complexity manageable. The issue redefinition step helps identify sub-problems, as well as the best angles from which to solve the overall problem.

Figure 7.1 shows the four-step innovative thinking process. This chapter explores in detail the approaches and techniques for Step 2: *Issue Redefinition*.

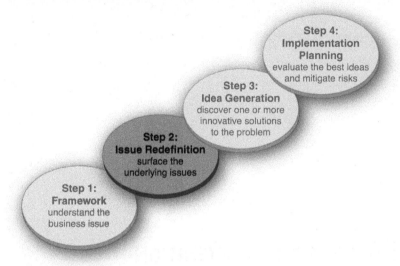

Figure 7.1: The Four-Step Innovative Thinking Process

THE FIVE AREAS OF FOCUS IN ISSUE REDEFINITION

One of the keys to success in innovative thinking is to "check twice and move once." It is essential that innovative thinkers make the effort and take the time to dig deeper into the question identified in the framework step before engaging in problem resolution. Innovative thinkers "check twice" by establishing the framework and also engaging in issue redefinition.

As a result of Step 2: *Issue Redefinition*, innovative thinkers are able to identify the real issue or issues to resolve, thereby maximizing the value of Step 3: *Idea Generation*.

The Five Areas of Focus in Issue Redefinition

1. *Clarify assumptions.* Expose the underlying assumptions and determine if they are facts or not.
2. *Map the system.* Understand how the issue fits into a larger and more complex system.
3. *Break down the issue into its parts.* Take apart the issue and determine if there are multiple aspects to the problem or opportunity.
4. *Gain insight into root causes.* Enter the problem and find the prime cause of the problem on which to focus idea generation.
5. *Validate the redefined issue.* Confirm the redefined issue with the owner of the problem.

This chapter explains the five focus areas for issue redefinition and describes one technique per area of focus. It is important to note that, although we present a number of very useful techniques, leaders do not need to use all of them for every issue. Rather, they should select the techniques most appropriate to generate the insight necessary to identify the right problem or problems.

Let's take a look now at the five areas of focus for issue redefinition.

Clarify Assumptions

Issue redefinition is fundamentally concerned with, and driven by, revealing the underlying assumptions to shape and reshape an issue. The innovative thinker always remains open to questioning the continuing appropriateness of all assumptions.

Nothing feels as real as a long-held assumption or belief. The problem is that one obsolete assumption can prevent a team from finding the best solution—the one that will address the root cause of the issue and not only solve the problem but prevent its recurrence. Assumptions are usually attached to memories and emotions, not only facts. This makes it difficult to separate them from reality. For example, the statement: "We believe something to be true because our previous CEO said it was true several years ago, and he was highly respected by all employees," could generate an assumption that is not true for a current situation and could distort the understanding of an issue.

The *clarify assumptions* technique helps distinguish fact from fiction. The team needs to clearly articulate the complete list of assumptions and challenge them where appropriate. This process focuses the issue on the facts of the situation (rather than false assumptions).

Here is a description of the *clarify assumptions* technique:

What it is
It is essential that the team separate facts from assumptions. They must create a complete list of their assumptions about the issue and then review the list.

The team should check the assumptions that can be verified with the most credible source, going outside the team if necessary. For example, most people on a team may believe that the majority of sales are from one customer group, even after a major shift happened that changed that customer dynamic. Checking this assumption with the sales department will alert the team to the change.

The assumptions that cannot be verified should be separated into two groups:

- The assumptions everyone agrees are true
- The assumptions that at least one person challenges.

Where at least one person has reservations about the assumptions, ask that person to express his or her concerns. Using a divergence perspective, ask everyone to find other possible reasons why the assumptions could be challenged. At this point, the group can decide if they accept the assumptions or if they need to collect more facts.

To eliminate obsolete assumptions that are widely held, start by challenging the simplest assumption first. Ask: "What if this were not true anymore? What would that mean and what would happen then?" This practice will help the group challenge more complex assumptions.

This process can be time-consuming, but it helps people realize that assumptions or beliefs are not facts and may or may not be accurate in the current reality. Once team members successfully challenge one strong assumption or belief, they are more likely to be willing to do so again in the future.

When to use it

This technique should be used for almost all issues, especially when the assumptions or the numbers do not feel right but are used to justify current problems. It also is particularly effective when change is happening so quickly that past assumptions may no longer be useful but the team has not caught up to the current reality.

Keys to success

The keys to success for the *clarify assumptions* technique are:

- Have the patience to list all the assumptions and then challenge one assumption at a time with the team.
- Check the facts that can be verified and make sure their interpretation is correct.
- Challenge all assumptions as much as necessary, without picking on any one in particular. This is important in a team, as some individuals are often attached to a particular assumption that others have no problem challenging.

Map the System

Understanding the issue thoroughly includes making an analysis of the larger system and determining where the issue fits within that system. Often, the process of exploring the larger system leads to the following:

- A more complete understanding of the issue and how it is interdependent or counterbalances other parts of the larger system
- A redefinition of the issue as a more complex, integrated problem, rather than as an isolated issue.

Often, the *map the system* process is instructive to an innovation team when they engage in Step 3: *Idea Generation,* because they will need to consider how the proposed solutions resolve the issue and fit into the larger system at the same time.

Here is a description of the *map the system* technique.

What it is

The technique of *map the system* assumes that all events (including events that may appear isolated) occur within a holistic system. It also involves the following:

- Seeing the total system and all its complexities
- Identifying important interactions, interdependencies, side effects, process disconnects, and leverage points
- Using mostly visual diagrams, rich in implications and thoughts, to facilitate dialogue and exploration of complexities
- Reducing ambiguities and miscommunication by making implicit knowledge explicit
- Facilitating questioning, dialogue, and the sharing of insights without "finger-pointing."

There are a number of methodologies for system mapping. Most often the process begins by drawing the system (with the name of the system in the center) to show connections and disconnects.[1] Here is an example of how one organization benefited from mapping the system.

---

1. System thinking and mapping is described in detail by Peter M. Senge, *The Fifth Discipline: The Art and Practice of the Learning Organization* (Doubleday, 1990). That systems mapping process identifies the reinforcing and balancing aspects within a system.

The team was exploring how to improve their approvals success rate from a regulatory body that controlled access for their patented drugs. They developed a map of the system to understand the broader drug approvals system and to determine how the regulatory body drug approval role fit into that larger system. The exercise clarified that the regulatory body was a piece of a larger puzzle and that the real hub of the issue was in the political part of the system that defined the mandate for the regulatory body. As a result, the team shifted their focus from trying to negotiate a new drug approval standard with the regulatory body to exploring how they could shape the decisions of the political policy makers who provided direction to the regulatory body.

When to use it

Mapping the system is particularly useful when the team understands that the issue is a part of a greater whole. Then, the team needs to understand how the issue contributes to or conflicts with aspects within its larger system, before they engage in issue resolution.

Keys to success

Some of the keys to success in mapping the system include the following:

- Openness to thinking outside the problem area
- Willingness to accept that the larger context and system within which an issue is occurring can directly influence the issue and its outcome
- Receptiveness to including team members who have an appreciation of the bigger picture and the entire system
- Awareness that some of the complexities in the larger system may not be relevant to the issue and to problem resolution
- Readiness to look at the issue from the points of view of all the key stakeholders. At this stage, the team can also apply the *focus exchange* technique we describe later in this chapter.

Break Down the Issue into Its Parts

The process of breaking down the problem into manageable parts usually focuses on two methodologies:

- *Sequencing.* Understanding the sequencing within the issue from beginning to end to assess where the greatest issues are located and if the various issues must be resolved concurrently or sequentially.

- *Atomization.* Breaking the issue down to its smallest components and seeing if there are specific parts that need to be studied separately or in greater detail.

The Sequencing Technique

What it is

Sequencing helps avoid the common problem-solving mistake of using the end goal as the definitive problem. When this occurs, it is possible that the innovation team may ignore the series of interconnected sequential problems that may exist. Some organizations use an elaborate process mapping exercise to describe the sequence of the process in extensive detail. In some situations, process mapping can add great value. However, many situations only require a simpler diagram of the sequence of events that occur within the issue.

Here is an example of how sequencing helped redefine an issue:

The senior executive asked an innovation team to explore how to cut the lead time of bringing their product to market by 50 percent. The group explored the sequence in the process from merchandising to manufacturing to delivering the product to the customer. They discovered that the processes of manufacturing, packaging, and delivery to the customer were accomplished at benchmark levels of excellence. The real bottleneck occurred in merchandising. They found that the merchandising group spent endless hours debating what they should do and where they should acquire the products. They also took lengthy trips overseas to purchase raw materials and often tacked on personal vacations, which further slowed down the merchandising process. The sequencing process helped the team redefine the problem so that it focused specifically on accelerating the process of merchandising.

When to use it

Sequencing is particularly useful for issues that have a starting and an ending point. The team needs to understand the areas of the sequence that are causing the greatest challenge before they engage in problem resolution.

Keys to success

Some of the keys to success in sequencing include the following:

- Including members on the team who know the entire process
- Identifying with candor the areas of the sequence where the bottleneck occurs.

The Atomization Technique
What it is

The *atomization technique* has been known in different forms for a very long time. It was popularized in the 1970s by Tony Buzan,[2] a British popular-psychology author. The technique is based on the theory that the way we learned to take notes and collect knowledge in school is not effective, as it does not mirror the way our brain functions. The traditional way to take notes favors the logical left brain. It is sequential and is written one way, horizontally—from left to right in English—starting at the top and ending at the bottom of the page.

In *atomization*, the note-taking starts with the main theme written in the middle of the page and can go in any direction, following the random patterns of the mind. The only rule to satisfy our rational mind is that each idea should be in a circle (or bubble) and should be linked to another idea. In the divergence phase, the individual or the team sets down their knowledge on a large piece of paper. They write whatever comes to mind that appears even remotely related to the issue. They do not try to be logical or sequential but simply connect the new idea to at least one other idea already on the page. In the convergence phase, the individual or the team can regroup all the useful elements of the information into meaningful clusters.

There are a number of approaches to atomization, including identifying the following:

- Areas of analysis of the problems (technology, political, customer, resources, locations, etc.)
- An alternative "fishbone" analysis of materials, people, processes, technology
- Identifying the answers to: "who, what, where, when, why, and how."

When to use it

The atomization technique is useful for almost any type of problem. It is a very fast way to gather a team's collective knowledge on the parts of a specific issue. It is most effective with rational problems and less effective with problems where the issue is mostly emotional.

---

2. Tony Buzan, *Use Both Sides of Your Brain* (Plume, a division of Penguin Books, 1991).

Keys to success

- Allow enough time to complete the *atomization process* and do the clustering. A good ratio is to use two-thirds of the time for writing all the ideas in divergence and one-third for clustering them in convergence.
- A good atomization will always have some elements that do not fit into any cluster. This usually means that the team has explored most of the possible ideas and that they have gone beyond the level of detail required.
- Groups often get better results when they start by asking individuals to do an atomization in pairs and then create a larger atomization with everyone's input.
- Atomization requires some practice before it can be really effective. If some participants have never used the technique, demonstrate it with a quick example. An atomization around all the concepts associated with an apple usually works well (Figure 7.2).

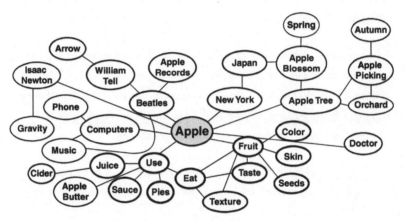

Figure 7.2: A Practice Example of an *Atomization* Process

Gain Insight into Root Causes

A primary purpose of Step 2: *Issue Redefinition* is to gain insight into the issue's underlying root causes. The first three areas of focus can yield that insight. However, it is often important to ask a direct question: why something is done the way it is done, or why not do it another way?

The best way to understand the root cause or the complex network of root that create an issue is to ask "Why?" or "Why not?" as often and in as many ways as necessary. The commonly made mistake is to ask "Why?" or "Why not?" just once or twice and then move on.

Here is a description of the *"Why?" or "Why not?"* technique:

What it is

The process of "Why?" or "Why not?" proceeds as follows:

- Ask "Why?" or "Why not?" and collect all the answers and document them on a flip chart.
- For each answer, ask: "Why is this so?" or "Why not?"
- Repeat the process until there are no more answers or the answers no longer make sense. The root cause of the problem is likely to appear in the last few answers.
- If the last answer obviously does not make sense, then ask: "Why do we do or think ABC when we all agree it does not make sense?"

Here is an example where the "Why?" or "Why not?" technique actually solved a problem:

A large newspaper publisher wanted to fix its door-to-door delivery process to ensure the papers were delivered on time to subscribers. For months, the paper had been delivered late more than 50 percent of the time. Subscribers were canceling in droves, and the publisher was ready to fire the vice president of distribution. A root cause analysis applying the "Why?" or "Why not?" technique to the delivery process showed the following:

- *The paper was late at the door because the local drivers did not get the papers on time. The local drivers had other day jobs and often couldn't wait to get the papers to complete the delivery.*
- *The local drivers did not get the papers on time because the trucks from the printer were late.*
- *The trucks were late because the papers were not on the dock when they were supposed to be.*
- *The papers were not on the dock because the printing presses frequently broke down. When the presses operated normally, the papers were on the dock on time.*
- *The printing presses broke down frequently because they were being run 10 to 30 percent faster than the recommended speed.*
- *The printing presses had to run faster because the printing plates for the presses were always delivered late.*

- *The plates were late because the articles and the advertising material were regularly delivered late to the plates department.*
- *The staff in the plates department accepted the articles and the advertising material past the required deadlines because they had a "can do" culture and had always accepted material after the written deadlines, often 30 to 40 minutes late. What had been an exception had become the new norm.*
- *The journalists and the advertising staff delivered their material late because they knew the plates department had moved the actual deadline forward by 30 to 40 minutes and would accept their material even if it arrived late.*

When the publisher uncovered the root cause of the late delivery, he could not believe that the "can do" culture he had promoted was actually responsible for the late delivery. He redefined the deadlines and asked the plates department not to accept any material after the deadline without his approval. The news content and advertising material started being delivered on time and the printing presses started delivering the papers on time 98 percent of the time. The vice president of distribution kept his job.

When to use it

"Why?" or "Why not?" is an effective technique when the key people who know the environment and the background for the problem are in the room. It is also useful for any team when time is limited.

Keys to success

- Involve people who are familiar with the problem or the situation.
- The key is to ask "Why?" or "Why not?" until it no longer makes any sense.
- Do not accept "Because it is so" as an answer.
- Write all the responses on a flip chart, and look for inconsistencies and logic gaps.

Validate the Redefined Issue with the Owner

All the work in Step 2: *Issue Redefinition* has one purpose: to better understand and define the problem or problems within a clear framework. It allows innovative thinkers to clarify what they are trying to achieve and the challenges they must overcome.

The analysis in Step 2: *Issue Redefinition* often changes one or more elements of the problem, including the context, the "How to . . . ?," the boundaries, and the type of solution. The outcome of Step 2: *Issue Redefinition* also can be the identification of more than one problem.

It is important to validate the changes with the owner of the issue before moving to the next step, Step 3: *Idea Generation*. If the team does not thoroughly validate the changes with the owner, the owner may not buy into them, and the time and resources the team spend on idea generation will most likely be wasted.

Often it is helpful to prepare for the validation process by considering what all stakeholders would say in response to the redefined issue. Of course, the innovation team could ask key stakeholders their viewpoint about a revised issue; however, sometimes there is not sufficient time, and in other situations there may be an unwillingness to let others know that the team is working on an issue until the owner confirms it.

An alternative way of achieving an approximation of stakeholder feedback is the *focus exchange* technique. This technique is often useful prior to the team meeting with the owner to seek confirmation for the redefined issue.

Here is a description of the *focus exchange* technique:

What it is

This technique asks individuals to look at an issue from other people's perspectives. The principle is simple, but it can deliver exceptional results. Here is the process for the technique of focus exchange.

Divergence

- Make a list of all the stakeholders who are or could be involved in the redefined issue or in the implementation of a solution.
- Individually or in small groups, role-play how each stakeholder might think of the problem and its context.
- Share each view with the whole team and discuss the findings.

Convergence

- Identify the useful findings that help the team understand the issue better.
- Document the stakeholder insights and reflect on how the stakeholder concerns can be addressed.
- Modify the issue or elements of the framework if necessary.

- Prepare how the team will seek confirmation from the owner, with the inclusion of the stakeholder analysis through the *focus exchange* technique.

When to use it

This is a useful technique when there are many stakeholders with significantly divergent interests and perspectives on the problem.

Keys to success

- Always include the problem owner and the customer as stakeholders.
- If possible, list specific people by name, instead of by title. It will be easier to imagine what they might say.
- Ask the participants to get into the role and be funny, clever, or dramatic in their comments.

LEVERAGING THE THREE INTELLIGENCES IN THE ISSUE REDEFINITION STEP

In addition to the techniques described above, the team can enhance Step 2: *Issue Redefinition* by applying either analytical or emotional intelligence. Here is how that can be accomplished.

Augmenting Innovative Intelligence with Analytical Intelligence

Analytical thinking is useful when assembling background data and looking logically at the current situation from a factual and reasoned point of view. However, the team must resist the temptation to draw conclusions prematurely. The analytical thinking process often assumes that all ambiguities can be reduced or eliminated and will have a tendency to aggregate different problems that would be better solved separately.

Augmenting Innovative Intelligence with Emotional Intelligence

Emotional intelligence is a powerful thinking process in Step 2: *Issue Redefinition* for three main reasons.

- **Complex problems always include people as contributors to the problem, as participants in the implementation of the solution, or as users or customers.**

   Teams can complement innovative intelligence techniques by drawing on emotional intelligence and asking questions such as: How do you feel about the situation? What does the situation feel like? What do customers (or employees) feel about the problem? When looking for the root cause, repeating the question "Why?" or "Why not?" will also often allow team members to go beyond the most obvious rational answers and access an emotional understanding of the issue.

- **Teams must often deal with emotional issues and barriers when applying the innovative thinking process to a problem.**

   One of the biggest causes of resistance to change is the difficulty individuals and groups have in admitting that the way they approached a problem in the past could have been a mistake in hindsight. The natural attachment to a past approach, especially if it was successful, must be taken into consideration when driving change. Solutions will only be implemented successfully if all the key stakeholders buy into the need for change at both an emotional and a rational level.

THE LEADER'S ROLE IN STEP 2: ISSUE REDEFINITION

Leaders have multiple roles in Step 2: *Issue Redefinition*. These include the following:

- Ensure that the team spends as much time as necessary to better understand the problem by using the right innovative thinking techniques.

- Ensure that the team genuinely challenges the problem and the framework and does not accept the problem as given, even if the leader gave them the problem directly. The team must assume that the problem can be improved, and the leader must constantly reinforce the team's efforts to do this.

Leaders also have a self-reflective challenge as they work on redefining the issue. Just as innovative teams need to challenge their own assumptions, leaders also must acknowledge that some of their assumptions may need to change. This sounds easy in theory but can be emotionally challenging. Leaders must be open to any challenges to their own assumptions and beliefs. If leaders respect different points of view, even if they conflict with their own, they will effectively reinforce the openness and trust that makes innovative thinking possible. It takes courage for leaders to give up strongly held assumptions, especially if those assumptions are part of what made them successful.

CONCLUSION

Step 2: *Issue Redefinition* is an essential step in the innovative thinking process. Teams often have a strong desire to skip this step and rush to idea generation once they identify the framework. It is important for innovative teams to realize that the desire to solve the problem is a well-trained automatic response that most people learned in schools. Accessing innovative intelligence often means slowing down and staying with the issue long enough to ensure the right problem or opportunity is being worked on. Only after innovative thinkers complete the process of issue redefinition, do they proceed to idea generation and problem resolution.

The next two chapters complete the explanation of the four-step innovative thinking process by describing how to engage in idea generation and problem resolution (Chapter 8) and how to engage in implementation planning of the innovative solution (Chapter 9).

CHAPTER EIGHT

STEP 3: IDEA GENERATION

The executive vice president of HR wanted new, breakthrough ideas for the department and asked one of her directors to develop them. The department needed more visibility in the organization and had become complacent. It was time for "big" ideas. The director invited 10 of his best managers for a day of brainstorming. The team started with a series of crazy exercises to warm up their creativity before they really got down to business. For hours they had great fun. They threw ideas on flip charts, picked the best, and started developing them in a second round. Before long they had over 50 good ideas to improve not only the HR department but also the rest of the organization. They presented their favorite five to the EVP. Her response was disappointing. She liked the ideas, and she even said some were very creative, but not one matched her definition of "breakthrough ideas."

The opening story describes one of the biggest mistakes in any innovation initiative. The HR director bypassed the framework and issue redefinition steps[1] and worked with the team on a fuzzy problem without the proper preparation.

The traditional underlying belief about idea generation is that if you let people think long enough without constraints and criticisms, they will eventually come up with new and useful ideas. However, developing the "right" answer to a fuzzy problem would have been sheer luck for this group, as they did not have a clear idea about what the vice president of HR was looking for. In no other situation would a leader waste so much valuable

---

1. The framework step is described in detail in Chapter 6, and the issue redefinition step is described in detail in Chapter 7.

time and energy on a process built on chance and serendipity, no matter how much fun it might be in the moment. The participants may have had fun, but the fact that the solutions were not accepted left everyone with a bitter aftertaste.

The proponents of unstructured creativity tell fascinating stories about how a group of random people had great fun playing music or creating art and produced an innovative business idea. What they do not talk about are the many sessions spent arguing the issue rather than resolving it or the sessions where brilliant ideas were later shot down because they did not answer the real problem.

Many books have been written about brainstorming or creativity sessions, which have become a regular feature in almost every organization. Despite all the history, starting with Alex Osborn[2] and Sidney Parnes in the 1950s, there are still misconceptions about how brainstorming processes really work and why they can sometimes be effective and at other times a complete waste of time. Our experience with these situations is that, without a proper process, success generally depends on having a very skilled and inventive facilitator who can generate great ideas with any group of any size, based on the facilitator's own creativity and techniques. These talented and rare facilitators sometimes teach their processes to others, but the problem is that they retain the secret ingredient—themselves. Without them, the results can rarely be reproduced. The lessons they teach are quickly forgotten as teams cannot replicate the magic on their own. This does not have to be the case.

Figure 8.1 shows the four-step innovative thinking process. This chapter explores in detail the approaches and techniques for Step 3: *Idea Generation*.

We use the term *idea generation* instead of the more commonly used, and frequently misused, "brainstorming" or "creativity session" in order to differentiate the right way to follow this process from the way it is too often performed today. Effective idea generation ensures that innovative thinkers systematically identify solutions to the real issue or issues within clear boundaries, thereby maximizing the value of the whole innovative thinking process.

Our objective in this chapter is to present the core processes that leaders must apply to enhance every idea generation session and to correct some

---

2. Alex Osborn, *Applied Imagination: Principles and Procedures of Creative Problem Solving* (Charles Scribner's Sons, 1953).

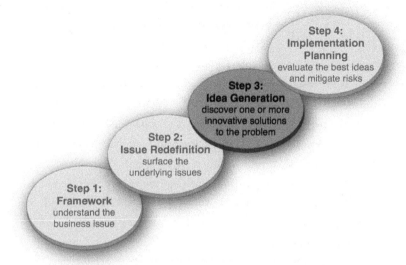

Figure 8.1: The Four-Step Innovative Thinking Process

common misconceptions. Considerable detail is offered, as the process must be applied rigorously to be effective. This is one place where simplifying or cutting corners can be costly.

IDEA GENERATION IS A RIGOROUS PROCESS

New ideas do not appear out of nothing. Most great ideas, inventions, and innovations result from combining existing and unconnected facts in a new way to solve a clear problem or opportunity. Success almost always involves the application of a rigorous planning and thinking process.

Most great ideas, inventions, and innovations are the result of combining previously existing and unconnected facts in a new way to solve a clear problem or opportunity.

Through our experience with both structured and unstructured idea generation sessions over many years, we have come to a clear conclusion—that a structured approach to resolving complex issues is essential. It produces a larger number of innovative ideas that can solve clearly defined business problems effectively. We have developed this approach as the *four stages of idea generation.*

The Four Stages of Idea Generation

Stage 1: Prepare thoroughly. Come to the meeting prepared with the right problem, participants, facilitator, agenda, and techniques.

Stage 2: Introduce the process. Introduce the "How to . . . ?" question, the boundaries, the goals, and ground rules for the meeting, and make the participants comfortable with the process.

Stage 3: Generate many ideas through divergence. Generate many possible and impossible ideas without any convergence of ideas.

Stage 4: Discover meaningful solutions through convergence. Spend enough time to transform the many ideas into meaningful solutions and select the ones that best answer the original *"How to . . . ?"* question within the framework.

Idea generation is usually a group activity, and proponents of unbridled creativity suggest that this is the only way to do it. There are two main benefits associated with group idea generation. First, the group has a greater sum of knowledge and experience than any one individual, and this can be used to create new combinations of ideas. Second, when used effectively, the planned combination of different thinking and problem-solving styles creates more value than simply adding randomly selected individuals. We have found that individuals can successfully implement the same processes as well. However, the best creativity sessions combine the power of the individual and the group.

This chapter first explains the four stages of idea generation with groups and then it describes how individuals can work alone and follow the same stages. We also identify how accessing innovative intelligence in the idea generation process can be augmented by applying emotional and analytical intelligences. We conclude with how leaders can assist groups and individuals in the process of idea generation.

STAGE 1: PREPARE THOROUGHLY

Creative and productive innovative thinking does not happen automatically when participants walk into a meeting room. In fact, the outcome of an idea generation session is mostly sealed by the time the participants come into the room. The process of clearly preparing an idea generation process for a group usually takes as long as or longer than the idea generation session itself.

As we explained in the previous two chapters, preparing for group idea generation involves making sure that the problem, boundaries, and ownership are clear. It also includes defining the objectives for the session, selecting the right participants, and ensuring that the logistics for the session have been arranged. Preparing thoroughly for an idea generation session is the best investment a leader can make to increase the chances of success.

There are three key elements involved in preparing thoroughly for a group idea generation session.

Key Elements in Preparing for a Group Idea Generation Session
- Set the objectives for the session.
- Select the participants and define the roles.
- Arrange the logistics for the session.

Set the Objectives for the Session

It is important to clarify the objectives of an idea generation session. These objectives are the logical outcome of a well-defined Step 1: *Framework*. The process of establishing the framework that is used as the foundation of idea generation has been explained in detail in Chapter 6. The framework includes:

- An understanding of the context for the issue
- The "How to . . . ?" question the participants must resolve during the idea generation session
- The boundaries for a successful solution and the type of solution expected
- Clarification of who owns the problem and how the final decision will be made.

In addition, the leader needs to clarify the level of precision expected for a proposed solution in this process. Here are some questions the leader should consider when preparing for an idea generation session:

- Should the group generate one solution or many solutions?
- Should the group identify one practical solution that can be implemented immediately, or should they identify revolutionary, long-term solutions?

If the expected outcomes are not clear, the participants will make their own assumptions about the leader's expectations. The chances that the participants will get it right are negligible. Participants will waste valuable time arguing about what the problem is, its boundaries, and its expected outcomes. The probability of finding effective solutions to the real issue will be very low.

Select the Participants and Define the Roles

During the idea generation process, every person can be creative and can help to resolve complex problems. However, careful selection of the participants most appropriate for the specific complex problem or opportunity can improve the quality of the solutions dramatically.

The number of participants in an idea generation session should be between four and seven people for each group, excluding the facilitator. If a session has less than four members, the opportunity for a broad range of ideas may be limited. On the other hand, even experienced facilitators find that having more than seven participants may compromise the chances of a successful outcome because group dynamics may get in the way. If a session must involve more than seven people, the answer is to have two parallel subgroups working on the same problem using the same techniques in the same room.

Consider three guidelines when selecting participants for an idea generation session designed to resolve a complex issue:

1. Balance experts and non-experts

One of the mistakes leaders often make when organizing an idea generation session for a complex issue is to use the existing team of experts who are working on the project already. This approach is often effective with complicated problems that need to be simplified, but it will likely be ineffective with complex problems. This is an example of a situation where well-developed analytical intelligence can block access to innovative intelligence. The team of experts who are working on the issue will often rely on their past experience and knowledge to discover solutions that are familiar to them. However, complex issues have their own uniqueness and ambiguities that differ from complicated situations.

As a result, the participants in the group idea generation session should include non-experts who bring a different perspective to the complex issue. The non-experts often identify ideas that are not typical. That is precisely what is needed to stretch the experts' thinking in order to identify new and effective solutions. Of course, experts can also contribute innovative ideas, but their main contribution occurs at the convergence stage, when they can assess whether the excellent idea can be implemented.

Non-experts should not be selected at random or simply because they happen to be available at the time. If the challenge is to find new and original solutions to an old problem, most of the participants should be people who have never been directly involved in the problem or in previous solutions but who have relevant expertise or skill. If the group is looking for immediate implementation, it is important to include participants who will be critical in the implementation, as they will feel much more ownership of the solution. If the problem targets a specific age group, it is useful to invite at least some representatives of that age group.

2. Balance the different individual creativity styles in the group

A good idea generation session always needs a blend of two different types of personalities: adaptors and innovators.[3] *Adaptors* tend to stick to the defined problem and are more likely to identify solutions that require incremental changes. They also tend to be more focused on implementation and on making sure the results will be practical. *Innovators* tend to challenge the problem statement and identify solutions that are more radical or revolutionary. Innovators are usually more naturally outgoing and spontaneous, instantly volunteering new ideas or different solutions to any type of problem.

The balance of adaptors and innovators will vary depending on the type of problem. If the solution requires incremental changes for immediate implementation, the team should have more adaptors than innovators. If the solution requires revolutionary thinking, the majority should be innovators.

3. Define roles in advance of the session

Group idea generation also is most effective when all participants know their roles in the process. It is important for the leader to decide what the

---

3. We are using the definition of Adaptors and Innovators used by Michael Kirton in his research on individual problem-solving styles – See: Michael Kirton, *Adaptors And Innovators: Styles Of Creativity And Problem Solving* (Routledge, 1989).

roles will be and to clarify them in the introduction to the process. Here are some examples of common roles:

- *The decision maker.* The decision maker is responsible for resolving the issue or simply for taking the solutions to the next step. Often, the leader is the decision maker, but someone else may have this role. To avoid inadvertently influencing the process or the outcome, the decision maker should not be the facilitator. In addition, facilitators should be aware of how they contribute through verbal or non-verbal messages. Their behavior influences the participants, and an enthusiastic outlook about the group's output rather than a demeanor of boredom enhances the success of the process.
- *The facilitator.* The facilitator's goal is to generate the best possible result from the group. The facilitator is responsible for the process, for capturing the ideas on flip charts, and for allowing the participants to focus solely on the content. The facilitator's role starts with the discussion of the framework for the problem or opportunity and ends when he or she has ensured that the group has assessed the solutions and that the implementation process is under way. Ideally, the facilitator should be independent of the team working to resolve the issue, as this will allow the necessary distance to focus on the process without getting involved in the content or, worse, giving personal opinions and attempting to influence the group. This is why the decision maker or any strong, opinionated individual should not facilitate idea generation sessions.
- *The participants.* The participants' primary role is to have fun, generate innovative ideas, and contribute to transforming intriguing concepts into possible solutions. Their role is to be free to think in new directions within the defined boundaries without the responsibility for achieving the outcome. As soon as the participants think they are responsible for the outcome, their capacity for unrestrained creativity will be reduced dramatically.

Arrange the Logistics for the Session

Although it may seem trivial, planning the logistics for an idea generation session is very important. It is comparable to the precision required when preparing a theater production. The space has to be large enough for the performance, the stage scenery must be prepared, all the props must be in the right place, and the actors must know when to enter and when to leave.

Idea generation sessions are no different, even if they are conducted in regular meeting rooms. Careful planning of logistics will set the stage for an idea generation session that runs smoothly and where the logistics will enable rather than block the idea generation process. The logistics include the following:

- **Space and props:**
  Ensure the space is large enough that people can move around in the room during divergence and that it has enough wall space to post flip chart pages on the walls. One of the simplest but most costly mistakes untrained facilitators make is to fold flip chart pages back when they are full, hiding the content from the participants. This has two unintended consequences: (1) participants will quickly start to repeat the same ideas, and (2) participants cannot use the previous ideas to build new ideas. Posting every filled page of ideas on the walls ensures that all the ideas are available to everyone at all times. For this reason, white boards and electronic boards are not as effective for the group idea generation process as paper flip charts.

- **Time allocations:**
  Allocate the proper amount of time for the idea generation session. Usually, the minimum time required for an effective session is about 90 minutes. Some sessions for more complex issues may be as long as one to two days. Also, identify how time will be allocated to the stages of the idea generation process—the introduction to the process (Stage 2), divergence (Stage 3), and convergence (Stage 4). Respecting the time allocated for each stage is important. Divergence can be so much fun that teams often want to continue generating "crazy" ideas without leaving enough time to converge and generate implementable solutions. Conversely, individuals and teams can stop divergence too quickly and limit unnecessarily the identification of useful innovative ideas. Here are some guidelines for time allocations:
  - The introduction to the process can take as much as 10 to 15 minutes.
  - The amount of time dedicated to the divergence stage depends on the objective. If the objective is to generate revolutionary ideas or to solve a problem that has proven intractable in the past,

divergence can require as much as 60 to 75 percent of the total time available. If the objective is to quickly find implementable solutions, divergence can require as little as 30 to 40 percent of the total time available.

-   The amount of time dedicated to convergence is the balance of the time available and can vary from 20 percent when looking for a few long-term, revolutionary ideas, to as much as 60 percent if the objective is to identify one practical idea that can be quickly implemented.

• **Pre-session materials sent out in advance:**
Send out in advance a summary page with the context for the complex issue, the "How to . . . ?" question, the boundaries, the ownership, and the expected outcomes of the idea generation session. Also, include the agenda for the session with time allocations for each part of the idea generation process, as well as the start and finish times for the session.

STAGE 2: INTRODUCE THE PROCESS

The main difference between highly successful and average or failed idea generation sessions is the focus on the process and the details. In a group idea generation session, the introduction is critical for establishing the right tone for the process. It should introduce the question, the boundaries, and the types of solutions expected, and should identify the goals for the meeting. It should also clarify the ground rules, make the participants comfortable with the process, and clarify how decisions will be made.

Most people and groups cannot immediately move into a high-performance idea generation mode as soon as they walk into a session. It often requires 10 to 15 minutes for a group to become comfortable, and that time can be used effectively for the introduction to the process. Here are a few guidelines that will make the stage of introducing the process effective:

• *Post on the wall a flip chart page that lists the problem statement, the key boundaries, and the type of outcome.* The facilitator should refer to the wall chart in the introduction to the process, and the chart should remain on the wall throughout the idea generation session so that participants can refer to it whenever necessary.

- *Provide an overview of the process and the timing of each agenda item.* Introducing the overview of the process makes everyone feel more comfortable, but it is even more critical for individuals who rely mostly on their analytical intelligence. For them, understanding that there will eventually be a convergence stage where they can evaluate and select ideas is often necessary if they are going to be effective during the divergence stage.

- *Encourage the group to ask questions about the complex issue.* It is often very frustrating for groups to have to revisit the problem or opportunity definition late in the process of idea generation. Participants should be clear about the definition of the issue before the divergence stage.

- *Discuss and agree upon ground rules for the decision maker, facilitator, and participants.* Group dynamics is often a reason for the failure of traditional brainstorming sessions. This is because leaders and participants rarely understand fundamental group dynamic principles and how they apply to group idea generation. As a result, it is often useful for the team to discuss and agree upon ground rules for the decision maker, facilitator, and participants and to post the rules on the wall. It is sometimes useful to appoint a timekeeper as well. The ground rules often include agreeing that during divergence, no convergence is allowed, and that during convergence, the boundaries and type of thinking need to frame the preferred solution.

- *Be clear up front about how and by whom the final idea or ideas will be selected.* If they are not told otherwise, most participants will assume that they are responsible for selecting the preferred solution and making the decisions. Very often in group idea generation, the ultimate decision is made by one owner or decision maker, and it could be someone who is not in the session. To avoid any disappointment, be clear up front about how and by whom the preferred solution will be selected. It takes a few seconds, and participants rarely question it, but it can save a lot of frustration.

- *Conduct a warm-up creativity exercise to set the tone for the meeting.* It can sometimes be useful in the introduction to conduct a warm-up creativity exercise to remind the participants that this session is different from traditional meetings. The exercise should be fun and emphasize that divergence works best without any convergence. This is particularly useful when working with a group that is not familiar with the process or if the objective is to develop radical or revolutionary ideas.

STAGE 3: GENERATE MANY IDEAS THROUGH DIVERGENCE

The divergence stage requires participants to access their innovative intelligence. The objective is to generate as many intriguing ideas as possible in the time allocated and in the general direction indicated by the framework. This is the stage where participants' analytical intelligence often can get in the way by attempting to converge ideas too early in the process. The divergence stage is also where any criticism or negative comments are destructive, as they will stifle the flow of ideas.

There are four foundational ideas in the divergence stage.

Foundational Ideas in Divergence
- Balance individual and group contributions.
- Clearly separate divergence and convergence.
- Balance idea collection and free-flowing discussion.
- Bypass self-censorship during the divergence stage.

Balance Individual and Group Contributions

Most individuals believe that because they are on a team, they should work together all the time. However, this often is an ineffective way to manage the divergence stage, because there are always individuals who are more knowledgeable or who have more dominant personalities. These individuals may lack emotional intelligence and may take over the conversation. As a result, only a few people really contribute, and innovative ideas from quieter participants have very little chance of surfacing. A more subtle consequence is that people rarely challenge the dominant beliefs, represented by the experts. This is contrary to the group idea generation purpose.

To maximize the value from all the knowledge and creativity of all the participants, teams need a rigorous process to get everyone's full contribution. This can be achieved by sub-dividing the divergence stage into three parts: individual work, group display, and group brainstorming.

I. *Individual work:* The participants first work individually to identify a few ideas. For example, they may generate "crazy" concepts and write them down.

2. *Group display:* After each participant has generated a few ideas, the facilitator captures all the ideas and numbers them on a flip chart, going quickly around the table and getting one idea per person at a time. After each page is completed, it is posted where it can be seen easily and can trigger new combinations.

3. *Group brainstorming:* The group reviews the ideas and adds additional ones. The facilitator writes down each idea exactly as the participant said it, whether the idea seems like a good idea, a bad idea, a repeat of a previous idea, or even a joke. When the participants run out of ideas, the facilitator asks them to go back to individual work to see if they can generate any more ideas and start the process again.

In some situations it helps both the divergence stage and the convergence stage if the facilitator identifies *time within time*. Earlier we indicated that it is important to identify specific time allocations for both stages. *Time within time* means that the parts within the divergence stage and the convergence stage can be explicitly subdivided into time units. For example, in a one-hour divergence stage, the three parts described above could be subdivided into individual work (5 minutes), group display (25 minutes), and group brainstorming (30 minutes). *Time within time* allows a better control of the process and ensures each part is given the proper time it requires.

Clearly Separate Divergence and Convergence

In many meetings, including brainstorming sessions, facilitators make the error of not formally separating divergence and convergence. This potentially allows conflicts among the participants and does not maximize the use of the team's innovative intelligence. Here is a typical scenario:

*   The leader presents the problem to the group and asks them to generate many new ideas.
*   Very quickly, some participants start contributing and, operating in divergence, generate many ideas, good and bad, some reasonable and some not.
*   Other participants want to find the solution as quickly as possible, so they immediately operate in convergence and apply their analytical intelligence.

- Although the group is not aware of it, they are already unproductive and have little chance of finding good solutions. When the "divergent" participants give "crazy" ideas, the "convergent" participants wonder when they will start being serious. Also, they often openly criticize the divergent ideas and point to their flaws. In parallel, the "divergent" participants quickly tire of the criticism and stop generating divergent ideas. Very soon the two groups stop listening to each other and wait for the meeting to end.
- Usually, the meeting ends with a stalemate where both groups leave frustrated, and the organization loses.

This scenario highlights an intriguing question about the divergence stage: When a facilitator tells a group that there are no bad ideas in brainstorming and that people should not criticize ideas, why do people still challenge the ideas and judge them as either good or bad? It seems evident that the participants just can't help themselves. Some facilitators allow this convergence behavior to take place even when they clearly articulate the ground rules for brainstorming and post them on the wall after everyone agrees to adhere to them. What blocks people from staying in divergence?

Our analysis is that most people learned throughout their school years that good students know the answers to problems and that there is usually one right answer. Whenever someone begins to have convergence behavior in the divergence stage, the other participants stop engaging in divergence. Convergence trumps divergence all the time.

The facilitator and leader of the group need to protect divergence like a precious jewel that is very vulnerable. Group participants will stop engaging in divergence as soon as another person starts engaging in converging ideas. It is especially difficult to push back and stay in divergence if the leader engages in convergence.

Divergence and convergence need to be clearly separated. During divergence, one ground rule is that all the ideas are good and no criticisms are tolerated. If participants criticize an idea, either the facilitator stops them or asks them to find at least one or two valuable elements in that apparently unusable idea. During Stage 4 "convergence," the only new ideas should be those built from or inspired by the divergent ideas. Once again, the key is to allocate the right amount of time for each stage.

The basic ground rules of divergence are as follows:

- List as many ideas as possible
- Focus on speed and quantity
- Do not criticize any idea.

The more ideas available at the end of the divergence stage, the more potential there will be in convergence to combine ideas and develop a new solution that will solve the problem. Quantity is more important than depth or quality, and any idea is a good idea. At this stage, "crazy" answers are only ideas that are not immediately applicable. They are potential triggers or starting points for more useful ideas.

Balance Idea Collection and Free-Flowing Discussion

Most proponents of unstructured brainstorming suggest that the most valuable ideas come when the participants build on each other's ideas in a free-for-all. Experience shows that the most efficient way for participants to build on each other's ideas is to make the process systematic, rather than leaving it to unstructured chance.

For example, during the divergence stage, the goal is to generate many different ideas. However, individuals need to have the chance to identify and articulate their ideas in a systematic manner. Only after that should the facilitator have a free-for-all process of generating ideas. Similarly, in the convergence stage, the goal is to reflect on the many different ideas generated and identify how they can be combined and developed. Only when the most valuable ideas emerge should more unstructured conversations happen, usually to build on or combine complementary ideas. This careful balance achieves the best results.

Bypass Self-Censorship during the Divergence Stage

The difference between great and poor idea generation techniques is how individuals manage their own subconscious self-censorship during the divergence stage. In most social situations, self-censorship is very useful. It is driven by social needs and allows us to survive and fit into a group. However, when working in a team that is engaged in divergence, individuals are not always aware that they are stopping themselves from doing or saying something; yet they often adapt their behavior to the specific group. Their language and the spontaneity of their comments will be affected by who is in the room and how the meeting is proceeding.

This self-censorship significantly impacts individual behavior in idea generation sessions, as participants bring with them the social standards they subconsciously apply at work. Depending on cultures, backgrounds, and personalities, this can significantly inhibit their ability to generate divergent ideas. Some people will be quieter and more reserved than others, but some form of self-censorship will prevent all individuals from fully accessing their innovative intelligence in the session.

Understanding the role of self-censorship during the divergence stage and how to bypass it is critical. If individuals and groups (even those with limited inclination toward innovative thinking) know how to bypass their own self-censorship, they will be able to generate more new ideas.

There is an intriguing question about the stage of divergence: Why do most books about brainstorming present very unusual and sometimes bizarre exercises in the brainstorming or creativity process?

External creativity facilitators use these unusual techniques to help groups generate many ideas. However, after the external facilitators leave, the groups and the leaders often are unwilling to try an unusual technique because they consider it awkward, too gamey, or even childish. So the leaders revert to their standard method of posing a question, engaging in a group discussion, and then choosing the idea that makes the most sense to them.

What is really happening here?

It relates once again to school training. In school, crazy ideas that are not the "right" answer are often shunned. People may think about innovative ideas, but they self-censor themselves when they are asked to share these ideas in public. Instead, they offer the safe ideas that they are fairly sure are within the realm of good ideas.

The crazy techniques used by the creativity facilitators are all variations on the same trick. The processes are all methods to bypass the internal self-censorship so that participants express their innovative ideas without blocking them. For example, brainstorming processes are sometimes noisy, highly energetic, and fast-moving. The high levels of energy can sidestep the internal self-censorship because people do not have the time to block their ideas before they blurt them out. Another technique, *"brainstorm after the sillies,"* is a fun bypass process. It encourages participants to brainstorm ideas until they start expressing silly ones. Rather than stopping the brainstorming because of the silly ideas, the participants continue and see what new ideas emerge after their inhibitions are lowered. The same process is used if the facilitator asks participants to look at pictures and give ideas that are stimulated by the pictures—it's just another technique to bypass the self-censorship and access the innovative intelligence ideas.

One of our favorite techniques to bypass the self-censorship is called *"from worst to better."* The divergence process is based upon the observation that most people only have a self-censor for good ideas. They do not have a self-censor when they are asked to identify bad ideas. In *"from worst to better,"* the divergence stage has two distinct parts:

1. The question is: "What would be the *worst* possible ideas for the problem?" The key to success is that most participants have never been asked, especially in a business context, for the "worst ideas," and so they have not developed self-censors for bad ideas. Because of that dynamic, most participants are able to fully access their potential for innovative intelligence and can generate a lot of very bad ideas quickly.

2. The participants are then asked to "flip" the bad ideas or one word in each of the bad ideas into a divergent but positive idea. This process bypasses the self-censorship and generates useful divergent ideas that are the opposite of the worst ideas. Once the participants generate useful ideas, they produce *more* useful ideas. New ideas flow naturally because the participants have bypassed their own self-censorship.

Table 8.1 on the next page shows an example of the *"from worst to better"* technique applied to the question of "How to increase the use of bank machines by seniors?" It is a simple exercise that facilitators can use to explain the technique to a group and to give participants the chance to practice the technique before applying it to the real complex issue.

Many other techniques are effective in bypassing participants' self-censorship in divergence. Leaders and facilitators can select techniques that have worked for them in the past or those that are best adapted to their type of problem. Here are some examples of additional bypass techniques:

*   *Image maker.* Ask the participants to draw a picture of the solution they want. The less they know how to draw, the more they can access

Table 8.1: Example of a "From Worst to Better" Exercise

Question: "How to increase the use of bank machines by seniors?" (Within the boundaries of six months with a limited budget)	
Step 1: Divergent Worst Ideas (to bypass the self-censor)	**Step 2: Divergent Flip to Good Ideas**
• Very small type	• Large type • Voice activation
• Located on the sixth floor with no elevator	• Doorman • Automatic doors
• Open only from 2 a.m. to 4 a.m.	• Open 24 hours
• Random 24-character access code that must change at each transaction	• Voice or eye recognition
• Gangsters beside each machine	• Boy scouts or retired bankers beside each machine
• Machines in dark alleys	• Machines in retirement homes
• Grease on the floor in front of each machine	• Comfortable sofa in front of each machine
• Play loud punk rock music	• Play romantic music
• Keyboards six feet high	• Keyboard heights adjustable
• Give them $100 every time they withdraw $10	• Enter them in a contest when they use the machine

their innovative intelligence without self-censorship. The proof that the principle of bypassing self-censorship works is that participants who have artistic skills are not as effective with this technique as the ones with no artistic skills.

- *What if?* Ask the participants to solve a modified problem. For example, if a boundary is an idea to be implemented in two months, ask: "What if you had one day (or one year) to solve the problem?" If the boundary is a budget of $100,000, ask them "What if you had only $10?" or "What if it was your own money you were investing?"

- *Random words.* Ask the participants to use random words or pictures as a starting point. The more evocative the words or images, the more useful they will be.

As the second part for each of the above techniques, ask the participants to generate divergent ideas on the real problem, using the lists or images created in the first part as starting points.

STAGE 4: DISCOVER MEANINGFUL SOLUTIONS THROUGH CONVERGENCE

Convergence is the final stage of idea generation. The objective is to develop one new solution or a range of new solutions for the original question within the context of the framework and boundaries for the complex issue. During this stage, the group applies three intelligences—innovative, analytical, and emotional—to develop solutions. They do this by extracting the value from the large number of concepts and ideas they generated during the divergence stage.

Convergence is the easiest stage of idea generation for most people because it is more logical, and most participants have used convergence techniques in school and at work. The challenge is to prevent participants from using their analytical intelligence to push the group to conclusions too quickly, thus losing another opportunity to look for better answers.

At the beginning of the convergence stage, the link between the many ideas and the original problem may appear tenuous, but a small link can be built into strong solutions when the participants combine ideas with other ideas, including their own knowledge. The real power of convergence after an effective divergence stage is that, suddenly, the possibilities are greater, and an idea that could have appeared unusable on its own before divergence can now be put to good use.

The process for the convergence stage is as rigorous as the one for the divergence stage:

Part 1: Individual work

It is important to include individual work in the beginning of the convergence stage so that the group can identify as many solutions as possible from the many ideas. Otherwise, there is a tendency for the content experts to take over and control the identification of the solution. Here is what the facilitator should ask each participant to do individually in the first part of the convergence stage:

- *First revisit the problem statement and the boundaries.* This ensures all of the participants are clear about the question, boundaries, and type of solutions for the issue.
- *Work with the ideas generated in divergence and combine them, "play" with them, and "bounce" them off the problem.* The words "play" and "bounce" are used on purpose to indicate that the purpose is not simply to look at the ideas

and select the best one. The key is to continue playing with ideas, asking "Why?" and "Why not?" and looking at "What if?" combinations until new possible ideas emerge. To avoid a continuation of the divergence stage, the participants should rapidly convert totally new ideas or new directions to useful, convergent solutions.

- *Generate possible combinations or even totally new ideas inspired by the preliminary solutions.* It is important to suspend judgment about the solutions and say, for example: "What if I could combine solution A and B?" The individual should stay with the concepts instead of eliminating solutions simply because they are not immediately implementable. Rather, use individual reflection to help generate new combinations that improve the solutions.

Part 2: Group display

After each participant generates a few solutions, the facilitator begins by capturing one solution per person, and then repeats the process as many times as necessary. Alternatively, the participants can write their solutions themselves on the flip chart. The facilitator then reads the solutions to the group.

Part 3: Group generation of preferred solutions

Each individual explains his or her solutions to the other participants. Then the group discusses the merits of each solution and improves upon each of them. This process allows the group to use all the solutions generated during the individual convergence work, as well as the combined knowledge and experience of the group to improve each solution.

During the convergence stage, participants should listen to all the other ideas and combine them with their own ideas. The facilitator should encourage discussion only after all the participants have presented their individual solutions and the group understands them. The group then engages in open discussion to refine the solutions, combine them, and address possible flaws in the best ones.

A Note on the Use of Prototyping

With the growth of graphic design firms and through the application of design thinking, the concept of prototyping has become more common in all areas of innovation. Prototyping is the physical representation in rough form of a concept or an idea. The value of prototyping is that the participants in the team can play with the concept in almost real conditions. In particular, it is an excellent way to quickly "debug" a concept and identify the parts that will not work. This tool is an excellent complement to divergence and convergence.

WORKING ALONE ON IDEA GENERATION

Individuals working alone can also use the four stages of the idea generation process very effectively if they apply the process systematically. The main difficulty is to stay in the divergence stage long enough even when their analytical intelligence tells them to take the first answer that appeals to them. The key to success is to rigorously follow the process, including writing every idea down, even the craziest and apparently most useless ideas.

Here is the process for an individual who wants to work independently for between 30 and 60 minutes to develop a solution to a complex problem:

- *Stage 1: Prepare thoroughly:* Ensure that the framework for the problem has been confirmed.
- *Stage 2: Introduce the process:* Reflect on the problem to ensure it is clearly defined. If the framework has not been prepared, it is critical to quickly write a "How to ...?" question, validate the question, and add boundaries and the type of solution expected.
- *Stage 3: Generate many ideas through divergence:* The objective of the divergence phase is to generate as many possible concepts or ideas as possible. During this stage, the biggest danger comes from self-censorship, including thoughts such as: *That's crazy! It will never work! It is too silly! It cannot help!* To avoid these reactions, use all the time allocated and write down as many ideas as possible, as fast as possible.

    For example, using the framework as a starting point, generate a large number of random, connected, or unconnected thoughts and ideas and write them down. It can be useful to select random words (a dictionary or telephone book can be useful) and start playing with the words to help you look at the problem differently. Strange as it may seem, the individual can ask a question such as: "What do my problem and cell phones have in common?" The key is to quickly write down any thoughts that come to mind, whether useful or not, whether they make any sense or not. Another technique is to look at the problem from very different points of view. For example, ask: "What would a child think?" "What would an unhappy customer think?" "What would the CFO think?" If more time is available, you can also use the two-step technique, *"From Worst to Better"* described earlier.

- *Stage 4: Discover meaningful solutions through convergence:* The objective of the convergence stage is to use the ideas generated in the divergence stage to create real solutions for the actual problem. When working individually, it is useful to subdivide this stage as follows:

  - *Look at the question and the boundaries. Then, from all the concepts and directions, select the ideas or the combinations of ideas that could possibly make sense to solve the problem.* At this point, the objective is not to find finished ideas but to look for intriguing thoughts and potential directions. It is important to write down all the ideas. What we are looking for is perspectives such as "This is interesting!" or "If we could make this work, it would be great!" not simply ideas that are immediately implementable. It is probable that some of the ideas will have faults, but this will be dealt with in the second part.

  - *Combine ideas and move them to an implementable stage within the boundaries and the expected type of solution identified for the problem.* If an idea looks particularly useful but has one key flaw, ask "How can I eliminate the flaw while keeping what is positive about the solution?" The outcome of the process will be one or a few solutions that answer the original problem within the boundaries and the type of outcome expected.

LEVERAGING THE THREE INTELLIGENCES IN THE IDEA GENERATION STEP

Both analytical and emotional intelligence can augment innovative intelligence within the four stages of idea generation as follows.

Augmenting Innovative Intelligence with Analytical Intelligence

If participants use their analytical intelligence during the divergence stage of idea generation, it will interfere with the free flow of ideas because they are constantly thinking about why ideas will work or not work. However, analytical intelligence is helpful in combination with innovative intelligence during the convergence stage, when it can be used to discover and develop effective solutions.

Augmenting Innovative Intelligence with Emotional Intelligence

Throughout the idea generation process, it is important to leverage one's emotional intelligence. Sometimes participants have conflicts and differences of opinion in the divergence and convergence stages. In divergence, conflicts can arise if people want to interfere with the process and criticize ideas or converge while the participants are identifying ideas. During convergence, the participants may have disputes about what the preferred solution is. The emotionally intelligent innovative thinker can refer back to the framework to determine if the suggested solution responds to the framework effectively. It is important to manage the emotional intensity of the idea generation process so that participants can generate new ideas, individuals can bypass their self-censorship, and then the group can converge to identify the best possible solution to the complex issue they are resolving.

THE LEADER'S ROLE IN STEP 3: IDEA GENERATION

Leaders have an important role in idea generation. Here are some of their responsibilities:

- *Stage 1: Prepare thoroughly:* The leader must ensure that the group has a clear framework for the problem and has created a process that will maximize the chances of success. An example of one way a leader can maximize the opportunity to succeed would be to invite outside participants to contribute different perspectives and insights.
- *Stage 2: Introduce the process:* The leader must introduce the process to the team and hand off the facilitation of the session to the facilitator. The leader should encourage the team to apply the process rigorously, as guided by the facilitator. A leader should not allow personal bias of any kind to interfere with the process.

- *Stage 3: Generate many ideas through divergence:* The leader can influence the group's attitude and how they contribute. For example, if the leader offers "crazy" ideas, encourages the team to do the same, and explains that this will help the group to generate more and better ideas, the team will likely respond enthusiastically. On the other hand, if the leader sits back and frowns at the ideas during divergence, expressing doubt that the ideas can ever be useful, then the team may stop generating ideas that seem unreasonable, extravagant, unconventional, or simply not immediately valuable.

- *Stage 4: Discover meaningful solutions through convergence:* The leader should encourage the team by recognizing original ideas, even if they are not immediately implementable in their current form. The leader should also prevent the group from quickly jumping to one solution that looks like it answers the "How to . . . ?" question. Instead, the leader should encourage the group to build further and improve on the solution. Finally, often the leader is the decider for the group. If the group does not reach consensus on the preferred solution, it is the leader's responsibility to make the decision about which solution best resolves the complex problem in the interest of the organization.

CONCLUSION

Step 3: *Idea Generation* is the step in the innovative thinking process that relies most intensely on innovative intelligence. Leaders need to prepare thoroughly, introduce the issue and process to the group, engage in a divergence process to generate ideas without criticism or judgment, and then converge the ideas to identify the preferred solution to the complex issue. Leaders play a very important role by helping their teams access their innovative intelligence as they proceed through the idea generation process.

Chapter 9 explores Step 4: *Implementation Planning,* the fourth and final step of the Innovative Thinking process. In implementation planning, leaders guide groups through the process of confirming the preferred ideas, engaging in a risk analysis, and presenting the innovative solution for approval. They then ensure there is a proper handoff to an implementation team that takes responsibility for implementing and continuously improving the innovative solution to ensure that it resolves the complex problem effectively.

CHAPTER NINE

STEP 4: IMPLEMENTATION PLANNING

For three weeks, the innovation team worked hard on a project. They identified the key insights to unlock the issue. They generated great ideas and selected one that was sure to be a success. They were so excited that they decided to present it immediately to the Chief Marketing Officer. The CMO's response was: "How much will it cost, what is the expected pay-off, and what are the risks?"

The team members had not anticipated the questions and were not ready to answer them. This was despite the fact that the CMO always asked the same questions when new ideas were presented. The CMO's impression was that the team had not done a thorough job. As a result, they had to go back, assess the cost, the pay-off, and the risk. By the time they proposed the idea again, most of their excitement had worn off.

When they reflected on what had happened, they recognized that the CMO's questions were totally predictable. They had just failed to factor them into their process.

This situation is, unfortunately, all too common. It is a typical application of analytical intelligence. The team found the right question. They found the only possible answer—now they had to "just do it."

This is when leaders need to stop the strong instinct to "just do it" and follow the last step in the successful resolution of the original problem, Step 4: *Implementation Planning*. Innovation is successful only when a solution is implemented successfully, not when an idea or a solution is identified. This is the main difference between creativity and innovation.

Chapter 5 introduced the four-step innovative thinking process, depicted in Figure 9.1. This chapter focuses specifically on the tools and techniques for Step 4: *Implementation Planning*.

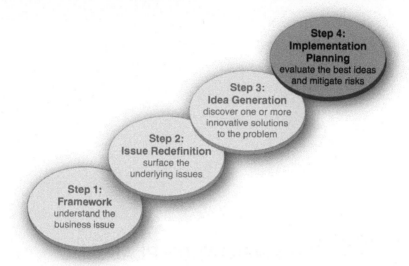

Figure 9.1: The Four-Step Innovative Thinking Process

As with every other step in the innovation process, innovative thinking needs to be applied to implementation planning. The problem that needs to be solved in this step is: How to successfully implement the innovative solution? Step 4: *Implementation Planning* helps identify and resolve potential issues and increases the chances of success. It maximizes the investment in the first three steps.

STAGE 1: CONFIRM THE PREFERRED IDEA

Issues with the implementation of an idea can come from two areas, the approval of the idea and the implementation of the idea. The adage "check twice and move once" applies perfectly to implementation planning. Instead of moving immediately to execution, a team should take the necessary time to identify any issues related to the innovative idea and its implementation. They should also identify more than one innovative idea because teams often find that their top idea, however brilliant, may have little chance of being implemented successfully.

In debriefings with teams that implemented a "great idea" that failed, we have found they usually recognized that the reasons for the failure were predictable but they either overlooked them or did not fully explore them.

There are four stages in Step 4: *Implementation Planning.*

The Four Stages in Step 4: Implementation Planning

Stage 1: Confirm the preferred ideas.

Stage 2: Engage in risk analysis and develop mitigation strategies.

Stage 3: Present the innovative solution for approval.

Stage 4: Ensure an effective handoff to the team that focuses on
change implementation.

There are two areas of focus for the first stage of Step 4: *Implementation Planning.* These are:

- *Identify the best team for implementation planning:* Ensure you include on the implementation planning team any stakeholders who will be critical to a successful implementation.
- *Confirm the best idea:* Screen the top ideas from Step 3: *Idea Generation* against the original problem, the boundaries, and the type of solution.

Identify the Best Team for Implementation Planning

The team that generated new and valuable solutions to the original problem is not always the most effective team for implementation planning. The implementation planning team should include internal stakeholders who will be involved in the actual implementation of the innovative solution. This will have two main benefits:

- *Commitment:* The new team members are more likely to understand the ideas and, therefore, be more committed to the success of the solution. Involving all relevant departments at this stage is the best way to prevent problems after an idea has been approved. In fact, the more difficult a department is to deal with, the more important it is to invite a representative from it to join the implementation planning team. They should be helping make the solution better, not attacking the idea from the outside.
- *Improvement:* Identifying potential risks before executing the idea should be highly valued. Some innovation teams are reluctant to invite departments that will be involved in the actual execution because they may fear that the other departments will find fault with their innovative solution. However,

the departments responsible for executing the idea often know what could go wrong during the actual implementation. They also can often identify the small changes that can convert a very innovative but flawed solution into a successful one. Once the solution has been approved by the project owner, departments such as IT, marketing, or finance usually find it is much more difficult to make the necessary changes.

Confirm the Best Ideas

The best innovative ideas the innovation team generated in Step 3: *Idea Generation* should always be reviewed during the implementation planning step because the original team's excitement and enthusiasm could have biased their judgment. This is no surprise. The team worked very hard on the process and developed great innovative ideas. They are justifiably excited about them.

Confirming the best ideas is particularly important if the top ideas selected involve significant change for the organization. It will also give new team members a chance to become familiar with the original objectives and boundaries.

There is no single technique that will work perfectly for all types of innovative ideas; therefore the team should use techniques only as a support to the decisions by the team and the owner. The team can use two simple tools to assist in selecting the top idea:

- **Selection Grid**
  The selection grid allows you to compare two or more solutions based on how well they score against the objectives, the boundaries, and the type of solution. It is particularly effective for tangible solutions that the team can easily compare.

  If one idea scores well on most criteria but poorly on one or two, it may be useful to go directly to Stage 2: Engage in Risk Analysis and Develop Mitigating Strategies. If the issues can be resolved, the idea should be evaluated again. If the issues cannot be resolved, it is better to know immediately and move the idea aside.

- **Positives and Negatives**
  This technique is frequently used but rarely effectively. Most teams can identify a large number of strengths for the innovative idea but usually

very few weaknesses. To use the positives and negatives technique effectively, the leader must ask the group to first identify all the idea's strengths. When they have finished, the team must identify the same number of actual and potential weaknesses.

This very simple technique confirms the strengths, but it also gives the participants permission to identify weaknesses they may not normally have mentioned. Interestingly, the number of distinct potential weaknesses teams identify is often higher than the number of distinct strengths. This is because most participants identify the same or similar strengths but frequently list different potential weaknesses.

After the implementation planning team evaluates the best ideas and identifies the top one, they will find it useful to look at the ideas that did not make the cut and search for what was unique and valuable in each of them. The team can then improve the selected idea by integrating one or more of the other ideas' unique elements.

STAGE 2: ENGAGE IN RISK ANALYSIS AND DEVELOP MITIGATING STRATEGIES

In complex situations, innovative ideas usually include actual or potential risks. Identifying the risks and mitigating them is the most effective way to implement innovative solutions successfully. Unfortunately, in our culture, where risks are always considered negatively, people often hesitate to point out the flaws or risks attached to an idea.

This is why it is so important to use formal techniques to counteract this natural tendency. The techniques allow team members to express what they know, believe, or feel about the idea.

There are three areas of focus in *Stage 2: Engage in Risk Analysis and Develop Mitigating Strategies*. These are:

- *Identify the top idea's actual and potential weaknesses.* Look at the idea from various points of view to identify possible weaknesses.
- *Identify the risks attached to the idea.* Identify the potential risks in the implementation of the idea and mitigate them.
- *Improve the idea.* Resolve the main weaknesses or risks in the selected idea.

Identify the Actual and Potential Weaknesses of the Top Idea

Two techniques are particularly effective to identify an idea's actual and potential weaknesses. We discussed the first technique, *positives and negatives*, in the previous section. The list of potential weaknesses is an excellent starting point for identifying weaknesses that could derail the innovative idea's implementation.

The second technique, *focus exchange*,[1] is more thorough and can be a lot of fun.

As we have seen, the participants on an innovative thinking team are often reluctant to find flaws in an idea they have developed and selected. The *focus exchange* technique allows individuals and groups to bypass their internal censorship by asking the participants to role-play what they believe other important stakeholders in the implementation of the idea would say about the idea. During the sharing phase, the participants will talk about possible obstacles and weaknesses very openly because they are "role-playing" another person. The result is always useful and frequently identifies potential weaknesses that had not been mentioned with the *positives and negatives* technique.

To identify the actual and potential weaknesses of the top ideas, the process for *focus exchange* is as follows.

1. List all the internal and external stakeholders who can have a positive or negative impact on the implementation of the idea. Select the stakeholders with the greatest influence on the approval or the success of the idea. It is always more effective to role-play an individual to represent a category. For example, it is better to role-play a well-known and opinionated executive rather than "the executive team."

2. Assign one or two stakeholders to each team member. Individually, each team member prepares a mini role-play of what he or she believes the stakeholder will say when presented with the solution. Humorous statements should be expressly encouraged.

---

1. See Chapter 7: Issue Redefinition, where *focus exchange* is used as a technique to validate the redefined issue with the owner.

3. Each individual role-plays the selected stakeholder to the group. During the presentations, the other team members listen for clues to other possible weaknesses in the solution. The key ideas from each role-play are captured on flip charts.
4. Individually, the participants summarize the conclusions they have drawn from all the role-plays and the potential impacts on the idea.
5. The group then discusses the possible impacts on the solution. Changes could include modifications to the solution, additional preparation for the presentation of the idea, or even questioning the validity of the idea and going back to look at alternatives.

If we look back at the example at the beginning of this chapter, we can see that if the participants had applied the *focus exchange* technique, they would have selected the CMO as a key stakeholder. In role-playing him, they would most certainly have asked: "How much will it cost, what is the expected pay-off, and what are the risks?" They would have realized that they did not have the answers. This would have saved them some embarrassment and might even have saved a great idea.

Identify the Risks Attached to the Idea

Most leaders and managers believe that risk is negative, and taking risks generally has a negative connotation. This is a result mostly of our school education, where taking a risk—for example, by giving a different answer—was a good way to get in trouble. In fact, most university students graduate from university without formally learning about risk and risk management. Too often in large organizations, formal risk management is only used for large investments.

Risk is not good or bad. We define risk as the probability that something will happen, multiplied by the potential consequences. In all complex situations, some level of risk exists because we cannot eliminate all uncertainties and ambiguities. The key is to understand the nature and level of the risks attached to an innovative idea.

- Is the risk known or unknown?
- Is the occurrence probable or not?
- Are the possible consequences important or minor?

- Is the risk manageable and can the probability or the consequences be reduced?
- How does the risk compare to the potential gain?
- What is the risk of not deciding or not acting now?

The risks in an innovative solution do not have to be large or dramatic. They are any elements that can get in the way of a successful implementation of the new idea. They can be as simple as "the CEO is very busy with a new acquisition and may not want to add another project" or "the customer may not understand our solution."

The most effective way to manage risks is to look at them as potential weaknesses that may need to be reduced, eliminated, or simply monitored. It is rare that a risk is so high as to eliminate a solution. If it does appear to be too high, the second choice idea can sometimes be a better solution if the risks attached to it are much lower.

In a complex environment, risk can sometimes be difficult to assess. Not only is it necessary to consider the direct consequences of an idea, but it is also important to consider the indirect consequences. The following example describes the challenge of assessing the direct and indirect risks in a complex situation and the importance of thoroughly identifying the possible risks and their probability and consequences.

The innovation team in a software company wanted to launch a new, low-cost solution with limited features. The direct benefit was clear—it would increase sales volume because the price would reach new potential customers who previously could not afford the full-featured product. The direct risk was also clear, beyond simply the product not selling, "If we implement the low-cost, simple solution, future customers of our full-feature solution may buy the simpler and cheaper solutions instead." The team had taken the risk of reduced sales of the more expensive product into consideration in their profit forecasts. When the team looked at the possible indirect consequences, the impacts were much more difficult to evaluate:

- *Current customers who do not use all the features in the more expensive product may want to switch and ask for a partial refund.*
- *The new customers will not fit our traditional customer profile, and we may not be able to cross-sell other products and services.*
- *The new customers may be less sophisticated and could require more help from our service desk.*
- *Our employees may not be enthusiastic about the simpler product.*

Based on the indirect risk assessment, the innovation team decided to survey employees and recommended a smaller and longer pilot project to better understand the new customers.

One of the possible dangers of this exercise is that the risk may appear so high and daunting that the team or the executives could decide that the idea is not worth the risk. To mitigate this possible scenario, it is also useful to do the risk exercise on "keeping the status quo." The team and the executives will likely realize that doing nothing can potentially be as risky as, or even riskier than, implementing the team's idea.

Figure 9.2 shows the "Risk Probability and Consequences" matrix, which is an easy way to represent risks for any idea or innovative solution. This exercise is not an attempt to eliminate the risks or the uncertainties of a solution but rather to recognize that they exist and manage the consequences. It is a powerful tool to trigger a meaningful discussion on the issue.

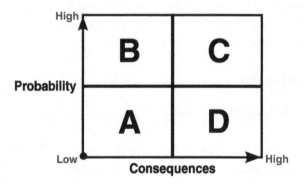

Figure 9.2: Risk Probability and Consequences

There are four options, one for each quadrant:

A   *A low probability and low consequence risk* means there is little probability that this risk will occur, and if the risk does occur, the consequences will be minimal.

B   *A high probability and low consequence risk* means there is a high probability that the risk will occur, but the consequences will be minimal. The team should look at ways to reduce the probability that the risk would occur.

C   *A high probability and high consequence risk* means there is a high probability that this risk will occur, and if the risk does occur, the consequences will be damaging. These risks must be mitigated, or the idea may have to be abandoned.

D   *A low probability and high consequence risk* means the probability that the risk will occur is low, but if the risk does occur, the consequences will be high. The team should look at ways to reduce the risk consequence in the event that the risk occurs.

To represent the uncertainty inherent in some risk factors, we recommend representing a risk, not as a point but as a line or a shape. This is particularly useful when there is a significant level of uncertainty on the probability or the consequences of a particular risk. It does not take away from the exercise; on the contrary it recognizes the fact that complex situations usually create high levels of uncertainty, without pretending that the risk can be accurately predicted.

Understanding and managing risks effectively is often the main difference between a creative idea that is not implemented and a successful innovative solution.

Improve the Idea

Consider the following situation:

The innovation team had identified a perfect solution to the executive's challenge. During the implementation planning step, they identified as a key weakness the need for a significant commitment from the IT department at a time when IT was working on a large project that was consuming all their resources. The innovation team created a problem statement for the weakness that read: "How to minimize the involvement of the IT department in the project?" They generated a range of solutions and selected one—to delay the implementation of the one feature that required significant IT resources but did not contribute much to the value of the idea. This enabled them to get a quick commitment from IT to do the minor modifications necessary to implement the main idea.

In this example, the innovation team preserved the main value of their great idea by delaying a minor feature. If they had gone to the executive team with the full idea, including the feature, the IT executive would have challenged the innovative idea, and it might not have been approved. The process of implementation planning is designed to reduce the potential weaknesses or risks of an idea and maximize the probability that it will be successful.

After the implementation planning team identifies the key risks and weaknesses, they must eliminate or mitigate them one at a time, always keeping in mind the key strengths. This process is similar to the overall innovative thinking process. While it includes some of the same techniques, it is usually faster.

The process has six steps that can be repeated if more than one weakness or risk needs to be addressed. The steps are:

1. Identify all the potential weaknesses and rank them in order of potential impact on the successful implementation. Select the top weakness, define it clearly, and identify the root causes.
2. Identify the strengths of the idea, which will then be the boundaries of the problem-solving exercise. The problem becomes: "How to eliminate 'weakness A' without losing the key strengths of the idea?"
3. In divergence, generate possible solutions to eliminate "weakness A."
4. In convergence, identify the best solution to resolve "weakness A" while still solving the original problem and without losing the strengths of the idea.
5. Modify the original idea by integrating the solution and verifying that the weakness has been eliminated and the strengths retained. It is not uncommon at this stage to see the idea evolve significantly, to the point of being almost a different idea.
6. Identify the strengths and the weaknesses of the new solution, and repeat Steps 1 through 5 until every significant risk and weakness has been removed or minimized.

Only after all the key risks are mitigated and the key weaknesses have been eliminated can the idea be presented to the owner of the problem.

STAGE 3: PRESENT THE INNOVATIVE SOLUTION FOR APPROVAL

The approval of an innovative solution is the most important milestone in any innovative thinking process. In fact, without the approval, all the work in the previous steps is a waste of time.

Unfortunately, in too many innovation projects, the presentation of the solution is an afterthought, and planning the presentation is something the team does on the way to the meeting. To ensure that an innovative solution will be approved, the innovative idea is certainly important, but a solid presentation is essential. Too many times a team presents an innovative idea without referring to the problem they solved, including its importance, and without anticipating the questions from their audience. In this situation, a simple question can endanger the innovative idea because the team will appear unprepared.

There are two areas of focus in *Stage 3: Present the Innovative Solution for Approval.* These are:

- *Plan the presentation.* Often the preparation for the presentation can take as long as or longer than the presentation itself.
- *Present the innovative solution using the decision presentation document.* The presentation should be done in a systematic manner to increase the likelihood of approval.

Plan the Presentation

When planning the presentation, the team must go back to the original problem and be clear about the original mandate. A good, executive approved framework can be invaluable. Experience indicates that the preparation for a presentation should take at least as much time as the presentation itself. The preparation should include creating the *decision presentation document* described below and answers to the possible questions from the audience. The *focus exchange* technique, described earlier, is a useful tool to prepare for this task.

Present the Innovative Idea Using the Decision Presentation Document

Over the years, we have designed and refined a focused *decision presentation document* that leaders and teams can use as a starting point for the innovative solution presentation. There are seven key elements included in the *decision presentation document.* While it is possible to add other elements, we have found it risky to omit any of the seven key elements.

Table 9.1: The Key Elements of a Decision Presentation Document

---

The Key Elements of a Decision Presentation Document

1. *Problem the solution must solve:* This section describes the situation that triggered the problem or the opportunity. It can be phrased as a "How to …?" question with boundaries and type of solutions expected.

2. *Risks with the current situation:* What will probably happen if no solution is implemented? For example, a competitor may launch a similar product and have first-to-market advantage.

3. *Root causes and key insights on the issue:* Refer to key findings from Step 2: *Issue Redefinition.*

4. *Recommended solution:* Present the recommended innovative idea for approval.

5. *Strengths of the recommended solution:* Propose why the solution is recommended.

6. *Potential weaknesses and risks of the recommended solution:* Identify the internal and external risks associated with the solution, and the risk mitigation strategies.

7. *Main alternatives considered:* Present the top alternative solutions considered and explain why they are not the preferred solution.

The *decision presentation document* is a very helpful format that can be used for the innovative solution presentation for approval. It demonstrates the depth of the team's work. It also improves the quality of the decision-making by the owner because the owner will be able to consider three distinct options: retaining the current approach, implementing the recommended solution, or approving an alternate solution.

STAGE 4: ENSURE AN EFFECTIVE HANDOFF TO THE TEAM THAT FOCUSES ON CHANGE IMPLEMENTATION

Implementation planning teams need to take accountability for the proper transition of the innovative idea from development to implementation. Often the implementation planning team does a handoff of the approved innovative solution to another team that focuses on change implementation, which we refer to as the "change team." This handoff must be planned carefully. To achieve an effective handoff, the implementation planning team should do the following:

- Ensure the change team members understand the innovative thinking process so that they can apply the same thinking process, can separate divergence and convergence, and can assess risks even as they implement the change.
- Ensure that the change team understands the context, the problem, the urgency for the solution, and the vision of its successful implementation so that they can communicate the change effectively.
- Ensure that the change team understands the issue's insights and appreciates why the innovative thinking team recommended the specific innovative solution.
- Ensure that the change team understands the analysis of risk associated with the innovative solution, especially the risks that relate to implementation.

The handoff is often improved if there is some overlap of membership between the implementation planning team and the change team. In addition, the implementation planning team should prepare an *Implementation Planning Report* to ensure that the change team has a clear understanding of the work that has been done, the contents of the *decision presentation document*, the innovative solution that was approved by the owner, and the best way to implement the innovative solution so that it resolves the problem that was originally identified.

LEVERAGING THE THREE INTELLIGENCES IN THE IMPLEMENTATION PLANNING STEP

Both analytical and emotional intelligence can augment innovative intelligence within Step 4: *Implementation Planning* as follows.

Augmenting Innovative Intelligence with Analytical Intelligence

Analytical intelligence can be useful during implementation planning to identify possible weaknesses or risks in an idea and to plan its implementation. Because the situation is usually complex, the team members must be careful to respect the divergence phases in each of the exercises to ensure they explore all the alternatives. This should be easier for people who have been with the team from the beginning, but the leader and the team must be aware that new members added for Step 4: *Implementation Planning* may not be as familiar with the innovative thinking process.

Augmenting Innovative Intelligence with Emotional Intelligence

Emotional intelligence is critical during Step 4: *Implementation Planning*. The team members and their leader must recognize that the team is likely to be excited about receiving approval and implementing their idea. They need to distance themselves to look at what potentially could go wrong. The team members who identify potential weaknesses or risks should be encouraged to do so, even though nobody likes criticism of their innovative idea.

The four stages of Step 4: *Implementation Planning* can generate conflicts and differences of opinion. The emotionally intelligent innovative thinker must balance the excitement about the great idea with the emotional maturity and intellectual rigor necessary to look at it critically.

THE LEADER'S ROLE IN STEP 4: IMPLEMENTATION PLANNING

The role of leaders in Step 4: *Implementation Planning* is to ensure that the group thoroughly analyzes all the potential weaknesses and the risks during each stage of the step, as follows.

- *Stage 1: Confirm the preferred ideas.* The leader must be certain that the team selects the ideas based on their value to solve the problem successfully or take advantage of the opportunity, rather than because the team is enamored with the ideas. During this stage, the leader must ensure that the team creates an objective *positive and negative assessment* of the innovative ideas.
- *Stage 2: Engage in risk analysis and develop mitigating strategies.* The leader must work with the team to identify all the idea's possible risks and weaknesses. By helping the group stretch beyond the obvious answers, the leader can make sure that the team has carefully examined the idea

and that the idea is as strong as possible. The leader must guide the process to make sure the team members work effectively to solve each key weakness and also to preserve the strengths of the original idea. The leader should encourage the team to apply the process rigorously so that they address all important weaknesses and risks. The team may want to stop after resolving one or two weaknesses, but they must be encouraged to continue until the level of risk is acceptable.

- *Stage 3: Present the innovative solution for approval.* At this stage, the leader must remind the team that however great the idea is, it has no value until it is approved and successfully implemented. The leader has an important role in making sure the team is well prepared for the presentation of the innovative solution.

- *Stage 4: Ensure an effective handoff to the change team.* The leader must remind the team that only when the approved solution is successfully implemented will their work really deliver tangible value. As a result, the leader needs to encourage the team to make an effective handoff to the change team so that the knowledge transfer from the designers of the implementation to the team that focuses on change implementation occurs seamlessly. Finally, the leader must inform the innovation planning team about how the implementation of the innovative solution is progressing and celebrate its success with all the people who helped create and implement it. This celebration is one of the main motivators for employees to participate actively in the next innovation project.

CONCLUSION

Step 4: *Implementation Planning* may not be the most exciting step of the innovative thinking process, but how well it is done determines the value of the whole process. This step is most often shortchanged as time runs out or leaders do not want to focus on an idea's possible negatives. Too many great innovative ideas are rejected or fail because the team and/or the leader do not consider their innovative solution's potential flaws, and they do not spend enough attention making sure they have properly considered and mitigated the risks. It is especially important to remember that innovation in organizations is about successfully implementing new ideas that create value. Everything else is creative, fun, and exciting but not beneficial to the organization in the long run.

We have now looked in great detail at the four-step innovative thinking process that enables individuals and teams to access their innovative intelligence. While it is detailed and rigorous, the four-step process can be completed in as little as an hour for a simple problem or as long as six months or more for a major disruptive innovation. The process is effective for all the types of innovation; the main differences are the time and the number of people involved. Most innovative thinking projects will use only a portion of the techniques presented here. What counts is that the leader and the team apply the logic and the sequence of steps to "check twice and move once." This is the best way to get it right the first time, and if leaders are tempted to think it may take too long, just remember how much time it would take to fix it or to redo it.

Some critical success factors to remember in the innovative thinking process are as follows:

- Ensure that the problem is well defined and that the team is working on the root causes, not simply a symptom, before looking for solutions.
- Apply divergence and convergence at every step of the process to maximize the use of innovative intelligence.
- Ensure the innovative solutions are thoroughly evaluated and the risks and weaknesses mitigated.

Part Three of *Innovative Intelligence* focuses on the key enablers that are essential for employees and teams to have access to their innovative intelligence. In particular, it explores the following:

- How leaders have a central role to lead and enable their employees' and teams' innovative thinking
- How to create and support a culture of innovation
- How organizational practices can make it much easier for innovative thinking to occur.

Finally, we explain how an effective organization-wide innovation plan is essential in order to align the entire organization so that it focuses on closing the innovation gap in a systematic, aligned, and effective way.

PART THREE

MAKING INNOVATION HAPPEN

CHAPTER TEN

MAKING INNOVATION HAPPEN: AN OVERVIEW

The executives of a food manufacturing company were frustrated when they saw the results of their employee survey. The company had invested heavily in innovative thinking training programs in order to close their innovation gap. However, their employees indicated in the survey that they were unable to apply what they learned. The executives were worried that their investment might be wasted if they did not do something quickly. More importantly, their organization would continue to lose its competitive advantages if it did not become more innovative.

The executives decided to investigate the root causes of this problem. While they believed that leaders were more innovative as a result of the training, innovation was still not happening. They found that leaders and employees were very frustrated that they could not use what they learned about innovative thinking.

Essentially, there were two primary dynamics. First, the leaders were indeed more skilled at innovative thinking, but they did not know how to help others access their innovative intelligence. The leaders misunderstood their role in innovation. They believed that they should be the most innovative people, rather than the catalysts to draw out their team members' innovative intelligence. As a result, team members felt stifled by their leaders, and they were discouraged because their innovative ideas were not explored.

Second, the organization had a very rigid annual budgeting process that required leaders to identify all new initiatives and budgets one year in advance. However, the complex customer and supplier challenges the company was encountering required innovative solutions throughout the year. Their innovative ideas were often blocked because they lacked budgeted funds and didn't have the ability to reallocate resources to make the innovations happen.

The executives knew something had to be done quickly or else their leaders and employees would lose the confidence that they could close their company's innovation gap.

This story illustrates that leaders should not expect that they must be the most innovative thinkers. Their role is to help their employees and teams access their innovative intelligence. The story also shows how leaders and organizational processes (in this case, budgeting) can be barriers to innovation and frustrate efforts to make innovation happen.

Table 10.1 shows the interaction between innovative thinking skills and an enabling organization that is set up to facilitate innovative thinking.

Table 10.1: The Interaction between Innovative Thinking Skills and Organizational Enablers

	Organization Stifles Innovation	Organization Maximizes Innovation
Employees Skilled in Innovative Thinking	**High Skills – Disabling Organization** Frustrated individuals Innovation can happen in spite of the organization	**High Skills – Enabling Organization** High innovation continuously supported by an enabling organization
Employees Not Skilled in Innovative Thinking	**Low Skills – Disabling Organization** High risk of organizational demise	**Low Skills – Enabling Organization** Wasted opportunities and potential Need to develop employee innovative thinking capabilities

Here are descriptions of the four scenarios in the table:

- **High skills – enabling organization**
  This is an innovative organization, where innovation, small and large, happens continuously. This organizational system is sustainable as long as the leadership ensures that the skills and the enabling organizational factors continue to be constructive and supportive.
- **Low skills – enabling organization**
  This is a less frequent scenario whereby an enabling organization does not have the employees to leverage the highly supportive organizational environment. This scenario is the easiest to repair, as leaders and employees can learn innovative thinking skills and, within an enabling organization, they can use and practice the skills and the organization will reinforce them.

- **High skills – disabling organization**

  This is the most frustrating situation for individuals and small teams. The employees know how to make innovation happen, but the organization interferes and inhibits it. Some organizations are not set up to promote collaboration among departments, so they block innovative ideas. Some organizational managers are more interested in "making their revenue numbers" than developing innovative solutions. Whatever the root cause of the problem, this organizational dynamic will eventually frustrate the individuals enough that some will leave to find another work environment where their skills will be recognized and utilized.

- **Low skills – disabling organization**

  Some organizations do not have the environment or the talent to be innovative. Often, in these kinds of organizations, leaders need a persistent and long-term perspective in order to turn things around. This scenario can also occur within organizations that were formerly in the "high skills – disabling organization" quadrant. Some innovative thinkers will have left the organization, and the employees that remain reinforce the status quo. This organizational scenario may be the most difficult to turn around because employees lose confidence that the organization will support any innovative efforts.

FOUR ESSENTIAL ORGANIZATIONAL ENABLERS TO MAKE INNOVATION HAPPEN

Organizations need to put in place four essential organizational enablers in order to maximize the potential of innovative individuals and teams, to remove barriers, and to foster innovation. Otherwise, innovation is stifled. Figure 10.1 depicts the four essential enablers.

The following is an overview of each of the four enablers. The next four chapters provide a more detailed explanation of how to put each of these organizational enablers to use.

Leading Innovation

Leaders directly influence whether or not innovation will happen by individuals and in teams. They help employees access their innovative

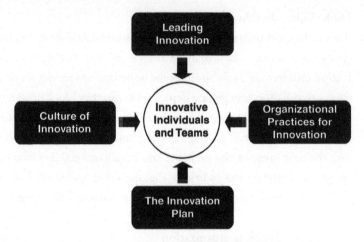

Figure 10.1: The Four Organizational Enablers to Make Innovation Happen

intelligence through innovative thinking. They assist individuals and teams in applying the processes described in Chapters 5 to 9 so that they are able to think innovatively. This responsibility exists whether leading groups of direct reports or cross-functional project teams working on innovation projects.

Leaders face many challenges in their role as leaders of innovation. The example presented in this chapter's opening story described how leaders can inadvertently block innovation. Many leaders are promoted to their leadership roles because they are experts, able to provide solutions to complicated problems their teams encounter. However, as more complex issues arise, leaders often do not know what solutions to propose, and they are often unclear about how to respond to new complex situations. As a result, some leaders struggle to define what their value is to their teams.

Leaders need to understand and use the tools at their disposal to enhance innovation. Their role is similar to that of a leader of an orchestra. Orchestra leaders do not make music. They select the right players, provide the musical conditions in which they can perform in an optimal manner, and continually guide the music through their conducting. In a similar manner, team leaders do not need to create innovation, but rather to provide the conditions in which innovation can happen.

Chapter 11 explores the new added-value role of leaders as enablers of innovative thinking and innovations. It identifies specific expectations of leaders to enable organizations, teams, and employees to be more innovative.

Culture of Innovation

An organizational culture either enables or prevents innovation. The term *culture* refers to the intrinsic individual and team motivators that exist in organizations. As organizations attempt to create a culture of innovation, they encounter many challenges, including the following:

- **Clarity about what is a culture of innovation**
  Leaders need to understand clearly what a culture of innovation is and how it can support them and their employees as they become more innovative. Some of the main cultural drivers of innovation are trust, response to risk taking, communication, and openness. Often, the lack of clarity is a barrier because without it, leaders will not know what kind of culture they need to create and what it will mean to their leadership approach. Leaders also may have a biased view of their current culture and believe that it is more enabling of innovation than it really is. Awareness is the first step to culture change.
- **Need to accelerate cultural transformation**
  Even if the culture of innovation is clearly defined, many leaders and employees have difficulty when attempting to change it. A major characteristic of culture is that it forms in an organization to give it stability and predictability. Challenges to that stability and predictability often create anxiety, which most leaders and teams will work vigorously to avoid. Leaders need to understand how their culture encourages or stifles innovation and how to accelerate cultural transformation.

Chapter 12 explores the culture of innovation and how to accelerate the transformation of a culture so that it functions as a key organizational enabler of innovative thinking.

Organizational Practices for Innovation

Organizational practices can either make innovation easier or more difficult. These practices function as extrinsic and explicit motivators for the kinds of behaviors that are required in an organization. Many organizational practices inhibit and block innovation rather than making it easier. The problem with most established organizations is that they created their practices based upon an industrial-era approach to encourage the repetition of the same task and to discourage variations and innovations around tasks.

Organizations have two primary challenges as they attempt to align their organizational practices to make innovation occur more easily:

- **Eliminate antagonistic organizational practices**
  Some organizational practices may be antagonistic to innovation. The opening chapter story about the budgeting process is an example of a practice that was an effective control of expenditures but was antagonistic and worked against innovation. Antagonistic practices make it difficult for people to be innovative, and often leaders will give up before they can achieve any meaningful innovative outcomes.
- **Foster synergistic organizational practices**
  Some organizational practices are highly effective in promoting and fostering innovation. These processes and structures are synergistic with innovation and make it easier for it to occur. For example, designing rewards, recognition, and performance management processes to promote and sustain innovation would contribute to making innovation happen more frequently.

Chapter 13 systematically reviews most organizational practices, the role each practice plays in innovation, and how each practice can make innovation easier or more difficult.

The Innovation Plan

When organizations want to succeed at a task, they develop a plan—except when they want more innovation. An effective organization-wide innovation plan is required to provide the direction that leaders, teams, and individuals need as they focus on innovation. The innovation plan functions as an essential organization-enabling process, but we highlight it separately because of how fundamental it is to an organization attempting to close its innovation gap.

As organizations attempt to develop an innovation plan, they encounter three primary challenges:

- **Deciding what to do**
  The innovation plan needs to focus the organization on innovations that will achieve important business outcomes. This role is often an

executive responsibility. In addition, executive leaders need to commit the necessary time and effort to promoting, measuring, and sustaining efforts that align with the innovation plan.

- **Deciding what *not* to do**
  Michael Porter wrote that "strategy is not deciding what to do; it is deciding what not to do."[1] The same applies to an innovation plan. It is sometimes more difficult to establish the boundaries for an organization-wide innovation plan and to decide what *not* to do, than to decide what to do. However, these boundaries are essential in order to keep the focus on the kinds of applied innovations that will deliver positive business outcomes. Also, it is important to manage the balance between the need for continuity and stability and the need for change.

- **Measuring and tracking progress**
  Most organizations develop performance measures and track progress on their strategic initiatives. However, because they rarely have an innovation plan, they also rarely have specific measures they can use to assess innovation progress and to track progress on those innovation metrics. Organizations need to include defined metrics, performance indicators, and the governance process in the innovation plan, in order to ensure that innovations are tracked on an ongoing basis.

Chapter 14 describes what should be included in an innovation plan, how to measure innovation, and how to track progress. It also explores some of the key implementation success factors that help expedite and sustain the innovation plan.

SUSTAINING INNOVATION

When innovation happens in organizations, it becomes embedded. It also becomes an invisible competitive advantage, consistently creating new value for the organization. It is reflected in how individuals and teams have access to their innovative intelligence and think innovatively as they redefine complex issues, generate new ideas, identify solutions, and mitigate risks. When leaders

---

1. Michael E. Porter, *Competitive Strategy: Techniques for Analyzing Industries and Competitors* (Free Press, 1998).

and teams are successful in applying their innovative thinking, they often enjoy the experience, foster it, and want to sustain and do more of it.

However, organizational innovation is often difficult to sustain. It is vulnerable—once you have it, it can slip away easily. Therefore, on an ongoing basis, executives and leaders need to be aware of five major challenges to sustaining innovation. These are:

- **Time**

  The innovation process takes time. In order for employees and teams to use their innovative thinking skills automatically, they need leadership support to practice innovative thinking for at least four to six months of continuous effort. If leaders do not support employees, then any excuse will cause them to revert to their former method of dealing with issues. In addition, leaders and teams need to have "think time" to explore complex issues, share ideas, think together, build trust, and discover innovative solutions. However, many executives and leaders are unwilling to invest the required time needed for innovative thinking.

- **Process**

  Teams cannot simply improvise to achieve effective outcomes in innovative thinking. They need to follow a clear innovative thinking process to help them work through issues in order to have an outcome that creates new ideas. Executives and leaders need to be persistent and champion the ongoing and effective utilization of the same innovative thinking process throughout their organization. They also need to protect team members by stopping peers who attempt to block or limit the team's capability to apply the innovative thinking process.

- **Ambiguity**

  Executives, leaders, and teams need to become far more comfortable with ambiguity and not rush to close down their discussions and resolve them too quickly. Leaders need to excel at leading through complexity, which includes a very high tolerance for ambiguity as teams explore issues and discover innovative solutions.

- **Commitment**

  Executives and leaders must commit to helping others access their innovative intelligence through the innovative thinking process. This includes sustaining the commitment to innovation when there is a change in the leadership of the organization or in its structure. Organizations need to sustain what they have and rebuild, if necessary, to ensure they can continue to achieve innovative thinking. They also need to commit to continuously removing organizational obstacles that are antagonistic to innovation.

- **Scalability**

  The term scalability refers to the need for plans that work on a smaller level to be able to be effective on a larger level as well. To sustain innovation, the innovation plan that is implemented effectively in part of an organization needs to be scalable for the more widespread application of innovation in the entire organization. The innovation plan should identify how the plan can be scalable to a more extensive group of leaders and teams. Also, innovative solutions need to be scalable so that isolated solutions can be applied broadly to maximize the benefit they can provide to the business.

CONCLUSION

Innovative thinking is necessary, but not sufficient, for innovation to occur in organizations. There are four essential enablers that are fundamental to making innovation happen. The next four chapters will explore these enablers in detail. Each chapter provides concepts, tools, and techniques to create a work environment that is conducive to innovative thinking, to making innovation happen, and to sustaining it.

Organizations need to maximize leaders' and teams' access to their innovative intelligence. By combining a highly effective innovative thinking process with focused organizational enablers, the innovation gap in organizations can be overcome. The innovation challenge may be substantial, but the benefits from delivering sustainable competitive advantage through innovation are worth the effort.

CHAPTER ELEVEN

LEADING INNOVATION

With the ever-changing media landscape, News Inc. had to evolve. Advertising dollars were decreasing, printing and paper costs were escalating, the customer base was declining and aging, and competition was increasing—mostly as a result of the digital age.

The president decided to put together a cross-functional innovation team to develop a plan to respond to the competitive challenges. Most leaders thought the president would choose a senior publisher of one of the largest magazines or newspapers or a member of the executive team to lead this strategic project. But instead, the president chose Tammy, a 35-year-old MBA graduate with experience in marketing, who had joined News Inc. as a director and had only two years of experience with the company. Tammy consistently exceeded expectations and her vice president identified her as a high-potential employee.

At the next executive meeting, several people questioned the choice of Tammy as the innovation team leader for this highly strategic project. They felt the project would be far too great a stretch assignment for her. After some debate, the president explained his logic. He felt this challenge required new perspectives. What had made News Inc. so successful in the past was not going to make it successful in the future. This innovation project needed fresh ideas and a different approach, starting at the top. He believed this was a complex problem that none of the executives had encountered before. He feared they would fall back on what they had done in the past to succeed, which would not work in this unique situation. The president concluded that "this project needs someone who can use our past experience and knowledge but who will not be constrained by it, so I have chosen Tammy."

The opening example describes the potential problem of excelling at analytical intelligence when what is required is innovative intelligence. All the executives had very well-developed analytical intelligence, which had worked well for them in the past. However, if they used that thinking to approach this new complex problem, it could block and inhibit innovative solutions. Tammy was an innovative thinker and was very open to new directions, so she could be free to explore issues without constraint or bias.

In Chapter 10 we introduced the four organizational enablers shown in Figure 11.1. This chapter focuses on how leaders like Tammy and the president of News Inc. need to function in order to lead innovation.

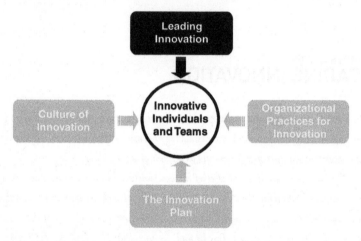

Figure 11.1: The Four Organizational Enablers to Make Innovation Happen

Our premise is that leaders are central to any innovation effort, whether at the innovation project level, the work unit level, or the overall enterprise level. Innovation rarely happens and certainly cannot be sustained without the active commitment and involvement of effective leaders of innovation throughout the organization.

There are four areas of leading innovation that we explore in this chapter.

Areas of Leading Innovation
- Leading self
- Leading innovation teams
- Leading intact work units
- Leading enterprises for innovation

We begin this chapter by exploring the foundational ability of leaders of innovation to be effective at "leading self." Regardless of the level in the organization, leaders need this skill in order to enable others to access their innovative intelligence. We then explore specific techniques for leaders of innovation teams (i.e., teams that are project driven to gain insight and discover solutions to complex problems) and for leaders of intact work units (i.e., managerial accountability for the ongoing deliverables of a work unit, department, division, etc.) as they draw out their teams' innovative intelligence and maximize their effectiveness. The chapter then explores how executives should be leaders of innovation throughout the organization.

LEADING SELF

Leaders need many personal characteristics in order to be effective leaders of innovation. We highlight three primary characteristics for consideration by leaders as they "lead self."[1]

Leading Self
- Think holistically
- Have a horizontal view
- Leverage conversations

Effective Leaders Need to Think Holistically

Complex problems are often characterized by information that is somewhat unclear, assumptions that may be unfounded and elusive solutions. Leaders may be in situations where team members from a variety of different areas are collaborating, trying to gain insight into an issue, and working to discover an effective solution. Collectively, the individuals on the team will always

---

1. David S. Weiss and Vince Molinaro, *The Leadership Gap* (John Wiley and Sons, 2005). Chapter 3 of *The Leadership Gap* defines "holistic leadership" as a "whole and complete way of thinking about organization and leadership." Chapter 9 of *The Leadership Gap* provides a more detailed description of the seven elements required of leaders to be capable personal leaders.

have far more insight and understanding about the details of the issue than the leader alone. However, each person will have his or her own perspective of the details that are important for any complex issue.

Some leaders fall into the trap of believing they have to know all the details themselves in order to be effective leaders of innovation. This may have been true for solving complicated problems, when the leader was usually the most experienced person and analytical intelligence was needed, but it is not true for solving complex problems. These leaders sometimes make the mistake of immersing themselves in the details, but, of course, they are far behind the team members who have been working with the details of the issue for a long time. Innovation team leaders will rarely succeed if they see their role as diving down into the details of complex problems.

Leaders need to orient themselves in the exact opposite direction. It is essential to have a holistic perspective and to understand the macro context within which the complexity is arising. Then, they need to lead the process to make sure they and the team maximize the value of their collective knowledge and innovative intelligence. Leaders are often exposed to overall business challenges, competitive issues, stakeholder interests, customer dynamics, regulatory requirements, and inter-divisional issues within the business, and they need to understand these macro variables to be able to frame the complex issue in its proper holistic context.

As we described in Chapter 3, intelligence exists in potential, and it is only within a context that intelligence can become reality. Leaders who are able to shift their focus to the macro and the holistic perspectives increase their ability to work more effectively and add value to their employees and innovative teams. At the same time, they will be able to function better as leaders in the organization across a wide array of other areas.

Holistic leaders need to have access to their three intelligences and to know how to draw all of these intelligences out of team members. They need to know when to apply analytical intelligence by using logic, current knowledge, and experiences to advance the understanding of a complicated issue. They also need to know how to ensure that teams work in an emotionally intelligent manner. Finally, the leaders must have a full understanding of the process of innovative thinking and how to help their employees and teams gain access to and utilize their innovative intelligence to solve complex issues.

Effective Leaders of Innovation Need to Have a Horizontal View

Leaders confronted with complex issues require diverse opinions in order to gain insight into the complexities and to discover alternative solutions that were not considered in the past.

To be effective at working horizontally (cross-functionally) and gain insight from all the organization's resources, leaders need to be oriented to the overall business. This may sound simpler than it actually is. Many organizations currently suffer from what are referred to as "silos." A silo occurs when deeply embedded subcultures in parts of the organization become much more dominant than the organization's overall culture. A major characteristic of a silo is the unwillingness of those in the subculture to collaborate horizontally and to share information with other groups. Members of silos are more focused on their own areas of responsibility than they are on the overall organization. As a result, rather than making decisions that balance the needs of their own local business environment and the overall needs of the enterprise, leaders of silos prefer to make decisions in the best interest of their own silo—even if those decisions sub-optimize another silo. Sometimes the leaders of silos feel they are doing a wonderful job when their silo is successful. However, the success of one part of an organization at the expense of the entire organization always generates dysfunction that should not be tolerated.

In companies that suffer from this condition, each department is like a storage silo, only in a business context. They store their own information and objectives rather than sharing common goals and information with other departments and communicating freely with one another. The common solution to the problem is to break down the walls of the silo—not a very encouraging image for most leaders. An image that better resonates with many leaders is to think of the various units as "islands." There are many departments in an enterprise that metaphorically live on separate islands. To become an integrated unit an enterprise needs to build bridges between some of the islands, while others may only need a fast-moving boat or a ferry to travel from one island to another to connect the overall enterprise. Leaders need to think about all the islands within the enterprise and determine how to connect the various parts so that the value of the total enterprise becomes greater than the sum of its individual departments. As teams work on complex issues, leaders need to be able to think horizontally by linking the various islands and offering that context to their teams. The enterprise also needs to set up forums within which leaders can exchange ideas and ensure that isolated islands are not encouraged. This approach will expand the leaders' access to resources from other parts of the enterprise, which can contribute to the teams' innovative thinking processes.

The benefits of the horizontal view apply equally well for innovation teams and for intact work units. For example:

- *Leading innovation teams.* Innovative organizations often form innovation teams with a diverse group of members who can view an issue from different perspectives and gain insight into the underlying complexities of an issue. A diverse group sees issues in many different ways, can more easily challenge assumptions, and can develop broad-based solutions. A mix of people working on a complex innovation problem is much preferred to a group of homogenous experts. Experts with similar backgrounds and perspectives may all arrive at a similar understanding of the problem and potentially the same answer as they gave previously, which may be simple, but wrong.
- *Leading intact work units.* When faced with complex problems, leaders of intact work units also need a horizontal view of the enterprise. Some simulate the horizontal view by bringing representatives from other departments (or key stakeholders and customers) into their teams to generate innovative thinking. We know of at least one organization that institutes this practice into their standard problem-resolution process. They require intact work units to conduct a meeting with a cross-functional group to vet ideas and assumptions before they permit the units to recommend a solution to a complex issue.

Effective Leaders of Innovation Need to Leverage Conversations

A primary challenge for leaders of innovation teams or intact work units is to know how to leverage conversations effectively. For many years, leaders were told they needed to coach their direct reports and teams rather than tell them what to do. However, many leaders struggled with that advice. After all, most of the problems they faced were complicated issues, and as leaders, they were supposed to know the answers. Coaching for complicated problems may slow down the process when leaders believe they know the answers already. However, for complex issues, coaching and leveraging conversations take on a new level of importance. Leaders do not know the answers to complex issues, and they need to coach employees and teams to help gain insight into the complexity and to discover new solutions.

To achieve that end result, leaders need to excel at "leading self" so that they can leverage conversations with individuals and with teams. They need to facilitate nonjudgmental conversations with others that will achieve the following.

- Make the implicit explicit. Sometimes, what is obvious to leaders is not obvious to others.
- Surface underlying assumptions, issues, and concerns.
- Accept challenges to assumptions or hypotheses.
- Suspend judgments and explore differences fully to achieve understanding.
- Accept that good ideas can come from anywhere and anyone.
- Emerge with a common understanding of the meaning of a situation so that it can be explored fully.

When leaders know how to leverage conversations, they are able to achieve a deeper, shared understanding of issues with their employees and teams. As a result, they consistently produce better decisions and outcomes for complex issues.

To leverage conversations, leaders sometimes need to extend themselves and communicate *in the language of the listener*. Most leaders assume that listeners should adapt their listening style and understand the way the leaders like to communicate information. However, the leaders who are effective at maximizing the capabilities of their innovation teams know how to adjust their communication style and language so that listeners are able to understand them easily.

Communicating in the language of the listener is particularly important for innovation teams that include cross-functional, as well as cross-cultural, groups. Innovation teams are often characterized by diverse representatives who approach issues from their perspectives gained from past experience. Cross-culturally, individuals might think about issues in a particular way and have different communication styles. Leaders need to adjust so that they can communicate in the language of their listeners. This is even more challenging in environments where innovation teams work together virtually and not in a common space where they can see each other. With these teams, leaders need to be very flexible in their communication styles—in how they write e-mails, how they communicate on conference calls, and how they work through video conferencing technology. Flexible leaders who learn to communicate in the language of their listeners are most likely to be able to lead innovation teams effectively.

LEADING INNOVATION TEAMS

Leading an innovation team involves leading that team to gain insight and discover solutions to a complex problem. Section 2 (Chapters 5 to 9) describes the rigorous innovative thinking process required of innovative thinkers and teams. Leaders of innovation teams need to excel at balancing the facilitation of the process of innovative thinking with the achievement of the goal of discovering an innovative solution to a complex problem.

There are 10 essential roles for innovation team leaders.

Leading Innovation Teams
1. Set the direction so all understand the required outcomes.
2. Set the boundaries within which the innovation team must operate.
3. Ask for innovation.
4. Ensure adequate resources for the team.
5. Reinforce the right behaviors constantly and consistently.
6. Build trust on the team.
7. Eliminate obstacles and protect the group.
8. Provide rewards and recognition.
9. Be the champion of the innovative thinking process.
10. Care about innovation and sustain it.

Here is a more detailed explanation of these 10 roles.

1. *Set the direction so all understand the required outcomes.*

   Leaders need to take the initiative to define the objectives and expected outcomes for the innovative thinking process. They must ensure that the team discusses the objectives so they fully understand the work that is required to explore the complex challenge.

2. *Set the boundaries within which the innovation team must operate.*

   Leaders must determine from the owners of the problem the boundaries that their innovation team is required to work within and communicate these specific boundaries to the team honestly and clearly. Also, in some cases, leaders may set their own additional boundaries, which they need to discuss with the team.

3. *Ask for innovation.*

   It is essential that leaders be explicit with their teams and ask the members to focus on innovative thinking within defined boundaries for complex issues. Sometimes leaders make the mistake of telling the team in detail what they should do and how they should do it. Instead, leaders need to explain the precise boundaries and then give the innovation team members the freedom and safety to explore the unique characteristics of the complex issue and to discover the best solution within those boundaries.

4. *Ensure adequate resources for the team.*

   Leaders often are responsible for negotiating and influencing executives to provide proper resources to innovation teams. Resourcing includes allocating diverse talent to the innovation team and providing a reasonable budget. Often, it also includes training the team members in innovative thinking so that they are able to have greater access to their innovative intelligence capabilities.

5. *Reinforce the right behaviors constantly and consistently.*

   Leaders need to ensure that their teams have governance structures and decision-making processes so that there are few opportunities for confusion and mistrust. Team norms are also essential, and leaders are responsible for establishing these norms and for ensuring that the innovation team works together according to them.

   We often refer to the team norms as a Collaboration Code. A *Collaboration Code* identifies how an innovation team will work together within their meetings, whether face-to-face or virtually, and how they will work together outside of meetings. Sometimes these Codes are signed by each of the team members. This helps to ensure that team members have confidence that the Collaboration Code is serious and that deviations from it will be stopped. The team can also openly discuss issues related to the Code if, in fact, it is impeding their ability to function as an innovation team.

The team governance structures, decision-making processes, and Collaboration Codes give leaders some measure of assurance that there will be few surprises as they facilitate the group, focus on the holistic context and cross-functional dynamics, and leverage team conversations. If these foundational elements are in place, then the innovation team members are likely to demonstrate the right team behaviors constantly and consistently.

6. *Build trust on the team.*

Building trust is essential in order to explore complex issues thoroughly. When team members operate in an environment of mistrust, it is very difficult for the leader to draw out their innovative intelligence. Building trust also has an impact on communication among the team members. When they trust each other, they are more open to each other's ideas, communication and openness increase, and the engagement of all participants is maximized. Trusting relationships contribute to opportunities to leverage conversations and to achieve meaningful outcomes for complex issues.

In contrast, leaders who create fearful environments, where mistakes or failures are punished, are rarely able to generate positive outcomes from innovation teams. Some leaders may be punitive when a team identifies incorrect answers or may reject innovative ideas during brainstorming processes. These leaders create guarded responses by team members and reduce the group's overall innovative thinking.

7. *Eliminate obstacles and protect the group.*

Leaders need to focus on eliminating obstacles that might reduce the team members' access to their innovative intelligence. The biggest obstacle to innovation usually comes in the form of interference or unreasonable boundaries from departments that would prefer to continue doing what they do currently. Too often, the innovation team does not have the authority to override or even negotiate with the resisting department. It is essential that the team leader make sure the obstacles are removed by escalating the issue if necessary. Another frequent obstacle is departments that put pressure on the innovation team to either follow a specific solution or develop solutions within a very narrow direction. In all cases, the team leader must act promptly and with conviction to ensure that the innovation team follows through on its mandate to gain insight into the complex issue and to discover innovative solutions to the problem.

8. *Provide rewards and recognition.*

Leaders need to reward and recognize the work of innovation teams. A fundamental way of doing this is to define their innovation work as part of their primary responsibilities. Leaders of innovation teams need to influence the organization to avoid the error of asking key talent to join innovation teams without reducing their day-to-day work. Innovation team members may feel honored and excited to be part of an innovation team but resent the added work required. Also, specific rewards should be identified to recognize the contribution of the team leader and the team members.

9. *Champion the innovative thinking process.*

Leaders need to be the champions of the innovative thinking process and must facilitate the process. Table 11.2 presents a summary list of the leader's primary roles at each step of the innovative thinking process.

10. *Care about innovation and sustain it.*

Leaders need to care about innovation and invest their emotional intelligence to sustain it. They should be relentless in their support of collecting individual team members' ideas and then expanding those ideas in group innovative thinking sessions. They also need to emphasize that innovative thinking requires divergent thought before convergence. It is essential that they be persistent with the innovative thinking process and commit to sustaining their team's innovative thinking for a minimum of four to six months.

LEADING INTACT WORK UNITS

Leading intact work units applies to a leader who has responsibility for the ongoing deliverables of a work unit, department, or division. This section presents four areas in which all leaders of intact work units need to

Table 11.2: The Leader's Primary Roles at Each Step in the Innovative Thinking Process

The Four-Step Process	Summary of the Leader's Primary Roles at Each Step in the Innovative Thinking Process
1. Framework	• Clearly articulate the overall goals for the team • Present the team governance structure and decision-making process • Establish ground rules and norms for the team • Clearly define the "How to …?" question and establish boundaries • Clarify the ownership of the issue and the accountabilities
2. Issue Redefinition	• Openly struggle with the ambiguity of the complex issue • Encourage a holistic view and systems-thinking approach • Share all the facts and knowledge about the complex issue • Challenge assumptions about the complex issue • Redefine the issue and engage in a review meeting with the executive sponsor who has oversight for the project to confirm the redefined issue
3. Idea Generation	• Ensure there is a safe and nonjudgmental environment in the group • Help achieve expansive thinking by ensuring initially that all members express their ideas openly • Ensure that the team separates divergence and convergence • Prevent early judgment or convergence before the team hears the ideas of all of its members • Champion the proper process to converge ideas to discover the preferred solution
4. Implementation Planning	• Help the team collectively anticipate and manage probable and possible risks • Refine the preferred recommended solution to mitigate or reduce the severity of the risk to an acceptable level • Develop backup alternative solutions with a lower or higher risk level than the recommended solution • Make an effective handoff to the change team, ensuring that the knowledge transfer from the designers of the innovation to the team that focuses on change implementation occurs seamlessly • Inform the innovation planning team about how the change implementation of the innovative solution is progressing and celebrate successes

be effective. It then concludes with the *Leaders' Innovation Readiness Survey* to guide these leaders as they prepare to enable their intact work unit teams to be more innovative.

Leading Intact Work Units

- Leverage the added value of teams.
- Encourage and model the use of innovative thinking.
- Understand when to focus on innovation and when to focus on stability.
- Ensure that the leaders at all levels are ready for innovation.

Leverage the Added Value of Teams

The concept that a team can generate new knowledge and value beyond its members' individual capabilities is an important insight in our knowledge economy. Organizations need innovation teams in order to survive and thrive in the rapidly changing competitive environment.

In the 1980s, many attempted to emulate the success of companies in Japan and developed new methodologies for businesses based upon teams. At that time, team-based management focused on innovations such as quality circles, continuous improvement, and quality of working life. These teams spawned several decades of gradual social change in organizations. The common model of one supervisor managing subordinates in one location was disrupted. There was new emphasis on working with virtual teams that were not co-located, working with teams that were self-regulated without a direct supervisor, and working cross-functionally so information was shared and decisions involved the collaboration of multiple leaders. Individuals on these teams needed to work in cooperative and collaborative ways across diverse disciplines. However, after many years of organizations attempting to build effective innovation teams, the results are still uneven.

One common error for leaders of work unit teams is functioning with the industrial economy mindset, in which leaders are expected to know all the answers to the issues that the team encounters.[2] This approach may be effective in work environments dominated by complicated problems, where past experience provides the expertise and knowledge to make those kinds of decisions. However, in the knowledge economy, a mix of complicated

---

2. See Chapter 2: "Leading Through Complexity" for a complete discussion of this concept.

and complex issues often exists, and many of the complex issues that leaders face have never been experienced before. As a result, the leaders do not know the answers to the questions. The challenge is for leaders to discover a new way to contribute value as they work with their teams and individual employees, in an environment where the answers to complex issues are not evident.

In dysfunctional situations, leaders create artificial methods to sustain their position of having unique knowledge and, therefore, value for the team. A common method these leaders use is to withhold information and knowledge. By doing this, they then have unique insights that their team members do not have, and they use that knowledge to create value falsely. In reality, this behavior creates mistrust because the team members often know that the leader had this information but did not share it.

In a work environment dominated by complex problems, knowledge no longer can be a source of power; rather, knowledge needs to be a shared resource. Leaders need to be actively committed to sharing knowledge and business developments with their teams so that all can work with the same information. This transparency of knowledge will maximize the trust on the team and, at the same time, will allow the team to collaborate in order to generate the most effective insights into complex issues and to discover the most effective solutions to the complexities.

Encourage and Model the Use of Innovative Thinking

A key role for leaders of work units is to encourage all their employees to use innovative thinking. Training employees in innovative thinking is important but not sufficient. Leaders must reinforce its use and model it so that everyone in the unit will be encouraged to apply innovative thinking when appropriate. In order to become effective at innovative thinking, employees must learn the theory, but they also must practice it in their own work environment for an extended period of time. Employees will internalize innovative thinking more rapidly if the leaders of their work unit reinforce the new behaviors and if executives use the innovative thinking tools when appropriate. If, on the other hand, leaders do not encourage and model innovative thinking themselves, then it will likely be ignored and quickly forgotten by employees.

Understand When to Focus on Innovation and When to Focus on Stability

Leaders of intact work unit teams face many kinds of issues—some are complicated, some are complex, and most combine elements of both. Leaders need to excel at understanding how to balance the need for stability and the need for innovation. Leaders of intact work units often are referred to as managers and leaders. These two roles are closely related to the challenge of balancing implementation of existing work with innovating to discover new ways of doing things.

Consider the following distinction between managers and leaders:

- **Managers focus on implementation**
  The four primary roles of managers are to plan, delegate, evaluate, and control. Managers of work units are in their roles to ensure the effective follow-through on specific deliverables and to ensure implementation effectiveness. Often, these deliverables are complicated, and effective managers are able to steer work unit teams to implement the work in a timely manner and with high quality. Many managers excel at analytical thinking in order to apply what they know and their past experience to the implementation process. They also need emotional intelligence to coach employees to fulfill their responsibilities in a positive work environment.
- **Leaders focus on innovation**
  Leaders need to think holistically and horizontally across the enterprise. They need to inspire teams to explore and gain insight into complexities and to facilitate the discovery of new ways of doing things. All these leadership roles are connected to innovation. Leaders need to use their own innovative intelligence and help teams to access theirs. Emotional intelligence also is of great importance because the ambiguity of the issues they are exploring could cause team members to panic or respond poorly. At times, analytical intelligence also is helpful to reuse some approaches that worked in the past and to avoid pitfalls that are already known.

Most individuals assigned to lead work units are expected to be both managers and leaders. They need to know when to wear the "manager's hat" and when to wear the "leader's hat." They also need to be able to shift gracefully from one hat to another so that the teams can switch to a different thinking approach as well. Leaders must guide their teams when they ask them to shift their focus from resolving complicated issues to exploring complex issues.

The key for leaders is to understand the process of innovative thinking well enough that they can effectively decide when to apply it. We validated this statement in our recent survey of HR executives.[3] We found that innovative organizations often have leaders who understand the process of innovation (68 percent) while non-innovative organizations rarely (6 percent) have leaders who understand the process of innovation.

Ensure That Leaders at All Levels Are Ready for Innovation

It is worthwhile to reemphasize that in order for leaders of work units to have a readiness for innovation, they do *not* need to be the most innovative. It is remarkable how relieved many leaders are when we mention this to them at our various sessions. There is a collective sigh of relief when leaders learn that they are expected to excel at drawing out their teams' and employees' innovative intelligence but that they do not need to be the most innovative individuals themselves. We interpret this collective sigh of relief as reflecting their feelings when they realize that their value as leaders will not be jeopardized if they are not the most innovative thinkers. Most leaders believe that with the right skills and knowledge, they can coach and facilitate any team to generate innovative ideas.

An example can be drawn from sports. The coach of a basketball team never touches the ball or shoots at the basket during a game. By definition, the coach's role is to draw out the players' expertise so that the team works together effectively and performs at the highest level of their potential. Often, the individuals who understand a sport well are the people who sit on the sidelines and observe what it takes to succeed and fail in the sport. They are conscious of every possible edge to succeed. Those individuals are often well suited to coach the team because they can spot the nuances to develop the team and individuals effectively. On the other hand, individuals

---

3. Based on the research by Ideaction and the Human Resources Professionals' Association (HRPA) in Ontario, Canada (2008).

who have always excelled in a sport often do not understand its challenges because they have been successful at it naturally. They also may not have experience with failure and may not know how to turn failure into a learning opportunity.

Most leaders have the personal capability to be facilitators and coaches of work unit teams and to draw out the team's collective innovative intelligence and insights through innovative thinking. As we have said, leaders do not need to be the most innovative on their teams. Indeed, if they are, then they have to be particularly careful not to overwhelm their teams or control them with their innovative ideas. They might weaken the team's overall ability to generate insights that will surpass what any individual would have been able to identify. It is important for leaders of work units to understand the four-step innovative thinking process so that they know how to access their own innovative intelligence, can help others access theirs, and can apply the process to complex issues.

Table 11.3 on the next page presents a leader self-assessment process we call the *Leaders' Innovation Readiness Survey*. This survey explores the extent to which leaders have created an environment for their teams that enables innovation when it is needed.

The survey can be used both as a self-assessment of the leader and as a feedback survey by team members to identify the developmental areas for the leader. Any areas that are marked below 75 percent of the time should become a focus for development for that leader. Any difference of 25 percent or more between what the leaders should do and what the leader currently does often reflects disappointment in his or her leading innovation performance. Also, many leaders benefit from the identification of the top priority leadership developmental areas that are required in order to lead intact work unit teams effectively.

LEADING ENTERPRISES FOR INNOVATION

Executives who lead entire enterprises, business units, countries, or significant functional departments all have the same responsibilities as other leaders to lead self, to lead innovation teams, and to lead intact work units. However, they have additional responsibilities by virtue of the executive positions they hold within their organizations.

Table 11.3: The Leaders' Innovation Readiness Survey

Instructions: Complete this survey using a scale of 1 to 5 as shown. Answer each question by writing an "X" on the number that describes what you *currently* do and an "O" on the number that describes what you believe you *should* do.

	Almost Never	About 25% of the Time	About 50% of the Time	About 75% of the Time	Almost Always
1. I always ask my team to be more innovative.	1	2	3	4	5
2. I understand how to help my team be more innovative.	1	2	3	4	5
3. I am clear about what prevents my team from being more innovative.	1	2	3	4	5
4. I personally model innovation consistently.	1	2	3	4	5
5. I encourage my managers to always look for better ways to do what we do.	1	2	3	4	5
6. I have a written plan on how to make my team more innovative.	1	2	3	4	5
7. I always ask my team to include innovative ideas in their plans.	1	2	3	4	5
8. I always give clear mandates within clear boundaries for each task.	1	2	3	4	5
9. I formally encourage my team to take time to think.	1	2	3	4	5
10. I always ensure we are working on the right problem before we look for solutions.	1	2	3	4	5
11. I encourage intelligent risk-taking.	1	2	3	4	5
12. I accept positive mistakes.	1	2	3	4	5
13. We are excellent at teamwork.	1	2	3	4	5
14. We always involve other groups when looking for innovative solutions.	1	2	3	4	5
15. We always look for root cause before implementing solutions to a problem.	1	2	3	4	5
16. I formally recognize innovation in my team.	1	2	3	4	5

17. Please circle the three most urgent items that need to be addressed now to improve the effectiveness of your team:

1	2	3	4	5	6	7	8	9	10	11	12	13	14	15	16

Leading Enterprises for Innovation
- Model the way of innovative thinking on the executive team.
- Ensure key organizational levers support innovation.
- Promote innovative executive leaders to the senior executive levels.
- Remove barriers to innovation.
- Create and sustain momentum for innovation.

Model the Way of Innovative Thinking on the Executive Team

The executive team's approach to innovation sets the tone and the example for others. Mid-level managers look to the executives to determine if they should take innovation seriously. If the executive team is a model of innovative thinking, then the chances are greater that teams throughout the organization will embrace innovative thinking. If the executive team is not consistent in the area of innovation, then managers often will not believe the talk about the need for innovation and will not focus on it. Essentially, the executive team will only be as strong as its weakest believer.

Consider the following situation in which an executive team often talks about the importance of innovation, but remains unaware of how their behavior contributes to stifling it.

The executive team often invites employees to be guest presenters at their meetings. Some of the executive team members have a bad habit of shooting down speakers before they have the opportunity to complete their thoughts. The team regularly prides itself on being critical of each other and trying to outsmart each other. When guests come into the executive meeting to present, the executives see it as their role to try to poke holes in the guests' ideas in order to demonstrate that they are smarter than the guests and that those employees should be working harder. They believe that this behavior enhances the quality of the result or outcome but, actually, all it does is make employees fear attending the executive meetings because they believe they will be embarrassed in the process and their credibility will be threatened. These executives do not know how to listen to each other or how to leverage conversations. Their entire process is short-sighted and ultimately stifles innovation in the enterprise.

When executives recognize the importance of innovation, they can have an immense influence on the leaders in their organizations by enabling them to focus on leading innovation. Executives signal what is important by their key decisions, such as who they promote, who leads key projects, and who exits the organization. They also indicate what they believe when the organization is under stress. If the executives panic and stop innovation activities during difficult times, employees will assume that innovation is nice to have but not fundamental to the way the business works and what it needs to succeed. If the executives respond to stressful events by sustaining and even increasing their focus on innovation teams, the message will be clear that innovation is not a passing fad but rather an essential way of doing business and part of the organization's current and future success formula.

Promote Innovative Executive Leaders to the Senior Executive Levels

Consider this story of an organization that chose not to promote an innovative leader to the executive level.

The vice president of sales in a large financial institution had completed his third major project in five years, building a business from zero to over a billion dollars in sales against all odds and successfully closing a major gap in the organization's operation. He was now the most experienced and the most successful executive at his level and was praised publicly for his successes by the CEO. Yet, over a period of two years, five executive peers were promoted to the senior executive level and the VP of sales was not chosen. Each time he was told that they were waiting for the right opportunity that would fit his style and expertise. The next year, another peer was promoted. This time the VP of sales approached a senior executive he knew well and asked her for the real reason he was not promoted. She said the senior executives as a group saw him as a maverick. They perceived his skills to be exceptional at solving complex problems that required innovative solutions, but he was too radical, and he did not have the right personality fit to be a senior executive in their organization.

Many surveys indicate that as executives rise in organizations, they tend to become more conservative.[4] This pattern is particularly true in large, more conservative organizations and can be attributed to the following two factors:

- As the responsibilities and spans of control of executives increase, the stakes become higher, and organizations perceive more conservative executives to be less risky.

---

4. Otto Kroeger and Janet Thuesen, *Type Talk at Work* (Dell Publishing, 1992).

- The majority of the current executive leaders of large traditional organizations rose through the hierarchy during the industrial economy. Many of them are experts at analytical intelligence and do not appreciate the value of innovative intelligence at the senior executive level.

The implication is that the senior executive level is often represented by a group of like-minded conservative leaders, while the innovative leaders are rarely promoted to the senior executive levels. In the above story, the financial institution referred to this VP of sales as a maverick largely because he was able to succeed at the toughest assignments despite the low odds given to him by the senior executives. But when it came time to be considered for promotion to the rank of senior executive, what happened in this organization is what often happens—the maverick was passed over in favor of other executives who managed traditional businesses with lower risks.

Understanding this factor is critical for senior executives in large and conservative organizations that want to commit to innovation and renewal. Unless they break the pattern and invite the mavericks into the senior executive levels, their enterprises will probably not become more innovative nor change fast enough to continue to be successful.

Ensure Key Organizational Levers Support Innovation

Executives have direct and indirect control over most of the key organizational levers for innovation. In the next three chapters, we explore three areas over which executives have direct influence. They are the following:

1. Creating a culture of innovation
2. Instituting organizational processes and structures that support innovation
3. Ensuring that there is an enterprise-wide innovation plan that is governed, measured, and continuously improved.

Perhaps the most commonly used organizational lever is the budgeting process. Even when organizations do not have strategic plans, they signal what is strategic by virtue of the amount of budget funds that are allocated to departments and projects. Innovation team projects that receive no budget are viewed by organizations as unimportant. When budget is allocated to innovation team projects, or when there is an unallocated fund available for innovations as they emerge throughout the year, that often sends a signal and motivates people to take innovation seriously.

Another key lever that is rarely utilized for the purpose of innovation is the development of an enterprise-wide innovation plan that is tracked and monitored on a regular basis. Chapter 14 explains how organizations can develop and track such a plan. It is surprising that even though many executives claim that innovation is of crucial importance to their organizations, they nevertheless do not develop a systematic plan to focus innovation efforts on priority areas. They also do not have a governance process to sponsor and track their innovation teams' developments. Executives need to apply the same managerial excellence they apply to the implementation of today's outputs to the leadership of the innovations for tomorrow's business.

Remove Barriers to Innovation

Executives have a unique role in removing barriers to innovation in their enterprises. They need to be keenly aware of what can constrain and block innovations. Some of the major barriers include the following:

- *People issues.* Some individuals may prefer the status quo and, therefore, look for ways to block or slow down innovations. These kinds of individuals are problematic if they operate independently, but the problem is magnified when they are in leadership positions or positions of influence. The executives need to identify the leaders who are barriers to innovation and innovative thinking and act quickly to address those barriers.
- *Process issues.* Sometimes the executives or various departments put in place organizational processes or structures that are antagonistic to innovation and innovative thinking. Some of these include the budgeting process, rewards and compensation processes, and compliance requirements. These barriers and what to do about them are described in detail in Chapter 13.
- *Inertia issues.* One of the greatest sources of inertia is enterprise success. Some executives in successful enterprises are reluctant to explore new and innovative ideas because they feel these ideas may erode their current success. However, more enlightened executives of successful enterprises recognize that success lasts for only a fleeting moment, and it

often erodes more rapidly because of inertia than as a result of ongoing systematic effort to introduce new innovations. The barrier that executives need to remove is the unwillingness to be innovative when they are succeeding. Innovation is not an event that is time bound. It needs to be a continuous process and part of the ongoing way of working.

Create and Sustain Momentum for Innovation

There are many pressures on executives that often motivate them to abandon longer range innovations in favor of short-term deliverables. Executives need to be the champions of the entire system so that their organizations do not forgo the future for short-term deliverables. Boards of directors should look closely at their models of executive compensation to ensure that they value innovation as highly as the implementation of current plans.

Sustaining innovation needs to be a way of life for executives and not a project that appears when a crisis arises. Executives need to have innovation on their agenda regularly, find ways to stimulate their thinking with new ideas, and allocate thinking time for the executive team to explore new ways of doing things. We indicated earlier that leaders of work units need to commit from four to six months to embed innovation in their work teams. Executives need to sustain innovation for an even longer time to embed it in the culture and in the organizational processes and structures.

It is particularly important for presidents or CEOs to be champions of innovation. The tone at the top shapes how the other executives approach innovation. CEOs must encourage and support the importance of innovation. They also must avoid creating an environment of fear that discourages innovation because of the perceived negative consequences of innovation failure. CEOs should be very aware of the messages they give through their reactions to innovation failures. They need to support innovation efforts even when their organizations are facing short-term deliverable crises.

CONCLUSION

In our rapidly changing work environment, most issues that leaders encounter are extremely complex and require sophisticated approaches to determine how to proceed. Complex issues are unique problems that leaders and teams need to understand thoroughly before they can consider a solution.

Leading innovation teams requires that leaders understand fully the unique elements associated with complex issues and be able to draw out their teams' innovative intelligence in order to understand the complex issues thoroughly. Leaders often need to guide their teams to spend extra time focusing on the uniqueness of the complexity and how it is distinguished from previous challenges, rather than looking for similarities. Once leaders help their teams understand the complex issue, they then need to facilitate the team to think innovatively in order to discover potential solutions that will best address the complex dilemma.

Leaders have a crucial role to play in creating, fostering, and sustaining innovation teams and in promoting innovation in their intact work unit teams. They must become champions of the innovative thinking process. They need to internalize the notion that, as good as individuals may be, and as good as their own personal ideas may be, a team can achieve a better innovation outcome than the leader can attain alone. Finally, leaders need to consistently model a commitment to innovation, both as leaders of their teams and as leaders of enterprises.

The next three chapters explore three essential enablers for leaders, with particular focus on how executives should lead enterprises for innovation. We first explore what an innovative culture is and how to accelerate cultural transformation (Chapter 12). We then discuss how to align organizational processes and structures to enable innovation (Chapter 13). Finally, we identify how to develop an enterprise-wide innovation plan that is governed, measured, and continuously improved (Chapter 14).

CHAPTER TWELVE

CULTURE OF INNOVATION

The executive team decided that the fastest way to create a culture of innovation would be to add "innovation" to the list of core values for the company. They announced the new values at the all-employees meeting, and they modified all the promotional and website materials to reflect the inclusion of the new value. They also found some examples of innovation in action and included those examples in their employee newsletters. Finally, they modified the performance management form to include a category on innovation.

However, after two years, this company was no more innovative than it was before. Employees did not really understand why innovation was a new value or what they were expected to do differently. They did not know how innovative thinking could help them solve problems or capitalize on the opportunities they encountered. On the rare occasions that innovation was a topic of discussion during performance reviews, the focus was often on how any attempts at innovation were undermined by the company's rigid approval processes and its lack of risk tolerance. The executives concluded that their approach to creating a culture of innovation was ineffective.

Let's begin by explaining why we use the phrase "culture of innovation" rather than "innovative culture." An innovative culture assumes that the culture, in and of itself, is innovative—but cultures cannot innovate. A organizational *culture of innovation* supports and encourages the use of innovative intelligence by individuals and teams. Organizations that want to become innovative systematically should enable a culture where most elements support innovating by individuals and teams and should have no elements that prevent innovation.

Executives are often told that a culture of innovation requires five to seven years before it can be realized. However, few executives have that much time to overcome the innovation gap. They then try superficial tactics, such as declaring that innovation is a new core value, with the hope that this will propel a focus on innovation, but that rarely works. This approach reflects a lack of understanding of what a culture of innovation is and how to accelerate cultural transformation to a culture of innovation.

Figure 12.1 shows the four organizational enablers that were introduced in Chapter 10, highlighting the subject of this chapter, "Culture of Innovation."

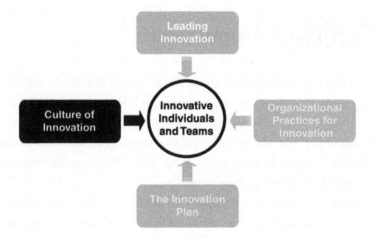

Figure 12.1: Culture of Innovation as an Essential Enabler to Make Innovation Happen

There is a critical need to demystify what a culture of innovation is and the techniques to accelerate cultural transformation to overcome the innovation gap, preferably within two to three years. This chapter will explore the following:

- What culture is
- How a culture can suppress innovation
- What a culture of innovation is
- How an existing culture can be transformed into a culture of innovation
- How to develop a "leadership culture" of innovation.

The objective of this chapter is to guide leaders to accelerate the transformation of a culture into one that enables and sustains innovation. It concludes with a challenge to leaders to actively pursue a culture of innovation rather than letting the existing organizational culture transform them.

WHAT IS CULTURE?

A study of 765 CEOs, senior executives, and public sector leaders from around the world found that "CEOs instinctively understand the need to play a prominent role in establishing a culture of innovation. But they are not always certain how to go about it."[1] Let's begin by clarifying what culture is, how it is formed, and how it can suppress innovation. We then will identify what a culture of innovation is.

Edgar Schein equates a group's culture to an individual's personality.[2] Schein argues that individuals develop a personality in order to achieve personal stability. To protect that stability, they create defenses for themselves and resist attempts at personality change. In a similar way, groups develop a personality, which is referred to as culture, in order to achieve group stability so that groups know who they are and how they do things. Groups also protect their cultural stability by creating defense mechanisms to guard against those who attempt to change their culture, and they often resist attempts to destabilize and change their group culture.

Based upon this analysis, culture can be defined as follows:

Culture = Group Personality

Chris Argyris identified a similar pattern of group defensiveness that he refers to as *organizational defensive routines*. He indicates: "These consist of all the policies, practices and actions that prevent human beings from having to experience embarrassment or threat and, at the same time, prevent them from examining the nature and causes of that embarrassment or threat." Argyris found this defensive theory "to be universal, with no measurable difference by country, age, sex, ethnic identity, education, wealth, power,

---

1. Marc Chapman, Saul Berman, & Amy Blitz, *Rethinking Innovation: Insights from the World's Leading CEOs* (Fast Thinking Books, 2008), p.25.
2. Edgar Schein, *Organizational Culture and Leadership* (Jossey-Bass, 2004).

or experience."[3] Organizational culture routinely defends the status quo. Argyris' defensive theory also explains how leaders in an organization may understand their problems and issues intellectually but are nonetheless incapable of creating the necessary change.

How Is Culture Formed?

Culture in organizations is formed through group problem solving—usually as a result of the following sequence of events:[4]

1. *The group experiences an urgent problem or opportunity.* A group faces a common problem or opportunity of how to work, externally or internally, that is compelling and urgent for the entire group to address.

2. *The group collectively discovers a solution that works well enough to be considered valid.* The group develops insight into a problem or opportunity and discovers solutions. The chosen solution works well enough for the group to consider it valid. Some of the other solutions are ineffective, and the group considers these solutions invalid.

3. *The group formulates explicit or implicit assumptions.* The group formulates assumptions—explicit or implicit—that they accept as valid methods of responding to similar and future problems and opportunities. The group then adopts these collective assumptions as the way it solves problems, and these assumptions begin to define the group's personality.

4. *The group teaches the assumptions to new members of the group.* The group then teaches the explicit or implicit assumptions to new members as the correct way to think, feel, and perceive when they work on current and future problems and opportunities. In order to belong to the group, the new members adopt these assumptions as the valid way to

---

3. Chris Argyris, "Good Communication That Blocks Learning," *Harvard Business Review*, July - August 1994, p. 81.
4. See Edgar Schein, *Organizational Culture and Leadership* (Jossey-Bass, 2004) where he defines culture as "A pattern of shared basic assumptions that was learned by a group as it solved its problems of external adaptation and internal integration, that has worked well enough to be considered valid and, therefore, to be taught to new members as the correct way to perceive, think, and feel in relation to those problems."

respond, sometimes without fully understanding how the assumptions developed originally.

One senior executive said it well when he defined culture in very straight-forward terms as: *"culture is what people do and say when no one is looking."*[5] Culture is not a demand placed upon the group by someone else. Instead, it is the group's self-directed and self-motivated method of responding to problems and opportunities. Culture only adheres when the group accepts the assumptions as the way they collectively perceive, think, feel, and do things, even without an external authority telling them to behave that way, or "even when no one is looking."

An organizational culture can form in a group of any size—whether it is a project team, an intact work team, or the entire enterprise. As a result, many larger organizations are challenged to transform their multiple sub-cultures into cultures of innovation at the same time as the overall organization is transforming into an enterprise-wide culture of innovation.

HOW A CULTURE CAN SUPPRESS INNOVATION

There is often tension between mature, well-established cultures and the new requirements for a culture of innovation. Most established organizations built their dominant culture during the industrial economy, when stability, order, productivity, and predictability made them successful. However, in the knowledge economy, where innovation and change are essential to success and need to be rewarded, many mature cultures struggle to adjust.

Several aspects of a culture can actively support leaders, individuals, and teams in their efforts to innovate, which we will describe in the next section. However, there are many other ways in which a culture can suppress efforts to be more innovative. Most of these aspects of culture were not designed to suppress innovation intentionally—they just were embedded in the culture at another time for another business purpose.

Here are a few examples of how cultural assumptions can impact innovation negatively.

---

5. This definition of culture was articulated by John Helou, General Manager Specialty Care Products, of Pfizer Canada Inc. It is quoted with his written permission.

- Executives choose prudence and the status quo over progress. They also exclusively focus on month-end and quarterly performance results.
- Senior leaders make all the decisions, and middle management mistakes are bad for your career. The more senior you are, the more right you are.
- Data are used frequently to confirm the current culture and not to stimulate change.
- Communication and information are controlled and given on a need-to-know basis.
- Decisions are driven by politics and not by insight. People get ahead by finding flaws in other people's ideas and projects, not by introducing new ideas.
- The organization's internal interests are placed ahead of the customers' interests. Looking busy and finishing a checklist at the end of the day is more valuable than thinking about new opportunities or customer needs.

WHAT IS A CULTURE OF INNOVATION?

We conducted research[6] to gain insight into the question "What is a culture of innovation?" We surveyed 550 HR professionals to explore the characteristics that distinguish organizations that are effective at innovation from those that are not.[7]

Perhaps it is important to first indicate what did not distinguish innovative organizations from non-innovative ones. We found that almost all organizations believe innovation is important to their future success and anticipate that they will require extensive or moderate changes within two to five years. This means that the business requirement for innovation and the need for changes do not necessarily result in the development of a culture of innovation.

Our research revealed seven major characteristics of a culture of innovation.

---

6. Based on the research by Ideaction and the Human Resources Professionals' Association (HRPA) in Ontario, Canada, 2008.
7. The primary question used to distinguish between organizations that were "innovative versus non-innovative" was the response to the statement: "My organization is effective at innovation."

Seven Characteristics of a Culture of Innovation

1. Everyone understands the organizational direction.
2. Innovation is a priority.
3. Executive team models innovative thinking and innovative practices.
4. Open and honest communication and trusting relationships.
5. Effective cross-functional teams that encourage diverse viewpoints.
6. Leaders who engage in risk-taking focused on delivering value.
7. Balance innovative thinking with the discipline to implement solutions.

Everyone understands the organizational direction

Leaders and employees must be clear about the organizational direction in order to be effective at looking for innovative ways to improve what they do. For example, if leaders and employees understand that all activities must create value for the customer, then they are significantly more likely to innovate in areas that improve customer satisfaction. When leaders and employees do not understand the organizational or departmental direction, their innovating efforts could potentially be dangerous because they could conflict with the direction of the organization.

Innovation Is a Priority

If innovation is not clearly positioned as one of the top three priorities, the chances of people believing that a culture of innovation is important are limited. In a 2007 survey of senior leaders in large organizations[8], about half of the executives who said innovation was a "top three priority" for their organization also said their organization was effective at innovation. On the other hand, those who said innovation was a "top 10 priority" or that innovation was "a value, not a priority," were much less likely to be innovative. When leaders at all levels talk about the importance of innovation but fail to place it on the top list of priorities, the message to employees is to continue doing what they did in the past.

---

8. 2007 Business Pulse Survey of senior leaders in Canada's five hundred largest organizations by the *Globe and Mail* newspaper, the Schulich Executive Education Centre, and Leger Marketing.

Executive Team Models Innovative Thinking and Innovative Practices

The executive team sets the tone for a culture of innovation. A culture of innovation is characterized by an executive team that:

- Believes innovation is crucial
- Is a model of innovative thinking
- Understands the process of innovation
- Functions as an excellent example of teamwork.

In addition, we have found that in cultures of innovation, the Human Resources executive is an active part of the executive team, since many elements of a culture of innovation involve excellence in people and organizational practices. Table 12.1 shows the data that support these insights.

Table 12.1: Characteristics of Organizations That Are Effective or Not Effective at Innovation

Percentages are the total percent that strongly agree and agree with the following statements.	Organizations That Are Effective at Innovation	Organizations That Are Not Effective at Innovation
All our executives believe that innovation is crucial.	86%	24%
HR is perceived as an integral part of the executive team.	73%	20%
Our executives model innovation practices in their own actions.	68%	2%
Our executives understand the process of innovation.	68%	6%
Our executive team is an excellent example of teamwork.	67%	12%

Open and Honest Communication and Trusting Relationships

Organizations with cultures of innovation foster open and honest communication and trusting relationships. They view information and knowledge as essential resources that are willingly shared. Leaders are not the people who have all the answers, but rather they are able to draw out the insights from their own teams and other teams in an open and trusting work environment.

Teams are open to divergent ideas and innovative thinking to gain insights into problems and discover the best possible solutions. The more leaders and employees understand where the organization is going and what is really happening in each area, the more they can contribute valuable ideas.

Effective Cross-Functional Teams That Encourage Diverse Viewpoints

Organizations with cultures of innovation excel at working cross-functionally. They value and encourage diverse ideas from other groups. Leaders see the holistic view and collaborate with other leaders and teams to discover the best solutions to complex issues. They view disagreements and conflicts positively, as opportunities to learn and to uncover the real issues that need to be resolved.

Organizations without cultures of innovation often view cross-functional teams as competitive opportunities to lobby for their viewpoint versus the other team's perspective. They see diverse ideas as threatening and creating tension. The separate groups often focus more on their power and on withholding information to strengthen their group's position.

Leaders Engage in Risk-Taking Focused on Delivering Value

A culture of innovation has leaders who encourage employees to take risks as long as they are smart risks that are focused on the business priorities and delivering external customer value. Leaders have the agility, flexibility, and authority to respond to shifting and emerging customer needs. There is trust and confidence that risk taking is done in good faith in the best interests of the external customer rather than for self-interest purposes.

Employees in organizations with a culture of innovation regard mistakes as learning opportunities, not something to be feared. They recognize mistakes quickly, learn from them, and move forward. They are confident that they will not be penalized or punished if they make thoughtful mistakes. Organizations that hide mistakes under the carpet struggle with innovation because they limit risk-taking, and their employees often repeat the same mistakes. In cultures of innovation, employees immediately report mistakes they notice, which enables quick remedies and reduces the impact of the mistakes.

Employees in cultures of innovation also are able to stop in a timely manner pilot projects and experiments that do not work. Non-innovative organizations often have many failed or insignificant experiments that no one stops because it would indicate that someone made a mistake. Organizations that *fail fast* and stop projects that do not work are much more likely to be innovative, because they can focus on projects that require innovation and free up space and resources to innovate. Table 12.2 shows some data that supports these insights.

Table 12.2: Factors Having a Positive Impact on Organizations' Effectiveness at Innovation

Percentages are the total percent for a factor's strong positive impact or positive impact on the organization's ability to innovate.	Organizations That Are Effective at Innovation	Organizations That Are Not Effective at Innovation
I am very clear about the long-term vision and goals of my organization.	79%	33%
Everyone in our organization feels responsible for the satisfaction of our customers.	78%	38%
My organization has a positive attitude toward risk-taking.	75%	33%
I am very clear about the risks I or my team can take in the company.	66%	32%
My organization trusts its employees to make appropriate decisions.	63%	20%

Balance Innovative Thinking with the Discipline to Implement Solutions

An organization with a culture of innovation understands that change is an integral part of work, not something to be avoided. It encourages these practices:

- The application of innovative thinking through open dialogue
- Information sharing
- Respectful questioning
- Divergent thinking.

At the same time, it encourages tough decisions, manages risk, and rewards performance. It blends the discovery and development of new ideas and insights with the discipline of implementing solutions that are required for the organization.[9] The key is for the leaders to understand how to balance the different elements of the process of innovation.

HOW AN EXISTING CULTURE CAN BE TRANSFORMED INTO A CULTURE OF INNOVATION

A common mistake in culture change is the belief that the *entire* culture must change for effective transformation to take place. In almost all situations, that is not the case. In fact, this expectation can be a source of anxiety that would make the task of culture change so daunting that it may not even be attempted.

The preferred approach to transforming to a culture of innovation is a targeted one that focuses on two activities:

- Reinforcing the current cultural elements that should be sustained
- Transforming the current cultural elements that need to be changed

We refer to this approach as a "laser beam approach" because, to be effective and implemented rapidly, cultural transformation requires the targeted precision of a laser beam.

There are five steps to the laser beam approach, as shown in Table 12.3.

Table 12.3: The Laser Beam Approach to Accelerating Culture Change

Step 1:	Define the urgency and the vision for the desired culture of innovation.
Step 2:	Analyze the current culture and identify priority gaps.
Step 3:	Reinforce priority cultural assumptions that are consistent with a culture of innovation.
Step 4:	Change priority cultural assumptions that are inconsistent with a culture of innovation.
Step 5:	Take action and continuously reinforce the desired culture of innovation.

---

9. Shlomo Maital and D.V.R. Seshadri, *Innovation Management: Strategies, Concepts and Tools for Growth and Profit* (Sage Publications Inc., 2007). Chapter 1 argues that innovation requires a combination of creativity and discipline.

We will use an example of a printing company in this section to illustrate the five steps of the laser beam approach to accelerate cultural transformation. Here is the background to the case:

A printing company was successfully producing excellent products for its many multi-national customers. The culture was characterized by high-quality activities that employees and leaders maintained at all times.

However, the competitive landscape changed. The competition introduced innovative technological printing processes, and users were engaging in their own desktop publishing, which reduced sales for the printing company. Within a few years, some of their major product lines became obsolete. Their market share eroded rapidly, and there was great concern by all that the company might not be sustainable in its current state.

The executives recognized that they needed to change their culture to become far more innovative and that they needed to be willing to take risks.

Step 1: Define the Urgency and Vision for the Desired Culture of Innovation

In this step, leaders should define the compelling and urgent business reason for the culture of innovation and develop and communicate the vision of the desired culture.

When the desired culture of innovation differs from the current culture, the current culture will always trump the desired culture unless there is a compelling and urgent reason to adopt it. This is because trying to change the current culture's assumptions to the new desired culture of innovation will likely cause anxiety, and most individuals and groups will try to avoid anxiety wherever possible.

Groups often resist culture change if leaders decide to change a culture for the sake of culture change and not for important and urgent business reasons. If an organization deems it important to create a culture of innovation, it needs to clearly define the business urgency and the vision for it in order to justify the group's efforts to change.

As executives engage in cultural transformation, they often undervalue the importance of leveraging a sense of urgency. However, urgency is essential.[10] Employees and leaders need to understand and internalize the urgency for a

---

10. John Kotter, *Sense of Urgency* (Harvard Business School Press, 2008).

culture of innovation even more than they need to understand what the new culture of innovation would look like and how it would operate. The more deeply embedded an existing culture, the more urgent and compelling the reasons need to be to motivate employees to participate in cultural transformation.

In the printing company example, employees were willing to adopt a culture change because the business urgency for the change far exceeded the instability (and anxiety) that would be generated by abandoning the current culture. Here is what they did:

The senior leaders needed to clearly articulate the urgent business reasons for a new culture of innovation. They decided to run small group sessions for employees to discuss the urgent challenges that required solutions if the organization was to stay in business. They presented the competitive financial and technological information that showed the business was at a competitive disadvantage, and they articulated the compelling reasons for change. They also developed the "President's 100," which was a group of 100 highly respected employees at every level of the organization who went on competitive site visits and customer visits to see what innovations were actually happening in their industry. What the employees found compelled them to realize that something radical needed to be done.

The senior leaders then formulated the new vision of a culture of innovation with individual accountabilities and communicated it broadly to all employees and leaders. Through this process, most employees understood the urgency for a culture of innovation, and they had some idea of what that kind of culture would look like. However, they still needed more clarity about how they were expected to behave differently.

Step 2: Analyze the Current Culture and Identify Priority Gaps

In Step 2, the organization identifies the current cultural reality and specifies the priority gaps between the current cultural reality and the desired culture of innovation.

Usually the newest person in a group is the best person to describe the group's current culture. People who are new to an organization are most able to contrast the way the group operates, makes decisions, and resolves conflicts with the way other groups they have been associated with have acted and behaved.

A work group should take advantage of the experience of the newest group members and ask them to describe the behavioral aspects of the operations of the group in comparison with their previous work experiences. These aspects, or artifacts, can be obvious and tangible (such as dress code, office space, furniture, technology, locks on doors). They also can be more subtle and intangible (such as how the group utilizes meetings, how they make decisions, whether they defer to hierarchy, how they respond to conflict, whether they are open to diversity).

The next question the work group should ask is: "Do these observable aspects have any importance for the new culture of innovation that needs to be created?" If they are important, then there must be some assumption that explains why people are motivated to behave that way. Next, the group needs to analyze the gap between the current and desired culture.

Here is the process a group can use to surface the current cultural assumptions and to define the gaps between their current and desired culture:

1. Each individual records the visible aspects (or artifacts) of the current culture and reports to the group (starting with the newest member of the group).
2. The group then discusses the extent to which the visible aspects are consistent with the desired culture of innovation and the extent to which they are inconsistent, and then lists them.
3. The group identifies the underlying assumptions for the visible aspects in the current culture that are *consistent* with the desired culture of innovation.
4. The group identifies the underlying assumptions for the visible aspects in the current culture that are *inconsistent* with the desired culture of innovation.
5. The group summarizes the priority gaps between the current culture and the desired culture of innovation.

Let's see how Step 2 was applied to the printing company example.

Small groups met and identified the key aspects of the current culture. They identified that the current culture was a deeply embedded quality culture, with a strong commitment to team-based consensus decision making and the avoidance of any unnecessary risks. Employees were highly engaged; however, many believed there was a great deal of time wasted in meetings trying to reach consensus, individual innovative ideas were often not supported by the group consensus, too many decisions were delegated upwards, it was hard to pinpoint individual accountability for problems and failures, and overall the current culture was affecting the continued performance and success of the company.

They then identified the primary assumptions that motivated people to behave this way. The assumptions that were consistent with a culture of innovation included that people believed quality was of paramount importance, that teamwork was a key to success, and that consensus decision making was the best way to decide what to do. They also identified some assumptions that were inconsistent with the desired culture of innovation. These included that people believed it was important to avoid a making decision if it would hurt someone's feelings, that individuals who took personal accountability for projects were not really team players, and that it was better to defer to hierarchy than to make a difficult decision within a peer group.

Step 3: Reinforce Priority Cultural Assumptions That Are *Consistent* with a Culture of Innovation

It is important to identify what the group currently does that is consistent with the culture of innovation and to discover the top three to five current cultural assumptions to reinforce. These current cultural assumptions need to be retained and even celebrated.

Too often, executives do not exploit the current culture's assumptions that support the desired culture of innovation. Their focus is almost exclusively on what needs to change and not on what needs to be retained. This pattern is a significant missed opportunity in the process of accelerating the transformation of a culture for the following reasons.

- Employees and groups need to experience some positive reinforcement for the current cultural assumptions that helped them achieve stability and predictability in their work environment.
- Validating some current cultural assumptions motivates employees and groups to be more open to the desired culture of innovation because it will have some assumptions that are similar to the current culture.
- Retaining and reinforcing some current cultural assumptions will offset some of the anxiety generated from changing the current cultural assumptions that are inconsistent with a culture of innovation (which will be done in Step 4 of the laser beam approach).

There are three techniques that leaders can use to reinforce the current cultural assumptions that are consistent with a culture of innovation.

Reinforce Priority Cultural Assumptions
That Are *Consistent* with a Culture of Innovation
  1. Leader Modeling
  2. Building in Reinforcers
  3. Allocating Resources

Leader Modeling

Leaders sometimes underestimate their importance as role models of the desired culture. They need to think about what they do from the perspective of what employees and groups will learn from their actions. Without leader role modeling, culture change will lack integrity, and, as a result, employees will not change. This idea is supported by research that shows that working for an admired leader is the number one non-monetary incentive for employee motivation and retention.[11] If the leader who is admired is not a role model of the desired culture, then employees will interpret it to mean that the desired culture probably is not worth the effort.

Leaders also need to understand that their reactions to critical incidents during an organizational emergency will shape culture because their behavior defines how employees will react to urgent group problems. For example, in one organization, many leaders were fearful of the CEO because he had reacted angrily to a crisis incident five years earlier. The leaders internalized the underlying assumption that anger was the way to get quick action when under extreme stress. However, the CEO was shocked when he heard that interpretation of his behavior. He felt that he rarely got angry. He remembered that the event five years earlier occurred on a particularly problematic day on a personal level, and that spilled over into work. He regretted the outburst for a long time—and when he discovered that his leadership team learned from him that using anger was the preferred way to lead in crisis, he regretted the emotional outburst even more.

Building in Reinforcers

Leaders have many ways they can reinforce the current cultural assumptions that are consistent with the desired culture of innovation. A particularly powerful method for leaders to reinforce current cultural assumptions is to promote leaders who will function as role models of the culture they desire. The processes of hiring, promotion, assignment to special task forces, and so on, are very useful to reinforce the desired culture of innovation and at the same time to bring in the next generation of leaders who will continue to reinforce the desired culture.

Leaders also can reinforce the current cultural assumptions that are consistent with a culture of innovation by using monetary and non-monetary techniques, including the following.

- *Monetary reinforcers.* Leaders often use the allocation of rewards as essential tools to guide and reinforce employee behavior. These same reinforcers can be applied to groups.
- *Non-monetary reinforcers.* Leaders need to be effective at using non-monetary reinforcers for individuals and groups. These include giving enhanced profile and decision-making authorities, recognizing and appreciating employees both publicly and privately, including employees in important dialogue meetings, and giving time off.

Allocating Resources

Leaders often have control over discretionary funds and resources, which they can allocate to reinforce the cultural assumptions that are consistent with a culture of innovation. Employees watch the budgeting process closely and are aware of the departments and projects that receive additional funding. They also watch which departments and project teams are allocated the best internal people resources and the external consulting support to accelerate and achieve the successful completion of their work. These allocation processes send strong signals of what needs to be retained in the new desired culture.

The printing company example applied these reinforcing techniques to further embed their constructive underlying assumptions.

The leadership decided to use the three methods of role modeling, reinforcers, and allocating resources to reinforce the priority assumptions of the current culture they wanted to retain. They did the following:

- *The executive team decided they would work to become the role model of a diversified team and to find methods of making it known that they were engaging in innovative activities.*
- *The leaders and employees were supported with innovative thinking training and coaches in the workplace to help them think through innovative ideas and problems.*
- *They included criteria related to the desired culture in their leadership and employee hiring and promotional processes.*
- *The leadership also continued to allocate time and resources to their teams for idea generation.*
- *They allocated funds for video-conferencing so that groups from different offices wouldn't have to travel great distances for lengthy conference sessions. Instead, they could more regularly participate in shorter and more issue-focused group meetings to generate innovative solutions.*

By focusing on these initiatives, they were successful in reinforcing the stability the current culture provided. This also gave them some license to take away some aspects of the current culture that needed to be changed in order to achieve the desired culture of innovation.

Step 4: Change Priority Cultural Assumptions That Are *Inconsistent* with a Culture of Innovation

In this step, the leaders identify the top three to five priority assumptions of the current culture that are inconsistent with the desired culture of innovation and need to be changed.

The leaders need to find the least anxiety-provoking way to implement those changes. There are three techniques that they can use for changing the current cultural assumptions that are inconsistent with a culture of innovation.

Change Priority Cultural Assumptions That Are *Inconsistent* with a Culture of Innovation
   1. Rechanneling
   2. Counterbalancing
   3. Confronting

Rechanneling

Rechanneling is the process of redirecting the current cultural assumptions to achieve an outcome consistent with what the new culture of innovation requires. It is the least anxiety-provoking method of change for two reasons.

- It validates aspects of what the group currently does.
- It migrates the group's current cultural assumptions to the assumptions of the preferred culture of innovation.

Rechanneling is similar to the fencing technique of parrying a thrust blade. It is much more difficult to stop a thrusting blade than it is to redirect its power by parrying it to an area that would not cause any harm.

For example, in one situation, a marketing group was effective at the part of innovative thinking that focused on discovering solutions. However, once they discovered a solution, they became rigidly attached to their chosen solution even when it did not fully resolve the complex issue. They did not consider whether there were additional insights into the problem that would deepen their understanding of the complex issue. This group needed to rechannel their approach by first validating their skills at discovering solutions and then augmenting the approach with an equal or even greater emphasis on exploring insights into the complex problem.

Counterbalancing

This technique focuses on identifying alternative ways to model the desired culture of innovation, which counterbalances the existing culture. This is often the primary technique leaders use when they successfully change culture after five to seven years. They eventually succeed at culture change through employee attrition and turnover. In most organizations, turnover represents between 5 and 10 percent of employees per year, which means that approximately 25 to 50 percent of employees are likely to leave an organization within a five-year time frame.

If organizations are effective at selecting new employees who function according to the desired culture of innovation, then, within five to seven years there should be a critical mass of new employees that counterbalances the current culture of existing employees. At minimum, all hiring and promotions that occur within a business should include the consideration of how individuals to be hired or leaders to be promoted will reinforce the desired culture of innovation.

The counterbalancing technique is more anxiety provoking for groups than the rechanneling technique. Hiring and promoting employees and leaders who bring in new ideas and operate with the cultural assumptions of the desired culture of innovation will create tension and instability in the organization. However, as new employees are brought in and leaders are given the authority to model the desired culture, the culture will be reinforced, and it will eventually evolve to the desired culture of innovation.

Confronting

Directly confronting group behaviors that are inconsistent with a culture of innovation is the most anxiety-provoking technique to accelerate cultural transformation. Confronting tactics include reprimands, enforcing consequences, restructuring departments, and even terminations. Although some leaders may believe it is the fastest way to change a culture, it is risky, and it can backfire. After a confrontational act by executives, employees may superficially support the new culture. However, they may still operate according to the former culture whenever they have the opportunity. The former culture may just become a subculture that is preserved even more under executive siege. The employees experience the highest level of anxiety when confronted because of the instability it creates in the work environment. They are more likely to resist the newly imposed culture—if they can—if it is forced upon them. The new culture should be built upon shared assumptions that have solved problems or opportunities and work well enough to be considered valid, rather than being built on fear and intimidation.

The printing company example applied the three techniques to change the current cultural assumptions that were inconsistent with the desired culture of innovation.

The printing company leaders were respected as highly facilitative; however, they were also viewed as individuals who were reluctant to make decisions on behalf of the group and take personal accountability for those decisions. The executives made some decisive changes in this regard. They rechanneled the authority and trust that was vested in the leadership. They expanded the role of the leaders from being facilitators of discussions that generated new ideas to include being the final authority to determine direction and the persons accountable for the implementation of the decisions. They also enhanced the recognition for leaders who took personal accountability for team decisions and delivered results. They implemented a fail fast strategy that became a part of their company's approach to quality. The idea was that making mistakes would be supported if the failures occurred fast enough that employees could learn from those experiences and would be able to reduce the loss associated with the ineffective innovations. They also implemented a "lessons learned" process whereby they diagnosed successful and unsuccessful innovation projects to gain insight into what happened and to learn from those experiences. Finally, the executives did confront a few of the leaders who—after a certain amount of time—were still unable to adapt to the new culture of innovation.

Step 5: Take Action and Continuously Reinforce the Desired Culture

Cultural transformation requires diligent implementation approaches for it to adhere rapidly. Leaders need to develop the plan of action, define methods to measure and track the cultural changes and their direct impact on the business outcome they were designed to achieve, and continuously reinforce the new culture to sustain and deepen it.

Leaders should develop and communicate the cultural transformation action plan, which needs to include what will be done, by whom, by when, and with what resources. They also should communicate that the cultural assumptions that need to change are not bad; they simply are inconsistent with the desired culture of innovation that is required for the business. In most cases, the cultural assumptions that need to be changed were important assumptions of the former culture. However, in the desired culture of innovation, the former assumptions are actually problematic.

They also need to recognize that although cultural transformation can be accelerated, it still takes time to reinforce and sustain the desired culture of innovation. The executives need to exercise some patience so that the new culture can be solidly embedded in the organization and firmly established as the way things are done on a daily basis. It also must be planned in advance so that its implementation proceeds smoothly. A well-planned approach to creating a culture of innovation has another benefit: employees will find it more stable and, therefore, less threatening.

The printing company example applied the step of "taking action and continuously reinforcing the desired culture" as follows.

The executives developed an overall two-year cultural transformation target with measures that tracked indicators of progress to the desired culture of innovation. They correlated the progress toward the new culture with the company's positive developments in relationship to their competitive position in the marketplace. They assigned individual executive account-abilities to specific culture of innovation change initiatives and regularly reviewed the cultural transformation progress at executive meetings. They also held quarterly "all employees meetings" where they shared stories of cultural changes that occurred and celebrated group successes as they achieved interim milestones toward the new culture of innovation.

Through these efforts, the company was successful at remodeling their product offering and realizing the benefit of their investment in technology. They also acquired and integrated several smaller innovative printing technology companies to modernize their offering to their customers and to sustain their business. The newly acquired companies were accepted and welcomed as part of the solution to the printing company's challenges. The employees and the company were able to introduce the culture of innovation while retaining their legacy of high quality. They began to perform well against their competition based upon their new culture of innovation foundation.

HOW TO DEVELOP A LEADERSHIP CULTURE OF INNOVATION

Just like any group in an organization, a *leadership culture*[12] can be formed among the group of leaders. As a cross-functional, multi-level group, leaders can formulate assumptions of how they can solve problems that work well enough to be accepted as valid. As a group, leaders can have great influence on developing a culture of innovation through modeling innovative thinking and leading innovation.[13] However, many organizations have not attempted to build a leadership culture of innovation and therefore miss out on a key lever to accelerate cultural transformation to a culture of innovation.

The fastest route to culture change is to initially apply the laser beam approach to transform the leadership culture. The focus on the leadership

---

12. David S. Weiss, Vince Molinaro, & Liane Davey, *Leadership Solutions* (Jossey-Bass, 2007), explain in detail the concept of Leadership Culture.
13. See Chapter 11 for a complete analysis of the role of leaders in leading innovation.

culture will ensure that the leaders are in support of the cultural transformation and that they can play a leadership role in enlisting all employees and teams to support the culture change. Once the leaders are championing the change, then the probability that employees will follow greatly increases.

Here are some specific cultural assumptions that leaders need to adopt to lead the transformation to a culture of innovation.

- *Assumption about people.* Leaders need to adopt a basic belief about the human nature of employees—that innovative intelligence is a potential of every individual employee and that their potential is waiting to be accessed. More often than not, innovative intelligence exists, but is stifled by organizational culture, processes, and structures that are incompatible with innovative thinking.

- *Assumption about openness.* Sometimes individuals and groups do not believe that the leaders are open to new ideas and view them as barriers to innovative thinking and innovations. The leaders must model a culture of innovation, reinforce employees who think accordingly, and allocate resources to it. The leaders also should reinforce the employees and teams that are early adopters of the culture of innovation. They can do this by giving them additional opportunities and using their achievements to rechannel for innovative efforts and to counterbalance the existing cultural assumptions of the other employees.

- *Assumption about middle managers.* Leaders must pay particular attention to mid-level managers, as they are often essential to successful culture change. Mid-level managers often have control of communications and the daily work of a large majority of employees. They also see their role as making "the machine" work efficiently and delivering on objectives when everyone else keeps changing everything around them. If they are fully engaged in the culture change process, they can be very important contributors to making it successful. If, on the other hand, they are excluded from the process and resistant to the change, they can block the culture change and ensure that it will not be implemented.

- *Assumption about being proactive.* Leaders must be proactive and actively pursue a culture of innovation rather than letting the current organizational culture transform them. Leaders at every level need to become champions of a culture of innovation throughout the organization. As we described, many employees have a natural resistance to change when it generates personal anxiety and instability. The leaders need to rise above the anxiety and instability of culture change and be the enablers of the culture of innovation.

CONCLUSION

This chapter described what a culture of innovation is and how to accelerate the transformation of a culture to a culture of innovation. The laser beam approach highlights the importance of a targeted approach to accelerate cultural transformation. It focuses on establishing the urgency for a culture of innovation and defining how to diagnose the current cultural assumptions that are consistent and inconsistent with a culture of innovation. It also describes how to accelerate cultural change by focusing on the current cultural assumptions to be retained and reinforced and by changing any that will not be retained in the least anxiety-provoking manner possible. Ultimately, the key to successful cultural change is the commitment of leaders at every level to champion and enable a culture of innovation throughout the organization.

The next chapter will explore processes and structures that organizations should implement in order to enable innovative thinking and to help overcome the innovation gap. These organizational processes and structures function as external reinforcers that further drive innovation throughout the business. With the combination of effectively leading innovation, embedding a culture of innovation, and implementing the organizational processes and structures, the capability to overcome the innovation gap will be dramatically enhanced.

CHAPTER THIRTEEN

ORGANIZATIONAL PRACTICES FOR INNOVATION

When creating an organization that innovates systematically, it is important to pay particular attention to the organization's practices, including its structures, processes, and policies, which can inadvertently undermine innovation efforts. It is not enough for the senior leaders to commit to innovation, focus on the required skills and the culture, and then wait for innovation to flourish. Most organizations were not designed to make change or innovation easy. On the contrary, their organizational practices often work against innovation efforts by maximizing repetition and predictability and minimizing risk.

In Chapter 10, we introduced the four organizational enablers shown in Figure 13.1. This chapter focuses on how to develop organizational practices that support innovation rather than block it.

In most situations, organizational practices are the result of cumulative decisions taken by many leaders over many years. In the industrial economy, organizations developed practices to maximize the efficiency of work and its output. These practices led to an efficient standardization of work but also contributed to rigid processes to achieve consistency.

Organizations need to develop practices that make innovation easier. In most cases, it simply requires an adjustment to specific processes or rules. The real issue is that every department or function is affected, and just one reluctant department can jeopardize innovation in the whole organization.

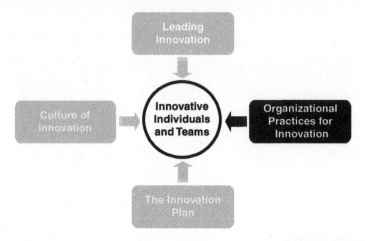

Figure 13.1: The Four Organizational Enablers to Make Innovation Happen

We explore the following four areas in this chapter:

Organizational Practices for Innovation
- Executive-level organizational practices
- Organizational practices in core functional areas
- Organizational practices in support functional areas
- Innovation-specific organizational practices

This chapter systematically reviews most organizational practices, the role each practice plays in innovation, and how each practice can make innovation easier or more difficult. It then asks a series of questions to help leaders ensure that each department fully supports innovation.

EXECUTIVE-LEVEL ORGANIZATIONAL PRACTICES

The first section of this chapter reviews the elements directly under the control of the executive team or usually associated with executive-level decisions. Also included are some organization issues, such as decision-making processes and communication, where the tone for the organization is set from the top. There are five executive-level organizational practices that can make innovation easier or more difficult.

Executive-Level Organizational Practices
- Structure
- Decision making
- Risk management
- Internal communication
- Executive-level innovation initiatives

Structure

Structures in and of themselves rarely have a positive or negative impact on innovation. They only become problematic when there is a lack of cross-functional teamwork or when compensation policies or internal politics convert structures into weapons against innovation. For example, if cross-functional teamwork is effective and encouraged between different parts of the organization, then structure probably has a minimal impact on innovation. On the other hand, if the department leaders are perceived as competitors or if compensation drives the wrong behaviors, then structure will have a negative impact on innovation.

There is no ideal structure for innovation, but a structure that focuses the organization on external customers will usually make innovation easier. The only general principle is that departments that need to collaborate every day should report to the same executive. For example, if product management and marketing are on different "islands" and connected only at the CEO level, effective innovation will require exceptional teamwork between the two teams. In this scenario, conflicts usually fester because the issues are rarely big enough to be escalated and resolved at the CEO level.

What leaders should pay attention to:

- Does the structure allow every part of the organization to focus on the customer?
- How good is cross-functional teamwork every day and for special projects?
- Do compensation systems favor "silo" behaviors or cross-functional teamwork?

Decision Making

Some styles of decision making can present potential problems for innovation. Organizations with multiple levels of decision making are usually deliberate but slow. Decisions can often be reversed by more senior leaders. Innovative ideas can be obsolete by the time they are approved. This type of organization may feel that it supports innovation, but the cumbersome processes often discourage the most active innovators.

Another version of slow decision making happens in organizations where consensus is so important that every decision must be unanimous. When a decision is finally reached, the innovative idea has been subjected to so many negotiations and compromises that it no longer resembles the original idea.

Organizations where every decision must be rational and justified by reams of data can also have a negative impact on innovation. Innovation can be stalled indefinitely, as there is always more data, however biased or obsolete, to support the status quo than to support a brand new idea. Chris Argyris clearly described the consequences of this attitude and how easy it is to remedy it:

"A CEO who had begun to practice his own form of management-by-walking-around learned from his employees that the company inhibited innovation by subjecting every new idea to more than 275 separate checks and sign-offs. He promptly appointed a task force to look at this situation, and it eliminated 200 of the obstacles. The result was a higher innovation rate."[1]

The most effective decision-making model is one in which decisions are made at the right level, with clear rules and a minimum of intermediaries. For big ideas, the innovative idea should be presented to the senior leader as quickly and with as few intermediaries as possible. For smaller ideas, it should be clear at which level in the organization the decisions must be made.

What leaders should pay attention to:

- How many decision layers are necessary to approve simple ideas?
- Are big ideas fast-tracked to be presented to executives without modifications?

---

1. Chris Argyris, "Good Communication That Blocks Learning," *Harvard Business Review,* July/August 1994.

- What are the accountabilities and responsibilities to approve innovative ideas at each level of decision making?
- What prevents the resolution of conflicts at the lowest possible level?

Risk Management

In organizations where innovation thrives, taking smart risks is recognized as a normal activity, and failure is accepted as a possible outcome of innovation. Both are discussed openly at every level, measured, managed, and, in the end, accepted. The most effective ways to reduce risk are to make risk assessment and project debriefing the norm, not the exception, and to regularly communicate successes and failures.

Leaders and teams at every level are very aware of how executives react to risk and failure. Executive support of or antagonistic reaction to innovation will send a clear signal to the rest of the organization about how acceptable innovation risk is.

What leaders should pay attention to:

- Are people always clear about the risks they can take in their jobs and for specific projects?
- Are risks approved at the right level and with the right information?
- Are all stakeholders debriefed about failures and successes to identify and share the learning?
- What happens to the careers of people who take risks and sometimes fail? Is association with a failed innovation project a career-limiting experience?
- How do executives react when projects fail? Do they look for scapegoats? Or do they look for ways to prevent the repetition of the failure and share the learning with the whole organization?

Internal Communication

Internal communication can impact innovation in four key ways.

I. *Executives set the tone for an organization by what they talk about repeatedly.* If the leaders talk primarily about short-term financial results, everyone will focus primarily on short-term financial results. Many of these executives know that innovation is important but often make it an afterthought in their communication. The inference is that innovation is something that is done only when there is nothing else to do.

2. *Executives need to be transparent about obstacles to innovation.* Some senior leaders talk eloquently about the need for everyone to innovate and have new ideas. However, they often neglect to give specifics, to provide new resources, or to discuss and address the obstacles repeatedly mentioned by their employees.

3. *Senior leaders need to listen to mid-level managers, not only to their direct reports.* Mid-level leaders and managers can be strong filters for information. They often feel they are the only ones making sure that the work gets done, while all the other departments and the executives are trying to change everything all the time. One of the ways mid-level managers make their unit work efficiently is by protecting the people working for them from all the distractions created by new initiatives. When new information comes down from the executives, employees will ask their manager, "What does it mean for us?" When employees come up with a new and innovative idea, their manager is the one who can either let them work on it or tell them to stay focused on their jobs.

4. *Every employee needs to understand the organization's strategic directions and priorities.* In organizations that innovate effectively, every employee understands where the organization is going and how their own area contributes. They also have a good understanding of the role played by other departments. Only when everyone is clear about the organization's direction can they innovate in the right direction.

What leaders should pay attention to:

- What do executives talk about when they address the whole organization?
- Do executives listen well to ideas from every level and every area of the organization, without hierarchical barriers?
- Is the role of mid-level managers clearly recognized and addressed in every communication?
- Does every employee understand the strategic priorities of the organization and of their department?

Executive-Level Projects

Role modeling is critical for innovation, as leaders and employees at all levels often emulate the behaviors of executives. The best way for executives to demonstrate that they are serious about innovation is to start applying innovative thinking to their key projects, for example, strategic planning or reorganizations. In organizations where executives avoid using innovative thinking, the leaders and employees quickly conclude that it is just a matter of time before innovation efforts will be canceled.

What leaders should pay attention to:

- Are the executives applying the principles of innovative thinking in their projects?
- Are the consultants who provide services to the executives applying innovative thinking principles?

ORGANIZATIONAL PRACTICES IN CORE FUNCTIONAL AREAS

Organizational practices in core functional areas can have a major impact on the overall ability of the organization to innovate. Core functional areas directly create customer value for the organization and can be different in various types of organizations. In business, core functional areas could include purchasing, sales, operations or manufacturing, and customer service. For non-profit or government organizations, core functional areas could include policy, operations, funding, and field services to constituents.

If core functional areas try to innovate on their own or do not collaborate effectively, then they will erode dramatically the organization's overall capacity to innovate. If, on the other hand, the core functional areas work well together and with support functions, then innovation will happen more easily.

There are seven primary areas for consideration by leaders. It is important to remember that these areas can have different functions and titles in different types of organizations.

Organizational Practices in Core Functional Areas
- Operations or Manufacturing
- Product Management
- Purchasing
- Marketing
- Sales
- Customer Service
- Research and Development

Operations or Manufacturing

Operations or manufacturing departments are critical for innovation, as ideas only create value if they are successfully executed. Operations and manufacturing have made huge strides over the past 20 years, mostly through the implementation of rigorous quality initiatives, including Lean and Six Sigma. Innovative thinking can be implemented as a stand-alone project in operations or manufacturing, but it is even more effective when it is combined with such quality techniques. Lean and Six Sigma apply when analytical thinking is required; innovative thinking is more effective when issues are ambiguous and involve multiple stakeholders.

Tensions between operations or manufacturing and the rest of the organization usually occur when the implementation of innovative ideas has the potential to negatively impact their efficiency and productivity. It is important to integrate operations or manufacturing early in innovation projects and work with them to manage the potential impact of new and innovative ideas. Failure to do so can result in the ideas not being implemented effectively.

What leaders should pay attention to:

- How open is the operations or manufacturing department to testing and implementing new ideas?
- How well is the operations or manufacturing department contributing to cross-functional innovation projects?

Product Management

Product management should be the most frequent and effective user of innovative thinking. After all, its role is to consistently come up with better products, services, or combinations of both in order to respond to customer needs.

In practice, product management too often manages existing assets, without much appetite for significant change because of the pressures from simultaneous conflicting demands in the organization. For example, in one organization, product management could not introduce new innovations because of the competing priorities. The manufacturing department was focused on maintaining productivity, the marketing department wanted exciting features they could promote, the sales department wanted a new version for each customer, the R&D department wanted to explore new and exciting directions.

Also, because of a lack of resources, product management departments often focus on multiple small changes that do not always create real value. To compound the issue, what is a small change for product management can keep the rest of the organization busy adapting for weeks or months. For example, a small change in a banking product can have major long-term implications in IT, HR, and in thousands of branches across the country.

Nevertheless, product management should be an innovation hub. On one side, they should work closely with sales, customer service, marketing, and strategy to generate the best possible insights. On the other side, they should work closely with operations, supply chain, sales, and marketing to determine how the organization will implement innovations successfully.

What leaders should pay attention to:

- Does product management have deep insights about current and future customers?
- Does the product management group have a balanced portfolio of innovations?
- Are they working closely and effectively with all other functions in the organization?

Purchasing

Purchasing contributes the knowledge and insight of their suppliers to the innovation process. They should be involved as much as possible. It is critical that they consider it part of their role to consistently bring new ideas from suppliers into the organization.

What leaders should pay attention to:

- Is the purchasing department consistently looking for new ideas from suppliers and bringing these ideas into the organization?
- Is the purchasing department actively involved with cross-functional teams?

Marketing

Marketing has a reputation for being the most innovative area in organizations, but too often they are mostly creative. Marketing is the most fertile ground for innovative thinking, as every project is different and deals with complex issues. To become systematically innovative, a marketing department needs to apply a process that blends a best-of-class marketing process with a rigorous innovative thinking process. Marketers usually avoid rigorous processes for fear they may stifle their creativity.

In addition, marketing departments play a critical role in cross-functional teams, as they often manage the knowledge about the organization's customers and markets.

What leaders should pay attention to:

- Is the marketing department fully contributing to cross-functional innovation projects?
- Does the marketing process encourage innovative thinking?
- Is marketing's output systematically innovative?
- Does the marketing department effectively manage knowledge gathering and dissemination?

Sales

The sales department is rarely cited as the most innovative department in an organization, and it is sometimes associated with resistance to change. Salespeople usually are "hunters." They are focused on short-term rewards and are always looking for the next good sale. Except in a few industries, they are rarely willing to take time away from selling for training or problem solving to address what they could do better. Their arguments are valid, as they could miss a big sale because of a two-hour meeting. If what they do works, they want more of it. If it does not work, they want to try something different as long as it can be quickly proven to be successful.

One of the ironies is that salespeople look at innovation as disruptive to their work, but they love the innovative products or services that will open new doors and allow them to close new sales and increase their revenue.

The second irony is that the best salespeople are usually very good at innovative thinking and problem solving. They regularly search for insight into what their customers want and repackage their products and services in innovative ways to satisfy them.

The sales department is essential to innovation because of the deep insights they can have about their customers and prospects. If the organization is successful at capturing the sales representatives' knowledge and insights, the sales department can be the originator of many innovative ideas. They are also necessary as the distribution channel for customer innovations.

What leaders should pay attention to:

- Are the knowledge and insights of the sales force being captured effectively and regularly?
- Are the salespeople participating actively in cross-functional project teams?
- Are the salespeople actively involved in the design and execution of pilot projects for new products or services?

Customer Service

Customer service has been the focus of many innovations over the past 20 years. In a recent survey of executives in Canada,[2] customer service was considered the most innovative area in organizations.

Customer service's main contribution to innovation is their knowledge of the customers. Positive comments and, more important, negative comments by customers and prospects are the simplest and one of the most

---

2. *Globe and Mail* newspaper and the Schulich School of Business survey conducted in 2007.

effective sources of knowledge for innovation. How well the knowledge gained from every contact with customers and prospects is translated into insight and how well the insight is disseminated in the organization can be a major competitive advantage.

What leaders should pay attention to:

- Is the insight from customers and prospects collected and analyzed in a timely manner?
- Is the insight regularly communicated to the key stakeholders in the organization?
- Is the customer service department actively engaged in cross-functional teamwork?
- Is customer service acting as a partner or an obstacle in the testing of new ideas?

Research and Development—R&D

In the past, R&D has been synonymous with innovation. The reality is that innovation in R&D is fundamentally different from innovation in the rest of the organization. R&D innovation practices are generally not transferable to the rest of the organization. For this reason, the R&D department should never be the starting point for an Office of Innovation. In addition, the research functions in R&D departments are rarely very effective at teamwork, either inside R&D or with other departments. This is because they have been trained in a scientific environment, where teamwork was often not well developed or encouraged. In contrast, the development function in R&D is more likely to be good at teamwork.

To maximize the contribution of the R&D department to organization-wide innovation, the department should be open to the knowledge and insights that the whole organization generates and be systematically involved in cross-functional teams.

What leaders should pay attention to:

- Is the R&D department fully contributing to cross-functional innovation projects?
- Is the R&D department focused on the customer?

ORGANIZATIONAL PRACTICES IN SUPPORT FUNCTIONAL AREAS

The organizational practices in support functional areas, such as Human Resources (HR), Information Technology (IT), and Finance can have a direct influence on innovation in an organization. There are six support functional areas that have an important direct or indirect impact on innovation.

Organizational Practices in Support Functional Areas

- Human Resources
- Information Technology
- Finance
- Strategic Planning
- Legal
- Project Management Office

Human Resources (HR)

The HR department has a significant impact on the organization's ability to innovate. This is because it works with the leaders, employees, and teams who are the main source of innovation. There are many ways HR can influence innovation. We have divided these HR organizational practices into two groups: people processes and organizational value-add processes.[3]

HR people processes
People processes focus on the employee life cycle at work (including HR's role in finding, developing, and retaining talent). Here are some ways HR can develop its organizational people processes to support innovation:

- *Recruitment.* It is difficult today to hire new leaders or employees who have competence in innovative thinking. When recruiting employees, especially at a leadership level, it is important to look for the characteristics of a leader of innovation. These include being competent in their work, good

---

3. See David S. Weiss, *High Performance HR: Leveraging Human Resources for Competitive Advantage* (John Wiley and Sons, 2000), for a detailed explanation and description of HR people processes and HR organizational value-add processes.

communicators, open-minded to new ways of doing things, confident, comfortable with uncertainty and ambiguity, good team players, intelligent risk takers, trustworthy, and able to resolve problems in different ways.

- *Job descriptions.* Innovation for individuals and managing innovation for leaders must be included in every job description. It is also critical to define innovation for the organization and for each unit.
- *Compensation.* Short-term and individual performance-based compensation can prevent innovation. Individuals at every level should be paid for a balance of short- and long-term results and innovation. The compensation plan should also specifically reward individuals for systematically contributing to their own team and, when called upon, contributing to cross-functional teams.
- *Performance management systems.* The performance objectives should include the practices, behaviors, and attitudes that foster systematic innovation. Leaders and employees should also receive concrete assurances that their work in innovation teams will contribute to their evaluation. To support innovation, the performance objectives can include items such as: applying innovative thinking, contributing to team performance, identifying problems, taking intelligent risks, and helping other innovation teams to succeed.
- *Promotions.* As we have seen, leaders of innovative teams are usually in short supply in established organizations. To create balance, especially in the senior leadership team, leaders skilled at leading innovation teams must be promoted to positions where they can influence innovation throughout the organization.

HR organizational value-add processes

Organizational value-add processes describe HR's role in systemic organizational processes, such as succession management, talent management, restructuring, change management, and employee engagement. Here are some ways HR can develop its organizational value-add processes to support innovation.

- *Executive development.* This entire book is about the role of leaders in innovation. Executive development is the first step toward building an organization that innovates. Leading innovation should be a cornerstone of the curriculum.

- *Talent management. Talent management* refers to the ongoing process of systematically identifying, acquiring, and developing talent in order to ensure that capability for all key positions continues to be available and developed. Innovative thinking and the management of innovation teams should be requisites for the identification and development of talent. The future of work demands that leaders be able to lead innovation teams. Future leaders should be selected, developed, and promoted, not only for their professional competence and attitude, but also for their ability to maximize innovative thinking in their teams.

- *Employee engagement.* Employee engagement reflects the degree to which everyone in an organization is deeply committed and personally invested in the success of the entire enterprise. Innovation can directly and indirectly impact employee engagement. Organizations that are more innovative are often more successful, provide more meaningful work, open up new opportunities, and often are more fun, all of which are variables associated with highly engaged employees.

- *Organization development and change management.* When organization development and change management embed the principles of innovative thinking into every structure, process, and change, then they can accelerate the organization's transformation into an innovation-ready enterprise.

What leaders should pay attention to:

- Is innovation clearly defined for the whole organization and for each department?
- Is the capability to lead innovation part of the criteria to recruit or promote leaders?
- Are individuals recruited, developed, and promoted based on their ability to succeed in a team-based, innovative environment?

Information Technology (IT)

The success of Information Technology (IT) is often predicated on eliminating uncertainties and ambiguities in projects. However, innovation projects are complex and usually include uncertainties that cannot be eliminated.

IT has two main roles in innovation. First, it needs to support the teams that are developing innovations. This support must start at the outset of the project—for example, by helping to set the right boundaries. The earlier IT can be involved in projects, the more it can contribute and ensure that the needs of IT are being considered. In the process of implementation planning, IT can play a strong role in helping the team keep the essence of an idea, while ensuring that it is implementable within IT boundaries.

The second role of IT is to introduce new and potentially useful technologies to their organizations. In the knowledge economy, new technologies are often the starting point or the enabler for innovative products, services, or processes. On their own, the new technologies may not create value or a competitive advantage, but within a culture that innovates systematically, they can be used to develop innovative solutions that will create value.

What leaders should pay attention to:

- Is the IT department fully contributing to cross-functional innovation projects?
- Is the IT department supporting the implementation of test or pilot innovative ideas effectively?
- Is the IT department systematically bringing in new technology ideas that can serve as the starting points for innovative ideas?

Finance

The finance department has a considerable impact on innovation through the development and implementation of the budget.

The budget development process is too often a lost opportunity for innovation. The process is often an exercise in incrementalism, adding a few percent to last year's budget. The preferred approach is to explore in the budgeting process the question "How to create additional value with the same overall budget?" The leaders and their teams would then have the opportunity to challenge the way things have been done in the past and to develop better and more innovative action plans.

Funding for innovation can be included either as a line in the overall budget or as a percentage of every departmental budget.

Be aware that the implementation of the budget can prevent innovation by making changes to budgeted items very difficult. For these organizations, innovation is only possible during a short window as the budget is prepared, usually shortly before the organization's fiscal year end.

What leaders should pay attention to:

- Does the budget development process encourage innovative thinking?
- Does the organization allocate specific funding for future innovation projects?
- Is the budget flexible enough to move funds from non-performing projects to innovation projects?

Strategic Planning

The most effective strategic planning and innovative thinking processes are very similar, as both must deal with uncertainty. In fact, the four-step innovative thinking process presented earlier in this book (Chapters 5 to 9) has been successfully used in strategy work for large and medium-sized organizations.

Strategic planning can contribute to successful innovation in organizations in two ways. It can be a model of applied innovative thinking, and it can make the mid- to longer-term knowledge and insight developed for strategic planning available to the organization.

What leaders should pay attention to:

- Does the strategic planning process apply the principles of innovative thinking?
- Does the strategy department communicate their knowledge and insight?

Legal

Legal departments are often ignored when innovation is discussed, but they can be strong contributors to the innovation process. They often have the reputation of only saying "no" or "it cannot be done." The best legal departments use the law to tell innovation teams what can and cannot be done, but also help the teams modify their ideas to make them fit within the boundaries of the law.

What leaders should pay attention to:

- Is the legal department helping or hindering innovation?
- Does the legal department help innovation teams modify their ideas to make them fit within the boundaries of the law?

Project Management Office (PMO)

Project Management Offices were created to manage large transformational projects. Their mandate is to bring rigor to projects and eliminate uncertainties and ambiguities. They can be dangerous for innovation if they try to make the innovation process too rigorous and eliminate uncertainties too early.

They can be an excellent partner in innovation if they look at innovation as a complement to rigorous project management, to be used in the right place and at the right time.

What leaders should pay attention to:

- Is the PMO using innovative thinking when necessary?
- Is the PMO stifling the freedom necessary for innovation to flourish?

INNOVATION-SPECIFIC ORGANIZATIONATIONAL PRACTICES

The last section of this chapter looks at possible innovation-specific organizational practices. Of all the priorities in organizations, innovation is generally managed with the least discipline and consistency. There are reference books and theories for managing every other practice in organizations but none, until now, about managing organization-wide innovation. Innovation is a rigorous process that enables individuals and teams to use their innovative intelligence, and it requires discipline and consistency to deliver value for an organization.

It is relatively easy to launch innovation programs and departments, but it is more difficult to make them work effectively. The most important lesson from innovation successes and failures is that success is totally dependent on the actions of the executives. If the initiatives start with a well-thought-out innovation strategy, if they are properly resourced over the long term, and if the executive team members are deeply engaged in innovation, then the organization is likely to be successful. When these characteristics are missing, the innovation results are at best mediocre.

There are five organizational practices that can be used to assist in the implementation of an innovation strategy. They are presented in order of commitment and investment and are cumulative, with each new element adding a higher level of commitment and increasing the chances of success.

Innovation-Specific Organizational Practices

Level 1: Employee suggestion or idea management programs

Level 2: Learning and development for innovative thinking

Level 3: Dedicated innovation resources

Level 4: Office of Innovation

Level 5: Chief Innovation Officer

Level 1: Employee Suggestions or Idea Management Programs

Simple employee suggestion programs have been around for decades, starting with the physical suggestion box near the employee entrance. The purpose of employee suggestion or idea management programs is to let all employees offer ideas that can be valuable for the organization. The concept is that if you ask employees for ideas, useful suggestions will flow in automatically. The reality is different. Without a clear overall innovation strategy and the right amount of internal resources, most idea management programs are not effective. The reasons include the following:

- Most of the ideas are for very minor improvements that are clearly the responsibility of the local manager.
- Managers are usually not involved or asked to contribute, and so they do not encourage their employees to submit ideas.
- Potentially valuable ideas are usually submitted unpolished. Their value may not be recognized, and they may be quickly discarded.
- The team responsible for managing the ideas does not have the resources to manage the flow. Delays in responding get longer, and the people who offered suggestions become cynical about the program.
- The program is often staffed part-time by relatively junior employees, and led by a junior vice president. The review of the ideas is not thorough, and the best the idea management team can do is distribute them to the various departments. Since these departments did not ask for the ideas, they usually discard them without paying much attention.

These programs have seen a renewal in the past 10 years with the introduction of more sophisticated, web-based idea management programs, which focus not only on generating ideas but also on enabling online idea management to extract and capture their value. These programs are often promoted by software companies, and more experienced vendors can also be an excellent source of advice on their implementation.

Here are a few guiding principles to improve an idea management program.

- Engage every member of the executive team in actively leading and promoting the program in their area.
- Make a leader in each department responsible for managing the program in their department.
- Involve mid-level managers in promoting the program and working with their employees to develop the concepts and evaluate the potential of new ideas.
- Ensure that every idea is acknowledged and reviewed quickly. For example, ideas should be acknowledged within two days and first comments given within two weeks.
- Focus the idea collection around simple and clear questions relevant to the organization's strategic priorities.
- Create a process to evaluate the real potential value of interesting ideas and transform them into practical innovations.
- Create reward and recognition programs to motivate employees and their managers.
- Resource the program with the appropriate budgets and staff.
- Communicate successes regularly.

What leaders should pay attention to:

- What are the goals of the current employee suggestion and idea management programs?
- Are there enough resources to make the process effective?
- Is there a process to mine the rough ideas and identify the potential diamonds?
- Is there a better way to capture the innovative intelligence of leaders and employees?

Level 2: Learning and Development for Innovative Thinking

Training leaders and employees in innovative thinking is necessary to ensure they can access their innovative intelligence. Organizations where leaders and employees are trained in innovative thinking or managing innovative teams are almost 10 times more likely to be innovative than those that do not offer these programs.[4]

The challenge with innovative thinking training is that learning experts do not always appreciate the amount of effort necessary to acquire a new thinking process. Innovative thinking is too often compared with creativity. It only takes two hours to learn how to run an efficient brainstorming session and two days to be good at facilitating one. But this will never make an organization better at innovation.

Learning the theory of innovative thinking often requires a minimum of two days. It needs to be done in intact teams (intact functional teams or innovation project teams) to ensure they have the opportunity to practice the new tools continuously for at least three months after their training. In addition, the team or project leaders must be trained in leading innovation teams before their team is trained in innovative thinking. Without reinforcement and practice, the time and resources invested in training will be wasted.

As well as developing individual and team innovative thinking skills, the learning and development team should include some of the principles of innovative thinking in other programs, making the repetition even more frequent and the impact on the participants greater. Two principles that can easily be embedded in other programs are: (1) focusing on the problem first and (2) ensuring divergence before convergence.

What leaders should pay attention to:

- Are we offering learning programs on innovative thinking and leading an innovation team?
- Is innovative thinking training part of an overall plan for innovation?
- Are the leaders always trained in innovative thinking before their team?
- Are the learning sessions for innovative thinking conducted with intact teams or random mixed groups?

---

4. Ideaction and the Human Resources Professionals' Association (HRPA) in Ontario, Canada, 2008.

Level 3: Dedicated Innovation Resources

Dedicated innovation facilitators, coaches, or mentors have two functions in an organization. The first is to create a critical mass of experts who can make innovation projects more effective. The second is to act as coaches and mentors when individuals and teams start applying the innovative thinking process.

To successfully utilize dedicated innovation resource people they must be facilitators, never owners of a project. Their job is to help functional teams innovate and solve problems more effectively. They should be perceived as added-value resources with a unique and valuable skill. If they are responsible for innovation projects, they become competition for the functional leaders.

Dedicated innovation resources should have a full-time leader to implement the innovation agenda. The leader should be located in a highly credible support department. This will not be an issue if the organization decides to establish an Office of Innovation or a Chief Innovation Officer.

The innovation leader and resources should mostly be current employees with a good knowledge of the organization and the willingness to learn and practice an important new skill. Dedicated innovation resources can have different levels of knowledge and experience with differing certification level credentials. They must, however, use a common innovative thinking process to ensure their skills are transferable.

Innovation resources can be centrally located or be part of each department. There are pros and cons to these two options.

- If they are centrally located, innovation resources are more likely to focus on their innovation work and to share their expertise more easily, but they will not be as close to core and support functional group problems and may miss opportunities to help on specific projects that could use an innovation process.
- If they report within each department, they will have a direct link to the department's leadership, which will ensure that innovation is actively practiced. This will give them better access to projects where innovation can be effectively applied, as well as to employees who want to improve their innovative thinking skills. However, it will be easier for the department leaders to tell them to do non-innovation work when their department is overworked.

- In both cases the team of dedicated innovation resources should have a full-time leader responsible for continuous learning, for bringing in new resources as others move on, and for creating a community of practice where expertise and experience can be shared and where team members can assist each other on larger projects.

In many organizations the cost of innovation resources is recovered through internal charges. While this can be a good solution in the right culture, it should never be the operating mode at the outset of the program. When the program is launched, innovation resources should be made available without internal charges, until their credibility has been established.

What leaders should pay attention to:

- Is the organization ready for a team of dedicated innovation resources?
- Are all the executives ready to support dedicated innovation resources in their area?
- Who is the best person to lead the team of innovation resources and which department should they report to?
- Should the dedicated innovation resources work in a central group or in each department?

Level 4: Office of Innovation

For larger organizations or organizations where innovation is a top priority, an Office of Innovation can be a powerful statement, a permanent reminder of the commitment to innovation. The Office of Innovation should be responsible for delivering and driving the innovation agenda throughout the organization. It must focus on delivering short- and mid-term tangible value for the organization and for the various departments. This is the most effective way to ensure it will be sustained.

The Office of Innovation must be, and must be perceived as, a resource for the core and support functional areas, available to help them solve complex problems and develop innovative solutions. If the Office of Innovation or any dedicated innovation resources own any functional project, they will be competing with functional departments for resources and budgets. They cannot win in such a situation.

The Office of Innovation must be rigorous and disciplined to eliminate any potential remaining stigma attached to previous, unsuccessful efforts at creativity or innovation. They must look and feel like any other support functional department and become part of the fabric of the organization.

It is often useful to have a mix of both centralized and decentralized resources working in the Office of Innovation. Training and innovation process experts can reside in the Office of Innovation, while facilitators and coaches can report into each department, with a strong link to the Office of Innovation.

The Office of Innovation functions should include:

- Continuously securing active commitment to innovation from each member of the executive team.
- Promoting changes in the culture and organizational practices to make the organization innovation compatible.
- Facilitating major strategic innovation projects at the organizational level. It can also facilitate very large projects in key departments.
- Introducing best practices and outside innovations into the organization.
- Coordinating the broader list of innovation projects and eventually tracking the progress on all approved innovation initiatives.
- Removing obstacles to innovation in the organization.
- Collaborating with the HR department to be responsible for skills training and coaching in innovative thinking and innovation management. This can include working with internal resources as well as external suppliers, clients, and distributors to build a strong knowledge foundation for innovation initiatives.
- Creating a group of *corporate innovators* in addition to the Office of Innovation facilitators. This group should be leaders and employees across the organization who are interested in and skilled at innovation. The corporate innovators can be valuable resources to work on major cross-functional innovation teams. These employees can receive special training to be highly effective in innovation teams. The Office of Innovation should also be responsible for managing this community of innovation practitioners.
- Maintaining an innovation factory; for example, providing meeting rooms specially designed to make research, innovation, and prototyping easy for innovation teams.

- Managing rewards and recognition programs for innovation.
- Soliciting innovations from leaders and teams, and matching people with ideas with the right groups that can implement those innovations.
- Organizing *innovation forums*, where leaders and corporate innovators throughout the organization can meet and discuss new ideas.
- Coordinating and enabling skunk work, or any projects developed outside of the regular channels, if it is part of the organization's strategy.

The two key decisions regarding the Office of Innovation are where it should report and who should lead it.

- *Where should the Office of Innovation report?* Ideally the Office of Innovation should report directly to the President, CEO, or COO. If this is difficult, the second best choice is for it to report to a credible support area. If the Office of Innovation reports into one of the core functional departments, such as marketing or operations, it will spend considerable energy asserting its independence when working with other core areas. The only place where it should not be located is the Research & Development department, as the operation of the two functions is fundamentally different.
- *Who should lead the Office of Innovation?* The leader of the Office of Innovation should be an innovative, trusted, and respected leader and should have direct access to the President or CEO. Although the person appointed may not have the greatest expertise or experience in innovation, he or she should have a solid understanding of the organization, its leaders, its culture, and its organizational practices. It is easier to learn innovation than to learn an organization's internal environment. In many successful organizations, the position of head of the Office of Innovation is a stepping stone to an executive function. The leader of the Office of Innovation also should have a title that reflects the importance of the role.

What leaders should pay attention to:

- Do we have enough innovation initiatives to justify a central Office of Innovation?
- Does the mandate of the Office of Innovation potentially conflict with any core or support functional department?

- Does the Office of Innovation have the appropriate resources to succeed?
- Who would be the most respected person to lead the Office of Innovation?

Level 5: Chief Innovation Officer (CIO)

Creating a position of Chief Innovation Officer (CIO) will not make an organization instantly innovative, but it will send a strong signal internally and externally that the organization is serious about innovation. It also will make it more difficult to cancel the innovation push.

A CIO must be the voice of innovation at the senior executive table and the leader of the innovation strategy at the organizational level. To be effective, the CIO must be at the same level as the other C-level executives and sit at the executive table. The presence of a CIO does not reduce the whole executive team's accountability for innovation; it ensures that one member is responsible for its successful implementation. The responsibilities of the CIO should include leading and facilitating the execution of the innovation strategies with a single-minded focus to create value throughout the organization. The CIO is also responsible for challenging and coaching the other executives if the innovation strategy is pushed aside or simply paid lip service. The CIO needs to be expert in the organization's business but also a blend of strategist, executive coach, process expert, marketer, and communicator. He or she must influence all the other executives to make the necessary changes to become innovation compatible.

The best person for the CIO position is an up-and-coming executive, known and respected in the organization, and seen as an innovator. It should be a stepping stone for a promotion. We do not recommend bringing in a CIO from outside, as it is easier to teach innovation to the right person than to teach the nuances of the organization to an innovation expert. The best combination is a strongly committed internal executive with an innovation expert at number two, using the Office of Innovation to implement the innovation strategy.

What leaders should pay attention to:

- Is the executive team sufficiently committed to innovation to support a C-level Chief Innovation Officer?

- Who is the best internal resource to become Chief Innovation Officer?
- Is the Chief Innovation Officer pushing the executive team and the organization hard enough to implement innovation?

CONCLUSION

The implementation of innovation in organizations can take different forms, based on how much of a priority it is and the level of commitment. Every organizational practice cited in this chapter is important and needs to be included in the leader's thinking as he or she embarks on an innovation journey.

Success depends on:

- Executive commitment
- A rigorous review of organization practices from the perspective of whether the practices make innovation easier or more difficult
- The creation of innovation-specific organizational practices commensurate with the organization's innovation ambition

All the different forms and levels of organizational practices help every other department create real value, with new ideas and new practices that further the organization's strategy and long-term goals.

The next chapter integrates the ideas described throughout Part Three of *Innovative Intelligence*. It explains why an organization-wide innovation plan is essential to making innovation happen, how to develop the innovation plan, and what should be included in the plan to ensure that innovation can happen systematically in the organization.

CHAPTER FOURTEEN

THE INNOVATION PLAN

Although many organizations are trying to close the innovation gap, very few are successful—mainly because they fail to develop a formal plan. If senior leaders want better information technology or more productive marketing, they ask for a plan. And because most organizations are good at creating and implementing plans, they usually achieve their goals. However, if they need to increase innovation, leaders are more likely to make a few speeches and ask their employees to have more ideas. They rarely develop a specific innovation plan that is budgeted, resourced, and implemented.

It is only by creating a customized plan and implementing it rigorously that a leader can create an organization where innovation happens systematically. The plan gives focus and structure to the innovation effort and provides the long-term view required to be successful. In the absence of an integrated plan, an organization will find it is too easy to cut innovation resources when quarterly results demand cost reductions. The lack of a plan also has indirect effects. For example, leaders who are most likely to initiate innovation are generally uncomfortable with the status quo and strive to reach higher and achieve more. Their vision and drive, however, can also hold them back. As we have seen previously, they are perceived as mavericks—tolerated because they deliver but rarely promoted to the most senior positions. This sends an unintended signal to the rest of the organization that innovation is "risky change." As a result, the sporadic efforts of these individual leaders, however worthy and valuable, deliver only a small fraction of the innovation potential in their organizations. And because these leaders have to constantly fight a system created at another time for another purpose, they often get tired and leave.

Figure 14.1 shows the four organizational enablers introduced in Chapter 10. The subject of this chapter, "The Innovation Plan," is highlighted.

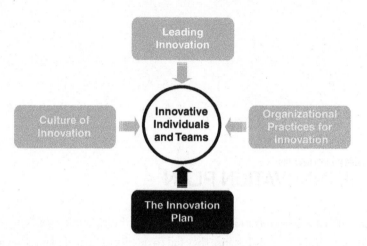

Figure 14.1: The Innovation Plan—Essential to Make Innovation Happen

This chapter focuses on the specific elements that should be included in a systematic innovation plan and the process to develop and measure its success. Specifically, it describes the following:

- Guiding principles for an innovation plan
- Key elements of an effective innovation plan
- How to develop the innovation plan and who should lead it
- When an innovation plan should be developed.

The final section of this chapter focuses on pulling it all together. In that section we integrate the ideas presented throughout the book and extend a challenge to governments, school educational systems, and multinational companies to do their part to help organizations close their innovation gaps.

GUIDING PRINCIPLES FOR AN INNOVATION PLAN

When organizations develop an innovation plan, they must follow six guiding principles. These principles ensure that the plan is solid, sustainable, and will achieve the objectives.

1. *Business focused.* The innovation plan must clearly state the specific business objectives on which innovation must focus. Innovation efforts will then contribute to creating real value, and the organization will not waste energy in directions that have no chance of being approved.

2. *Executive team driven.* The executives must be accountable for the development and implementation of the innovation plan. They must ensure that the scope of the plan spans only the area over which the leader or the leadership team has control.

3. *Top-down but open to bottom-up input.* The plan must be top-down but open to bottom-up initiatives and feedback. Business goals must drive strategies and actions. The top-down approach must be complemented by bottom-up input that gives all leaders and employees the opportunity to develop appropriate new actions.

4. *Boundaries and risk management.* Leaders must clearly establish boundaries in the innovation plan so that any risks are managed and efforts are all relevant and appropriate.

5. *Resourced and enforced.* The plan must only include strategies and tactics that the executive team is ready to resource and enforce.

6. *Metrics and tracking.* The innovation plan should include metrics so that progress can be tracked regularly. It is important that innovation results can be matched against any additional costs and that their effectiveness can be compared to the organization's other investments.

Within the innovation plan, there are often several sub-plans for each department and unit involved. Sub-plans should use the overall plan as a framework and follow the same format, but customize the boundaries and strategies to fit each unit's specific needs and unique situations. This cascading process can be done at every level until each team has an innovation plan.

KEY ELEMENTS OF AN EFFECTIVE INNOVATION PLAN

An effective innovation plan consists of seven key elements. The same format of an innovation plan applies for an entire organization, a department, or for a specific unit or team.

Elements of an Organization's Innovation Plan

Element 1: Business objectives

Element 2: Background and environment

Element 3: Boundaries for innovation

Element 4: Strategies and focus for innovation

Element 5: Possible actions and tools

Element 6: Sustaining efforts

Element 7: Measuring the impact of the innovation plan

Element 1: Business Objectives

The leader and team should identify the organization's business objectives and strategic priorities and, when appropriate, the business objectives and priorities of the specific unit for which the sub-plan is built. The innovation plan will need to deliver against these objectives and priorities. At this point, the focus is on the business objectives without any direct reference to innovation. As we have discussed previously, innovation cannot be the goal—it can only be one of the means to the goal. Some of the key questions to ask are:

- What are the organization's business objectives and strategic priorities?
- If the plan is designed for a department or a unit, what are the team's objectives and how do they contribute to the organization's objectives?
- How do the objectives contribute to delivering external customer value?

The business objectives are the overarching goals for all innovation efforts. They will also be the touchstone against which the organization measures success for innovation.

This element also includes defining "innovation" for the entire organization and how it applies to various departments. In addition, it often is useful to define common terms such as "leading innovation teams," "culture of innovation," and "organizational practices for innovation."

Element 2: Background and Environment

The external and internal pressures in the environment give the context for the innovation plan. There tend to be two responses to dramatic change:

Either use the change to your advantage or be a victim of it. The innovation plan must focus on how the organization can create a sustainable competitive advantage in order to shape their environment or achieve competitive parity.[1] It must also focus on the organization's capacity to respond to change imposed from the outside.

- **External Environment**

  It is important to understand the external environment in order to create an innovation plan that can shape and also respond to it effectively. The key questions are:
    - How much pressure for innovation is there from the market and the competition?
    - How could future competitors change our market?
    - How will the pressure grow over the next three to five years?
    - How much pressure does the organization want to create on the market?

- **Internal Environment**

  Internal environment questions should focus on current internal strengths and weaknesses that can support or inhibit the organization's ability to innovate systematically. Some of the key questions that should be asked are:
    - How prepared is the leadership team to lead innovation?
    - What is the readiness of the organization and its culture to embrace and support innovation? For example, is there change overload?
    - Are there particular areas of weakness that need to be addressed before the innovation strategies can be implemented?
    - What current initiatives need to be coordinated to ensure a coherent overall approach to implementing innovation?
    - What is the history of innovation in the organization? What are the past and current successes and failures?

The most effective way to understand the internal context is to conduct one or a series of surveys on the innovation readiness of the leadership,

---

1. *Competitive parity* refers to a strategy designed to neutralize the sustainable advantage of a competitor. See David S. Weiss, *High Performance HR* (John Wiley and Sons, 2000), Chapter 1, for a detailed discussion of how to achieve competitive advantage and competitive parity.

the culture, and the organization. Insights generated from these surveys can guide this element of the innovation plan.

- **Identify Your Environment's Key Drivers**
  Of the many external and internal environmental issues, it is important to identify the positive or negative drivers that will have the greatest impact on the implementation of innovation. The key questions are:
  - What are the key *external* elements that will have the most impact on the implementation of innovation?
  - What are the key *internal* elements that will have the most impact on the implementation of innovation?

Element 3: Boundaries for Innovation

Clearly defined boundaries are the most effective way to control the risk attached to an innovation plan and make every leader, even the most cautious, more comfortable with promoting innovation.

Executives are frequently unwilling to establish boundaries for innovation because they want to avoid the perception that they are constraining it. However, not communicating the boundaries will actually reduce the value-creating innovations because without boundaries, much of the team's efforts will be wasted. [2]

Boundaries are not good or bad for innovation—they are the reality of organizations. Leaders can choose to make them explicit or not. If they do not, leaders at every level throughout the organization will make up their own boundaries. In hierarchical organizations, most leaders and teams make up boundaries that are narrower than the real boundaries to reduce the risk of recommending a solution that will be rejected. Unfortunately, these leaders and teams limit themselves unnecessarily. A few leaders and teams make up boundaries that are wider than the real boundaries. As a result, executive leaders will reject many of the most creative ideas because they are outside the real boundaries. In all cases, the correct approach for executives and leaders is to identify and communicate the boundaries clearly and unequivocally.

---

2. See Chapter 6: Framework for a detailed discussion of how to use boundaries in the innovative thinking process.

The overall boundaries should apply to every project but should include special provisions for "disruptive innovation"[3] initiatives—such as the exploration of a radical change to the current business model—where different boundaries are usually required. Organizations are encouraged to have one or two targeted radical or disruptive innovation projects with very few constraints or boundaries, which will ensure they can shape the future directions of their business environment. These targeted disruptive innovation projects must be approved, owned, and governed by the senior executive team as organization-wide strategic initiatives that they resource, track, and evaluate regularly.

The discussion of boundaries within the innovation plan should include the following:

- The global boundaries, such as law, regulation, human rights, and so on
- Company-wide boundaries, such as corporate image, quarterly performance results, customer satisfaction
- Specific boundaries within divisional and departmental groups, such as specific budget and timing issues
- Level of approval for innovation projects, based on the levels of investment and risk
- Special rules for disruptive innovation strategic initiatives.

Element 4: Strategies and Focus for Innovation

The innovation strategies are the different ways in which innovation will contribute to the organization's objectives. There are two types of innovation strategies.

- *Core innovation strategies.* The leader and team should develop the core innovation strategies that are "value creating" first. These are strategies that will directly support the achievement of the organization's objectives—for example, sales, product, or manufacturing. The core innovation strategies usually result in tangible, value-creating outcomes—for example, a new disruptive business model or an improved service.

---

3. Clayton Christensen and Michael Raynor, *The Innovator's Solution: Creating and Sustaining Successful Growth* (Harvard Business School Press, 2003), introduced the term "disruptive innovation."

- *Supporting innovation strategies.* Supporting innovation strategies facilitate the capability to innovate consistently in the organization. They usually create new value indirectly for the organization. Some examples of supporting innovation strategies are:
  - Making the core enabling processes innovation-compatible.[4]
  - Ensuring all leaders can lead innovation teams competently.[5]

  Innovation strategies in the areas of finance, HR, IT, or marketing should not be stand-alone strategies, but should always support directly either the business objectives or the organization's core innovation strategies. Creating stand-alone innovation strategies for a support department such as HR or IT, for example, can be counterproductive for the organization. HR or IT might become very innovative, but its innovations may or may not be aligned with the organization's business objectives.

Often, organizations make the error of selecting too many strategies for innovation, which can make resourcing and implementation difficult. We often recommend, particularly for the initial innovation plan, that executives select no more than five organization-wide innovation strategies linked to their business objectives (including disruptive innovations). These strategies will become anchors for the entire innovation plan. In addition, the executives should select only the innovation strategies they are ready to resource and enforce. Failure to do so will have a significant negative impact on the plan and on innovation in general.

The key questions to assess which organization-wide innovation strategies to select are:

- On which business objectives does the organization want to focus its innovation efforts?
- Which innovation type (i.e., product or service, business model, process, or customer) will best support the organization's business objectives?
- What are the allocated resources and the budget required for the priority innovation strategies?

---

4. See Chapter 13: Organizational Practices for Innovation for a detailed discussion of how to develop enabling organizational practices.
5. See Chapter 11: Leading Innovation for a detailed discussion of this issue.

Element 5: Possible Actions and Tools

Only actions that have an organization-wide focus should be included in the overall innovation plan. Most of the specific departmental actions will be developed at the department or unit level.

Some of the key questions in this element are:

- What actions are needed to explore and implement solutions associated with each of the innovation strategies?
- What are the new cross-functional innovation teams that need to be developed?
- What does the organization need to do to support the approved innovation strategies that are occurring within teams?
- Based on the organization's strategies and current capabilities, what are the processes and tools required for the short- and long-term implementation of the priority innovation strategies?

The actions can include investments in the following five areas:

1. *Creating new project teams to develop organization-wide innovation initiatives.* Identify the best leader and the most effective processes to initiate and execute large-scale, value-creating projects such as business model innovation.
2. *Developing leaders to lead innovation teams.* Identify the investment in training and coaching required for leaders so that they can excel at drawing out their employees' and teams' innovative intelligence and facilitating innovation team discussions.
3. *Developing employees' innovative thinking skills.* Identify the investment in learning required for employees to be able to access their innovative intelligence and engage in innovative thinking independently and in teams. Identify how the principles of innovative thinking can be included in all learning programs.
4. *Accelerating transformation to a culture of innovation.* Identify how the organizational culture needs to change so that it can become a culture of innovation and identify the investments required to accelerate cultural transformation. Use the *laser beam approach* to target the areas to transform in order to achieve the changes to the culture as rapidly as possible with minimal anxiety and instability for the organization and its employees (See Chapter 12 for a detailed discussion of this process).

5. *Ensuring the organizational practices enable innovation.* Identify the organizational practices that need to change to enable innovation and invest accordingly. Also identify the organizational practices that are barriers to innovation and change them.

The executive team needs to champion the development of the organization-wide innovation plan and ensure that the following actions occur:

- *Allocating the budget and resources* for the implementation plan, including any permanent structure that will support the implementation.
- *Selecting the right leadership for the plan's implementation.* The executive team must lead the execution of the innovation plan and is collectively accountable for its successful implementation. It also is necessary to have a respected leader directly responsible for implementation. This does not always mean one leader is devoted to it full time, but it is critical that the innovation leader be known and respected in the organization and perceived as an innovative leader.
- *Announcing the innovation plan.* How the innovation plan is announced and by whom will have a major impact on how seriously it is considered and ultimately how successful it is. This does not mean that the plan should always be announced by the CEO with great fanfare. In fact, it is often more effective to start implementing the plan in some areas of the organization and achieve some preliminary results on short-term initiatives before announcing it at the organization level.
- *Developing the change management plan,* particularly for elements of the culture and the organizational practices that need to be changed to systematically support innovation.

Element 6: Sustaining Efforts

A major risk of any innovation plan is that the organization will not sustain its innovation efforts, particularly at the outset when there are not yet positive results. There is a need for a sustaining plan for the overall organization and for each of the individual teams. Often, successful short-term initiatives and close executive attention deliver enough momentum to sustain the focus on innovation.

The executive team should consider giving long-term funding to the innovation plan. Often, there is skepticism that innovation will be a short-term initiative for good times but will be cut as soon as times are tougher. By giving longer-term funding, the executives can dramatically improve buy-in.

The key questions in this element are:

- What initiative can be included in the innovation plan now to ensure your innovation initiatives will be sustained over the mid- to long-term?
- How will successes, and sometimes failures, be communicated and celebrated to maintain momentum and make innovation part of the culture?
- Would a Chief Innovation Officer or an Office of Innovation be helpful to facilitate the organization-wide priority strategic innovations and to coordinate, measure, and track the complete list of organization-wide and departmental innovation projects?

If innovation is only perceived as a cost, it will likely not survive the first cost-cutting measures. If innovation is considered an investment with expected results over the mid- to long-term, it has a much better chance of survival and success.

Element 7: Measuring the Impact of the Innovation Plan

Measurement is essential for the effective implementation of an innovation plan, but measuring organization-wide innovation is always challenging. Despite the difficulties, the measurements should still be clearly articulated and communicated so that the plan can be continuously improved based on successes and failures.

There are six main ways to measure innovation (other than in R&D):

1. *Achieve business objectives.* How well does the innovation help the organization deliver on its business objectives?
2. *Return on investment.* What is the real return on investment from the priority innovation strategies? Has the successful implementation of innovative solutions achieved new revenue gains (or cost avoidance) compared to the investment in the innovation strategies?

3. *Competitive or comparative advantage.* How does the organization compare with key competitors or benchmark comparators (i.e., industry standards, best practices, commitments to stakeholders)?[6]

4. *Leadership perception.* What are the executive and leadership teams' perceptions of the innovation strategies as contributors to the business success?

5. *Transforming the culture and organization.* Are the culture of innovation and the organization improving and transforming on key levers of innovation, such as teamwork, communication, employee engagement, and trust?

6. *Leader and employee engagement.* What are the innovation activities, such as training programs and innovation projects, and are leaders and employees engaged with the innovation activities and asking to participate?

HOW TO DEVELOP THE INNOVATION PLAN AND WHO SHOULD LEAD IT

The organization's executives are accountable for the development and implementation of the overall innovation plan, but they can decide to delegate the responsibility for its development. The leader and the team they select and the attention they pay to the development of the plan will send a clear message about how important innovation really is and whether employees should take it seriously.

Ideally, the innovation plan should apply to the whole organization. Each department and unit can then create their own departmental innovation plan. It is also possible to begin the process by developing a plan for a department or a unit without an overall organizational innovation plan. It is not as effective, but it is better than no plan at all.

The process we recommend for developing an effective innovation plan is similar to the development of a strategic plan and combines top-down and bottom-up approaches. The more leaders and employees are involved in each step of the development, the more buy-in there will be during the execution. The process should include the following:

• Select a respected leader with a strong reputation as an innovator and solid credibility in the organization.

---

6. Organizations in the private sector often assess whether the innovation strategies achieve sustainable *competitive* advantage or *competitive* parity. On the other hand, organizations in the public and non-profit sectors often assess whether the innovation strategies achieve sustainable *comparative* advantage or *comparative* parity.

- Assign a cross-functional team responsible for developing the innovation plan.
- Create an innovation plan development process that mirrors the four-step innovative thinking process (See Chapters 5 to 9) as follows:
    1. *Framework:* Develop a framework and project charter.
    2. *Issue redefinition:* Redefine the issue and the opportunities by involving a large number of leaders and employees from across the organization.
    3. *Idea generation:* Generate options for innovation strategies and select the best.
    4. *Implementation planning:* Engage in a risk analysis and develop the organization-wide innovation plan.
- Ensure that the executive team buys in at every step of the development of the innovation plan so that they will be fully committed to its execution.
- Ensure buy-in from key leaders and stakeholders in the organization by asking for their feedback before the plan is announced and implemented.

WHEN SHOULD AN INNOVATION PLAN BE DEVELOPED?

The timing for the development of the innovation plan is important. For example, if it is developed soon after the budget planning process, it will have less impact, as the key budgetary decisions will have already been made. Leaders at all levels in the organization will pay greater attention to the innovation plan if it is developed in advance of the budgeting process, and if it clearly influences budget and resource allocation decisions.

The plan should also precede any significant investment in employee and leader training. A plan will increase the chances that the participants engaged in the training will recognize that innovative thinking is not another training course they can leave on the shelf. Instead, they will realize that it is fundamental to the success of the business, their teams, each of the leaders, and, in fact, each individual within the organization.

The innovation plan also needs to be renewed regularly as part of the organization's overall strategic and operational plans. The plan increases the chances that targeted innovations will have the proper budget, resources, and sustained efforts to ensure that they succeed.

✳ ✳ ✳

PULLING IT ALL TOGETHER

Our intent in writing *Innovative Intelligence* is to develop a systematic approach that will enable organizations to close their innovation gaps.

Organizations must invest in their leaders in three significant ways:

- Ensure leaders develop their own innovative intelligence and innovative thinking capabilities so that they can lead innovations effectively.
- Be sure leaders have the capability to develop their employees' and teams' innovative intelligence and innovative thinking skills.
- Help leaders learn how to apply their innovative intelligence and augment it with their emotional and analytical intelligences.

We also argue that organizations need to design their culture and organizational practices to make innovation easier. We advocate a well-developed organization-wide innovation plan to establish a focused approach to organizational innovation. An organization-wide innovation plan enables local teams to focus their innovative thinking activities and align their innovations with the organization's overall requirements for innovation.

We also encourage governments, school educational systems, and multinational companies to do their part to close the innovation gaps. Our recommendations for each of these entities include the following:

- *Governments* need to invest resources to close the innovation gaps within their jurisdictions. Government systems can apply the same processes described in *Innovative Intelligence* to build sustainable cities and countries and to support underdeveloped countries. Governments also need to support the non-profit sector by funding their innovative efforts to deliver vital societal services. Finally, governments should expand innovation funding for multi-industry innovations to achieve societal benefits, such as funding joint innovation projects of universities, hospitals, and pharmaceutical companies to deliver integrated healthcare solutions for citizens.
- *School educational systems* need to continue to change how they prepare students at all levels—from primary schools through universities—so that when graduates enter the workforce, they will be able to resolve complex issues using their innovative intelligence. The role of teachers should evolve in the same way that the role of leaders must evolve in

organizations. Teachers should understand how to develop their students' capacity in analytical, emotional, and innovative intelligences. They also should ensure that students have full access to their innovative intelligence and that they are skilled at innovative thinking. They need to focus on developing the students' leadership capacities so that they can be ready to become the next generation of leaders.

- *Multi-national companies* need to have a higher level of social responsibility. They need to invest in innovations that focus educational institutions on the development of their students' innovative intelligence. They also need to allocate innovation budgets to their subsidiaries in other countries so that they can develop innovation plans that achieve local business strategic objectives.

Our hope is that *Innovative Intelligence* will become the practical road map for executives and leadership professionals to close their organizational innovation gaps. Our systematic approach will help leaders, teams, and employees develop their innovative intelligence through innovative thinking. It also will make innovation within organizations easier by doing the following:

- Accelerate cultural transformation to achieve a culture that systematically supports innovation.
- Create organizational practices that make innovation easier.
- Ensure there is an enterprise-wide innovation plan that guides innovation strategies and activities.

The end result will be that organizations will close their innovation gaps, achieve sustainable customer value and employee engagement, and remain vital into the future.

Index

About the Authors

Dr. David S. Weiss, President & CEO of Weiss International Ltd.
Affiliate Professor of the University of Toronto, Rotman School of Management, and former Chief Innovation Officer

Dr. David S. Weiss is President and CEO of Weiss International Ltd. David and his team of organizational and training consultants apply innovative intelligence to generate effective strategy, leadership, and HR solutions for boards, executives, and senior leaders throughout North America and Europe. Previously, David was a Partner in a human capital consulting firm and then he worked for a multinational consulting firm as their Vice President and Chief Innovation Officer.

David is a highly sought after keynote speaker at major conferences throughout the world. He is also very committed to and involved with executive continuing education through major universities. He is an Affiliate Professor of the University of Toronto, Rotman School of Management, a Senior Research Fellow of Queen's University, and a visiting faculty member of the Schulich School of Management, and the University College of Cayman Islands.

David received his doctorate from the University of Toronto and has two master's degrees from Columbia University in New York. He is also an Institute Certified Director (ICD.D) with the Institute of Corporate Directors. He has been honored internationally by a number of organizations. He was the recipient of the "HR Leadership Award" by the Asia-Pacific Human Resources Congress, the "Human Resources Distinction Award" by the Israel Human Resources Association, and the "Fellow Certified Human Resources Professional (FCHRP) Award" by the Human Resources Professionals Association in Canada.

David has written 40 journal and trade articles, including "Leading through Complexity," "Innovative Team Learning," "Leadership Capacity: The New Organizational Capability," and "Driving Employee Engagement." Business books David has written include: *Leadership Solutions* (Jossey-Bass, 2007, coauthored), *The Leadership Gap* (Wiley, 2005, coauthored), *High Performance HR* (Wiley, 2000), and *Beyond the Walls of Conflict* (Irwin Professional Publishing, 1996). *Innovative Intelligence* is his fifth book.

For more information, see www.weissinternational.ca.

Claude Legrand, President of Ideaction Inc.

Claude Legrand is the President of Ideaction Inc. For over 20 years he has been one of North America's leading experts in practical innovation and is an acclaimed and frequent conference presenter. He leads a team of experienced consultants who specialize in making organizations innovation- and change-capable and in delivering major innovation projects.

Claude has extensive experience in teaching and consulting on innovation, strategic planning, and culture change, mostly for large North American and European organizations. In 2007, he founded and was the first program director at the Centre of Excellence in Innovation Management at the Schulich Executive Education Centre, where he created the curriculum and taught the first Masters in Innovation Management program course in North America.

He is the founder of the Association of Innovation Professionals. He also developed a new program to teach innovative thinking in primary and secondary schools which will be piloted in 2011.

Born in France and a graduate of the École Supérieure de Commerce de Paris (ESCP), Claude has worked in Canada for over 30 years.

Claude started Ideaction in 1983 as a training company specializing in creativity and brainstorming. After 1992, realizing that the programs were only delivering short-term fixes, he used his experience to transform the methodology and developed the current processes for sustainable innovation and change management. In addition, Ideaction has used the methodology to develop effective models for Innovative Strategic Planning and Innovative Marketing Planning.

For more information, see www.ideaction.net.